The Stories We Tell

Stories give meaning to our lives and make us who we are. They shape our self-awareness, thus helping make sense of personal experiences, no matter how complex or difficult. Stories can also have a profound impact on our behaviours, values, and attitudes. This exciting new book examines the powerful role stories can play in schools both as a curriculum/teaching tool and as a framework for school improvement.

The Stories We Tell looks holistically at the uses of story in schools and sets out the ways it can be used to support teaching, including by:

- Organising the curriculum and helping to structure lessons

- Aiding students' memorisation

- Promoting inclusion

- Preparing students for future success

    In addition, it offers four ways of using story and storytelling in the school improvement process to:

- Consult, communicate, and collaborate with stakeholders during the school improvement journey

- Articulate a vision for the future and foster a set of shared values

- Build trust and adopt ethical leadership behaviours to create a no-blame culture that encourages risk-taking

- Resolve conflict and manage people, and lead change and manage PR

    Providing a fresh and stimulating approach to teaching and learning, curriculum-development, and school improvement, this will be valuable reading for teachers and school leaders across the primary and secondary phases.

Matt Bromley is an education journalist, author, and advisor with 25 years' experience in teaching and leadership. Matt is a public speaker, trainer, initial teacher training lecturer, and school improvement advisor. He remains a practising teacher, currently working in secondary, FE and HE settings; as well as writing for various magazines, authoring numerous best-selling books on education, and co-hosting an award-winning podcast. Find Matt on X @mj_bromley and at bromleyeducation.co.uk.

"In this thoughtful and inspiring book, master-teacher Matt Bromley reminds us of the unique power of stories to engage hearts and minds – not just as part of lessons, but as a framework for curriculum design and transformational school leadership. The style is highly readable, drawing on the author's own engaging personal stories as a practical way of modelling his message, as well as on a wide range of research and a deep knowledge of how schools work."
– Jean Gross, CBE

"It's very encouraging to see the power of story set out in *The Stories We Tell: How to Use Story and Storytelling to Improve Teaching and School Leadership*. Stories and storytelling are an underdeveloped aspect of the curriculum and of school development and Matt Bromley has made a compelling case for using them to help us refine the curriculum and school improvement. A welcome addition to the field."
– Mary Myatt, Education Consultant

"Matt Bromley is quite-simply a must-read for the classroom teacher. Clear, practical, insightful – his advice draws upon years spent in the classroom and is immediately useful and inspiring for teachers of all levels of experience. That is why he has long been one of *SecEd*'s most popular authors. This new book is no exception and offers a range of great ideas that you will feel inspired to adapt and adopt in your classroom. Matt remains one of the most important – and most useful – voices in teaching."
– Pete Henshaw, Editor, *SecEd* and *Headteacher Update*

The Stories We Tell

How to Use Story and Storytelling to Improve Teaching and School Leadership

Matt Bromley

Routledge
Taylor & Francis Group

LONDON AND NEW YORK

Designed cover image: © Getty Images

First published 2025
by Routledge
4 Park Square, Milton Park, Abingdon, Oxon OX14 4RN

and by Routledge
605 Third Avenue, New York, NY 10158

Routledge is an imprint of the Taylor & Francis Group, an informa business

© 2025 Matt Bromley

British Library Cataloguing-in-Publication Data
A catalogue record for this book is available from the British Library

ISBN: 978-1-032-73694-5 (hbk)
ISBN: 978-1-032-73693-8 (pbk)
ISBN: 978-1-003-46549-2 (ebk)

DOI: 10.4324/9781003465492

Typeset in Gill Sans
by KnowledgeWorks Global Ltd.

Contents

Acknowledgements

Although there is one name on the cover of this book, its story could not be told were it not for the many heroes and heroines who populate my life.

I'd like to thank my wife, Kimberley, for her unwavering love and support. The day our plot-lines converged, and *my* story became *our* story, the narrative got all the richer for it! And I cannot wait to turn the page and see what happens next!

Thanks, too, to our daughters Matilda, Amelia, and Harriet for keeping me, well, if not sane, then certainly grounded!

My parents are, of course, the authors of my life story and they have kept my narrative true since page 1.

Also keeping my story true are the friends I've known since I was at school and those with whom I was at university as an undergraduate, plus the partners and children who've joined this cast of characters over the years. They've been there through all the plot twists and turns, and will no doubt remain till the denouement. There are too many to name, but they know who they are!

Professionally, I've been fortunate to work with many inspirational people over the course of my career. Fellow teachers and education leaders, trainers and speakers, writers and editors, and the many unsung heroes who work behind the scenes keeping the story unfolding. Again, the dramatis personae is too long to list but I am truly thankful for your continued kindness, contributions, and support!

I'd like to thank the team at Routledge for helping to bring this book to print, including my commissioning editor, Annamarie Kino, senior editorial assistant Sophie Ganesh, copy editor Katie Finnegan, and senior production editor Helen Strain.

PART I
Learning through storytelling

The power and the story

Story is as old as civilisation.

Before the invention of writing, people told each other stories as a means of passing important information from branch to branch down the family tree, and stories have long been used as a conduit to convey a society's values, morals, and customs. In fact, storytelling has played an important role in every society throughout history. In ancient Greece, for example, storytelling was integral to the culture, with myths and legends passed baton-like between generations. In medieval Europe, troubadours and minstrels travelled town to town, telling stories and singing songs.

The earliest forms of storytelling were likely oral traditions, whereby stories were shared through the spoken word and memorisation. But, with the invention of writing, storytelling took on new forms. Epic poems such as the *Iliad* and the *Odyssey* were written down, allowing them to be preserved and more easily shared. In the Middle Ages, stories were often written down in the form of manuscripts, which were painstakingly copied by hand.

The advent of the printing press in the 15th century enabled stories to be shared on a much larger scale, leading to the rise of the novel as a popular form of storytelling. In the 20th century, radio, television, and film provided more media for storytelling, allowing stories to be told to larger audiences and on a more epic scale.

Today, the art of storytelling continues to evolve with the rise of digital media and the internet. Social media, blogs, podcasts, short-form videos, and other types of digital content have given people new ways to share their stories with the world and have democratised storytelling, giving many more people a voice with which to tell their own tales.

As such, despite myriad changes in technology and media – or perhaps because of it – storytelling remains a fundamental part of human culture, connecting us to each other and to our shared history.

Stories give meaning to our lives and make us who we are. They shape our self-awareness, thus helping us to make sense of personal experiences, no matter how complex or difficult. Stories can also have a profound impact on our behaviours, values, and attitudes – as well as on our very belief system.

DOI: 10.4324/9781003465492-2

Stories don't just help us make sense of ourselves; they teach us important lessons and convey complex ideas, thus helping us make sense of the world around us.

And stories help us connect with other people. When we hear a story, we often identify with the characters and their experiences, even if they are very different to our own. This connection can foster empathy and understanding, helping us appreciate different perspectives and experiences. In short:

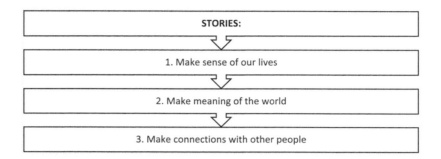

Thus, story can be a powerful tool in education because, surely, this is also the purpose of schooling: to help learners make sense of their lives, make meaning of the world, and connect with others. Schools do not exist simply to shepherd learners towards certification, but rather to prepare them for the next stage of their lives. The product of a good education, in my estimation, is a well-rounded, happy, healthy, informed, and compassionate citizen of the world. Story is the secret to achieving these success criteria.

You may well be thinking this is nothing new: stories have always played a part in school life. And you'd be right. When I was at primary school, I remember sitting cross-legged on a carpet in the corner of the classroom while my teacher read a story to the class. But this book is not about that. Reading stories to children in class is not new and there are plenty of other books on the art of storytelling. Instead, this book is about using story and storytelling techniques in more innovative ways. And it's not just about teaching through storytelling; it's also about the use of story in school leadership.

Secreted in the pages of this book, you'll find practical ideas and strategies you can put into immediate practice in your school and classroom. But you'll also discover lots of stories, including many of my own anecdotes. This isn't an act of navel gazing; rather, I want to practise what I preach. I want to tell stories that bring my arguments to life and ground theory in sensory reality. I want to prove the power of narrative, including analogy. I also want to make a personal connection with you because isn't this what great teachers do? They are knowledgeable in their subject disciplines and have excellent pedagogical content knowledge – in other words, they know their stuff and know how to teach their stuff in a way that makes sense to learners. But they are also friendly, approachable, and willing to listen; they are positive, enthusiastic, and have a sense of humour; they encourage and help learners to succeed. Great teachers are relentless in their pursuit of excellence and their language is infused with a sense of urgency and drive. They need not argue about expected standards; they achieve this in different ways – sometimes through the gravitas of maturity and experience, sometimes through warm, interpersonal interactions with every learner.

To help you navigate this book, I've used the following icons:

Inspiration
Telling my story

Whenever you see this icon, you'll find a personal anecdote that I hope will help relate my argument to real life and add hue and texture to the topic at hand, thus aiding your memorisation.

Into practice
Writing your story

This icon tells you that I'm about to share some practical, tangible tips for using story and storytelling in your teaching or leadership so that you can go forth and tell your own story.

This book is in three parts:

In the remainder of Part 1, I will argue the importance of stories to our everyday lives. I will explain how the stories we tell ourselves shape our self-narrative and lend meaning to our lives. I will advocate telling stories to our children to help them make sense of the world. And I will argue that stories aid the development of literacy skills and thus are vital to helping children access and understand texts and engage with the world around them. I will share some practical ideas for helping learners develop reading comprehension skills, as well as reading fluency, to ensure they can access the stories we tell in class and can craft their own stories to help them navigate the world around them.

In Part 2, I will assert that stories and storytelling can play a crucial role in teaching. Specifically, I'll argue that stories can help teachers to:

● Organise the curriculum and structure lessons.

● Aid learners' memorisation.

● Pique learners' curiosity and wonder.

- Relate the curriculum to the real world.

- Help promote inclusion.

- Prepare learners for future success.

In Part 3, I'll assert that stories can give meaning and structure to the process of school improvement. Specifically, I'll argue that stories can help school leaders to:

- Consult, communicate, and collaborate.

- Articulate a vision for the future.

- Build trust and create a no-blame culture.

- Resolve conflict and manage people.

- Lead change and manage processes.

By the end of this book, I hope that you will have developed the tools to use story and storytelling techniques to:

- Plan an ambitious, engaging curriculum that talks to learners' lived experiences.

- Structure lessons around a compelling narrative or idea, lending purpose and focus to learners' studies, helping them to manage the cognitive load.

- Help learners remember (retain and apply) information and make sense of what you teach them.

- Connect what you teach in class to the real world and to learners' future lives.

- Ensure every learner, irrespective of their starting points and backgrounds, is included at school and helped to achieve.

- Communicate more effectively and compellingly with colleagues and others, thus fostering a collective will.

- Frame the future and articulate shared values and beliefs, promoting collaboration over competition.

- Lead on school improvement, overcoming setbacks and resolving conflicts.

What you do with these tools is up to you. You can use them in our own teaching and leadership, you can share them with colleagues through mentoring or via a planned programme of professional development, or you can use them to audit your current provision and identify better ways of working. All I ask is that you do something! Make a change, tell your own story and, with it, make the world a better place one lesson at a time.

What have we learned?

In this chapter, we have discovered that:

Stories can help us make better sense of our own lives as well as give meaning to the world around us. They can also help foster closer connections with people. As such, stories can play a crucial part in education.

In teaching, stories can be useful tools because they can help us to structure learning. They can provide context and predictability and thus help learners to remember information. As well as being interesting and inspiring a sense of wonder, stories can connect classroom learning with the real world. What's more, they can support inclusion and diversity and help learners prepare for their future lives.

Stories are not only useful teaching tools though; they can also be useful in school leadership. For example, they can give structure to the school improvement process and help school leaders to communicate their vision and strategy. Stories are naturally collaborative – we share stories to communicate ideas – and so they can help us bring colleagues together in the pursuit of a collective goal. By telling personal stories, we can engender trust among our colleagues, and we can model the taking of risks and the making of mistakes, thus creating a no-blame culture. Finally, stories can help resolve conflicts and bring people together.

What can we do?

To put the advice contained in this chapter into practice, it might be helpful to consider the following questions:

1. How do you currently use story and storytelling in your teaching?

2. How is narrative currently used to aid the school improvement process?

3. In what way(s) do you think story is used effectively in your school?

4. In what way(s) might you make better use of storytelling in your school in order to:

    a. Help learners make sense of their lives?

    b. Help learners make meaning of the world?

    c. Help learners make connections with other people?

2 The stories we tell ourselves

We only remember something once. Every subsequent memory is a memory of a memory and each time we 'remember' a memory, we change it, reshape it, polish it ...

As such, when we tell our stories, we are not simply recounting objective facts, but rather we are constructing a narrative that gives meaning to our experiences and helps us make sense of our past. We discern logic where none existed, and we find order in the chaos of our lives.

We do not learn from a direct experience; we learn from looking back and reflecting on that experience later. Through the act of storytelling, we can highlight certain experiences or aspects of our lives while downplaying or ignoring others. We can also reinterpret events in light of new information or insights, and we can assign different meanings or significance to the same events.

We process new information within the context of what we already know – making sense of the abstract and new by connecting it to the concrete and familiar. We call these connections 'schema', which is the name we give to the ever more complex web of information we spin spider-like in our long-term memories. The more connections we make, the more sense we assign to our life story.

What's more, the way we choose to tell our stories can have an impact on how we view ourselves and our lives. For example, if we focus on the positive aspects of our experiences, we may feel more optimistic and confident about our future, whereas if we focus on the negative aspects, we may feel more discouraged or pessimistic.

At the same time, it is important to recognise that our personal histories are not just a product of our individual narratives but are also shaped by the social and cultural contexts in which we live. In other words, the stories we tell are influenced by the expectations, social norms, and shared values of the communities we belong to, and they can both reflect and reinforce these broader cultural narratives.

Stories allow us to make sense out of otherwise puzzling or random events. Stories help us smooth out some of the decisions we make and create meaning and sense out of the tangles and complexities of our lives.

The stories we tell ourselves, also known as self-narratives, are the internal tales we create about our lives. These narratives are shaped by our experiences, beliefs, and values, and they play a significant role in shaping our identity and how we view ourselves.

DOI: 10.4324/9781003465492-3

The stories we tell ourselves can be positive or negative, and they can influence our emotions, behaviours, and self-perception. For example, if we tell ourselves a positive story about our abilities, we may feel more confident and motivated to pursue our goals. Conversely, if we tell ourselves a negative story about our abilities, we may feel discouraged and avoid taking on new challenges.

The stories we tell ourselves can also be influenced by external factors such as social norms, cultural expectations, and media messages. For example, if we are surrounded by messages that reinforce negative stereotypes about certain groups of people, we may internalise those beliefs and tell ourselves a negative story about our own abilities or worth.

In sum, it is important to recognise that the stories we tell ourselves are not fixed or unchanging. We have the power to rewrite and reinterpret our self-narratives, and in so doing we can change how we view ourselves and our lives. This process of *restorying* can involve challenging and reframing negative beliefs, focusing on our strengths and accomplishments, and seeking out new experiences that help us create a more positive self-narrative.

To explore this notion of self-narrative further, let's consider the school of structuralism...

Story and structuralism

Structuralism was built in the late 1920s and early 1930s on the foundations of Gestalt psychology, which maintained that all human conscious experience is patterned. Gestalt psychology posits that the human mind functions by recognising structures or, if none are present, by imposing structure on the random.

Claude Lévi-Strauss is widely regarded as the father of structural anthropology. In his 1972 book, *Structuralism and Ecology,*[1] he proposed that culture is composed of hidden rules that govern the behaviour of its practitioners. It is these hidden rules that make cultures different from each other. Lévi-Strauss proposed a methodological means of discovering these rules through the identification of binary oppositions. Some of these oppositions include hot/cold, male/female, culture/nature, and raw/cooked. Structuralists argue that binary oppositions are reflected in various cultural institutions and that we may discover underlying thought processes by examining such things as kinship, myth, and language.

As I explained in Chapter 1, before the invention of writing, people told each other stories as a means of passing important information from branch to branch down the family tree. The earliest forms of storytelling were likely oral traditions, whereby stories were shared through the spoken word and memorisation. Even today, in oral cultures the lore of the social group is preserved in living memories, which place a high value on storytelling techniques that aid memorisation. As such, techniques such as rhyme and rhythm are important in communicating a society's traditions. Formulae also play a crucial role. If important values, beliefs, and traditions can be encoded into a narrative which is formulaic and makes use of rhyme and rhythm then that lore can be more successfully preserved. This is why myths exist. They provide vivid and dramatic representations of important messages.

Rhyme, rhythm, and meter, formulae, analogy, metaphor, and simile are narrative techniques of considerable social importance for the preservation of memories.

Myths and fairy tales are often built on simple yet powerful abstract concepts presented in binary oppositions such as good/bad, safety/fear, courage/cowardice, and so on. Although the characters and plots of fairy tales are often far removed from our everyday lives, the messages contained within them are made accessible and meaningful because they are articulated through abstract concepts which are familiar to us.

Even very young children – four- and five-year-olds – can grasp the most powerful and abstract concepts we ever learn such as the binary oppositions I mentioned a moment ago. The first binary opposition young children tend to grasp is that of hot/cold because hot is the sensation of something hotter than body temperature and cold is colder than body temperature. Once these oppositions are grasped, children begin to mediate between them – in the case of hot/cold, children mediate 'warm' and 'cool'. By so doing, children can grasp a large range of phenomena in the world.

Thus, stories provide structure and meaning to our lives; stories order the arbitrary and impose logic on the haphazard.

Inspiration
Telling my story

An escape and an education

I remember stories from my own childhood and these memories are much more than vague recollections of plot and character. These memories take me back, sensorily, to a particular time and place. They evoke strong reminiscences of wonderment and discovery. Aged seven, for example, I lost a rainy Saturday to Enid Blyton. (I can still feel the thrill of it now.) I left a grey and drizzly northern town for a sun-streaked world of haunted castles, exciting adventures, and derring-do. After Blyton came Roald Dahl, who gifted me the keys to a magical factory wherein rivers flowed with chocolate and then took me into space in a great glass elevator.

Stories held a special place for me because they were my escape and my education.

They were my escape because, despite my humble circumstances, they afforded me infinite opportunities. I didn't need money or privilege to see the world or indeed explore the wider universe; stories were my means of transport; stories could take me anywhere I wanted to go.

Stories were my education because my love of reading fed my love of learning. I was schooled at a time when grammar wasn't explicitly taught and so learned to spell, punctuate, and understand grammar through reading well-written stories; stories were the best teachers I had.

Reading was my superpower, but sadly for today's children its powers are waning.

According to the National Literacy Trust's report on children and young people's reading in 2023,[2] levels of reading enjoyment are at a record low. In fact, they found that just 2 in 5 (43.4%) children and young people aged 8 to 18 enjoyed reading in their free time, which is the lowest level since the National Literacy Trust first asked the question in 2005. Fewer children and young people who receive free school meals said they enjoyed reading compared with their peers who do not receive free school meals (39.5% vs. 43.8%). Fewer boys than girls said they enjoyed reading (40.5% vs. 45.3%) and, while the gender gap in reading enjoyment has halved for those aged 8 to 18 between 2005 and 2023 (decreasing from a 10.7 to a 4.8 percentage-point difference in favour of girls), the National Literacy Trust claim this drop is largely because of a greater drop in reading enjoyment in girls.

Children are reading less frequently, too. The survey found that fewer than 3 in 10 (28.0%) children and young people aged 8 to 18 said that they read daily in 2023, matching levels seen in 2022. There has been a 26% decrease in the number of children and young people aged 8 to 18 who read daily in their free time since 2005 (decreasing from 38.1% to 28.0%).

Fewer children and young people who receive free school meals said they read daily compared with those who don't (24.1% vs. 28.9%). More girls than boys aged 8 to 18 said they read daily (30.4% vs 24.9%). Only 1 in 5 (21.5%) boys who receive free school meals read daily, compared with 3 in 10 (31.1%) girls who don't. However, daily reading levels increased for boys and decreased for girls between 2022 and 2023 regardless of whether or not they received free school meals.

The decline is, in part, down to the home environment. Nearly three times as many children and young people who perceived their reading environment to be supportive said they enjoyed reading compared with those who perceived it to be less supportive (63.9% vs. 25.4%), while twice as many read daily in their free time (41.7% vs. 17.7%).

We must do more, therefore, to buck the trend and get children reading again in order to rediscover this superpower. One way to do this is by using story and storytelling in our teaching, making great stories an everyday part of school life.

What have we learned?

In this chapter, we have discovered that:

The story we tell ourselves about ourselves has an impact on how we live our daily lives. Our self-story is our personal view on the 'good' and 'bad' experiences we've had, the choices we've made, and the people we've met.

Stories lend structure to the chaotic and lend meaning to the arbitrary. But to harness the power of story, we must first learn to read and write. As teachers, therefore, we must get children reading and we can do this by making great stories an everyday part of the classroom.

What can we do?

To put the advice contained in this chapter into practice, it might be helpful to consider the following questions:

1. To what extent do you teach learners about the importance of self-story?

2. How do you help learners tell a positive story of their past experiences to build resilience against future challenges?

3. How do you use story to help make the new and abstract familiar and concrete?

4. What do you do in your school to help every child learn to read with understanding and confidence? What more could you do?

5. What do you do to encourage all children to read for pleasure? What more could you do?

Notes

1 Lévi-Strauss, C (1976). *Structural Anthropology: Volume II*. Basic Books, Inc.
2 https://literacytrust.org.uk/research-services/research-reports/children-and-young-peoples-reading-in-2023/

3 The stories we tell our children

The stories we tell our children play a crucial role in shaping their understanding of the world and their place in it. Through nursery rhymes and bedtime stories, we can convey important values, beliefs, and cultural traditions, as well as teach children important life lessons and skills.

One of the primary functions of storytelling for children is to help them make sense of their emotions. By providing narratives that reflect their own experiences or that help them understand new situations, we can help children develop a sense of agency and resilience in the face of challenges.

It's important, therefore, that the stories we tell in school reflect children's own *lived experiences*, that children see themselves and their heritage represented in stories.

Storytelling can also help children develop important social and emotional skills such as empathy, compassion, and perspective-taking. Through stories, children can learn about different cultures, experiences, and points of view, which can help them develop a more nuanced understanding of the world around them.

At the same time, it is important to recognise that the stories we tell our children can also perpetuate harmful stereotypes or reinforce narrow cultural norms. Therefore, we need to be mindful of the messages we convey through our stories and seek out diverse and inclusive narratives that reflect the full range of human experience.

Thus, the stories we tell our children can have a powerful impact on their understanding of the world and their personal growth. By using stories to convey positive values, teach important life skills, and foster empathy and understanding, we can help children grow into thoughtful and compassionate members of society.

The balm of bedtime stories

One of the most powerful forms of storytelling in a child's early years is the bedtime story.

Bedtime stories are an essential part of a child's formative years because they offer numerous benefits that aid their cognitive, emotional, and social development. They are important for children in the following ways:

1. Language development: They help expand a child's vocabulary, improve their language skills, and aid their communication development.

DOI: 10.4324/9781003465492-4

2. Imagination and creativity: They encourage children to use their imagination and creativity, helping them to develop a love for books and reading.

3. Emotional development: They teach children about different emotions and help them develop empathy and compassion for others.

4. Bonding time: Reading bedtime stories can be an excellent way for adults and children to bond, creating a special moment that can become a cherished memory.

5. Relaxation and sleep: They can help children relax and wind down, leading to a better night's sleep and improved physical and mental health and wellbeing.

Inspiration
Telling my story

The story train

If, when my children were younger, you were ever unfortunate enough to find yourself in a meeting with me towards the end of the day, you'd no doubt have clocked me clock-watching. As daylight disintegrated to dusk outside my office window, you'd have detected in me a growing unease, impatience perhaps, and – to your delight – a tendency towards shorter speech, even monosyllables. Why? Because I'd have been calculating how long I had left before the 'story train' left town – so called because it was the last train of the day guaranteed to get me home in time to read my daughter's bedtime story.

I used to work with someone who cunningly timed his daily departure from school so that he missed his children's bedtime. His view: he worked hard and wished to return home to quietude, a house free of children's screams, safe from the stresses and strains of bath-time.

But not me.

Reading my daughter's bedtime story was always an innocent act that knitted up the ravelled sleeve of care; it was my sore labour's bath, the balm of my hurt mind, and the chief nourisher in my life's feast. Our bedtime story made the world seem a better place; it was an oasis of calm and order in an otherwise cold, cruel world. After a stressful day of work, it reminded me what life was about and how precious our time on Earth was.

A book at bedtime is not just a literacy lesson – or indeed a literary one – it's a way of learning about the world around us, as well as a way of discovering new worlds and, with them, new hopes and dreams, and endless new possibilities. To climb inside the pages of a good book is to take a journey to paradise. Reading allows us to live a thousand different lives in a thousand different times rather than just the one we're given.

In the moment immediately before we descended, we used to perch on the edge of the book, excited, eager to fall headlong into the pages, to tumble down and disappear from the world for quarter of an hour and enter a timeless land of limitless opportunities. My daughter and I escaped for 15 precious minutes, leaving our house hand-in-hand to find a new home among the leaves.

As I explained in Chapter 2, when I was a child, stories were my escape and my education, and reading my children a bedtime story when I got home from work was always the best means I had of 'passing it on'; it was the best inheritance I could have bequeathed them. Well, that and the house.

The gift of reading

Research suggests that children who read for enjoyment every day not only perform better in reading tests than those who don't, but also develop a broader vocabulary, increased general knowledge and a better understanding of other cultures. In fact, there's evidence to suggest that reading for pleasure is more likely to determine whether a child does well at school than their social or economic background.

Parents are by far the most important educators in a child's life and it's never too early for a child to start, even if a parent only reads with their child for a few minutes every day, because even before they're born babies learn to recognise their parents' voices. Reading to a baby from the time they're born gives them the comfort of their parents' voices and increases their exposure to language.

Learning to read is about listening and understanding as well as working out the shape of letters and the formation of words. Through listening to stories, children are exposed to a rich and wide vocabulary, which helps them build their own word power and improve their understanding of the world around them.

Reading is also a gift that continues to pay dividends. A report by the Organisation for Economic Co-operation and Development in 2011 claimed that children whose parents frequently read with them in their first year of school continued to show benefits when they were as old as 15.[1] The OECD examined the long-term impact of parental support on literacy and found that, discounting social differences, children with early support remained ahead in reading. It also found a strong link between teenage reading skills and early parental help.

The study, which was based on an analysis of teenagers in 14 developed countries, found that active parental involvement at the beginning of school was a significant trigger for developing children's reading skills that would carry through until they were teenagers. On average, teenagers whose parents had helped with reading at the beginning of school were six months ahead in reading levels at the age of 15. The report said that parents did not have to be particularly well educated themselves for this impact to be achieved. What was important was that parents read books regularly with their children – such as several times a week – and that they talked about what they were reading together. This parental involvement superseded other social disadvantages and, in some countries, represented more than a year's advantage in reading levels at the age of 15 compared with children whose parents rarely read books with them.

If you're not yet convinced of the benefits of reading with children, and of the power of story in general, then consider a study by the Paediatric Academic Society in 2015,[2] which examined 19 pre-school children and their interactions with parents. Researchers attached brain scanners to the children as they listened to stories. The brain scans showed that reading at home with children from an early age was strongly correlated with brain activation in areas connected with visual imagery and understanding the meaning of language.

The study added weight to previous research that's shown that reading has many positive effects on young children, such as teaching the rules of syntax, expanding children's vocabularies, and helping children bond with their parents.

Reading to children and getting children reading to us is clearly important. So, how can we capitalise on this in school?

Into practice
Writing your story

It's good to talk

To maximise the chances of a child learning from reading aloud, we can use a technique called dialogic reading. According to Peter Watkins in a 2018 paper, "Dialogic reading draws on sociocultural learning theory to suggest that scaffolded interactions between children and adults during reading will result in language gains, particularly with regard to vocabulary development, oral complexity and narrative skills. There is also evidence that the experience of dialogic reading correlates with future literacy skills."[3]

At its simplest, dialogic reading is an adult and a child chatting about the book they're reading together. The conversation involves targeted questions which help learners to explore a book at a deeper level by unpacking new vocabulary – defining and exemplifying unfamiliar words; deconstructing a book's component parts to understand how it's structured and what makes it effective; and expressing a personal response to the text.

Dialogic reading is suitable for learners of all ages and working at all levels; it works for both fiction and non-fiction texts. It is an active, learner-centred process. It can help develop learners' literacy skills because it involves modelling how good readers think.

In practice, dialogic reading requires reading a text several times while using prompts and questions to stimulate thought. The four steps of dialogic reading form the acronym PEER, which stands for:

- **P**rompt the child to say something about the book.
- **E**valuate the child's response.
- **E**xpand the child's response with new information.
- **R**epeat the prompt.

There are five types of prompts typically used in dialogic reading, which form the acronym CROWD:

- **C**ompletion
- **R**ecall
- **O**pen-ended
- **W**h-questions
- **D**istancing

Completion prompts: Here, learners are asked to fill in a blank at the end of a sentence. For example: The boy's name was … His favourite hobby was … He found the time capsule in …

Recall prompts: Here, learners are asked to explain in their own words what has happened so far in a story. Recall prompts help learners understand a text or remember events. For example: What happened to the boy? What was in the time capsule? Who had buried the capsule and when?

Open-ended prompts: This works best when using books with pictures. Here, learners are asked, What's happening in this picture? Open-ended prompts help learners increase their expressive fluency and attention to detail.

Wh-prompts: These prompts are questions that begin with what, where, when, why, and how. For example: (Pointing to a picture) Who is this? Where is he here? What's the weather like here? Why is he looking puzzled?

Distancing prompts: Here, learners are asked questions that help them reflect on their own experiences, based on input from a text. These prompts help learners make connections between a text and the real world. For example: Have you ever found something unusual while out playing? What would you have done if you had found a time capsule? How would you feel if this happened to you?

One of the advantages of dialogic reading is that it expands learners' vocabulary. For this, it's useful to distinguish between Tier 1, Tier 2, and Tier 3 words:

Tier 1 – Basic words: These are high-frequency, everyday words that learners are expected to know such as *boy*, *name*, *time*, etc.

Tier 2 – High-frequency words: These are words that are used in a variety of contexts. For example: *analysis*, *capsule*, *coincidence*, etc.

Tier 3 – Context-specific words: These words are specific to a domain – often to a subject discipline – and are best learned in context when they are needed. For example: *onomatopoeia*, *polycarbonate*, *algebra*, etc.

Choosing which words to teach before a text is key to effective instruction. In general, learners benefit most from being *pre-taught* Tier 2 words that appear in a text because knowing these words helps them better understand the text. In their 2002 book *Bringing Words to Life*,[4] Isabel Beck, Margaret McKeown, and Linda Kucan suggest this sequence for explicitly teaching vocabulary:

1. Read a sentence in which the word appears.
2. Show learners the word and get them to say it out loud.
3. Discuss possible meanings of the word.
4. Identify any parts of the word that may be familiar (e.g. Greek or Latinate roots, common prefixes and suffixes).
5. Re-read the sentence with the word in it to detect any contextual clues.
6. Explicitly explain the meaning of the word through definition and the use of synonyms.
7. Provide several other examples of the word being used in context.
8. Ask learners to use the word in sentences of their own.

I would suggest that we not only make use of dialogic reading strategies in our lessons in school, but that we also teach parents how to utilise these techniques while reading with their children at home. We might also ensure any reading mentors we employ in school use PEER and CROWD, and that all teachers use a similar structure for explicitly teaching vocabulary in their subjects.

What have we learned?

In this chapter, we have discovered that:

Stories can play a crucial part in shaping children's understanding of the world and in helping them find their place within that world. Stories can help children make sense of their emotions, especially young children who are easily confused by new feelings. To maximise story's role in this process, it's important that the stories we tell children reflect their *lived experiences* and mirror the world in which they live. Children need to see themselves and their heritage represented in stories.

Stories can also be used as an aid to language development. And they can help foster a child's imagination and creativity, as well as help with their emotional development. What's more, stories can provide valuable time for bonding and can improve a child's ability to relax and their sleep hygiene. But to achieve these outcomes, as well as getting children to read, we also need to help them to read with speed, accuracy, and fluency.

What can we do?

To put the advice contained in this chapter into practice, it might be helpful to consider the following questions:

1. To what extent do you engage in dialogic reading in your school? Do you use PEER and CROWD? What else do you do to encourage active reading?

2. Do you explicitly teach learners the Tier 2 vocabulary they need to access your curriculum? When and how? Does it work? How do you know?

3. Does your school have a standard process for explicit vocabulary instruction? Do all teachers use it in all subjects?

Notes

1 OECD (2011). *Education at a Glance 2011: Highlights*. OECD Publishing. https://doi.org/10.1787/eag_highlights-2011-en.

2 Hutton, J S (2015). Home reading environment and brain activation in preschool children listening to stories. *Paediatrics*, 136(3), 466–478. https://publications.aap.org/pediatrics/article-abstract/136/3/466/61420/Home-Reading-Environment-and-Brain-Activation-in?redirectedFrom=fulltext

3 Watkins, P (2018). *Extensive Reading for Primary in ELT*, part of the Cambridge Papers in ELT series. Cambridge University Press, p. 9.

4 Beck, I, McKeown, M, & Kucan, L (2002). *Bringing Words to Life*. Guilford Press.

4 The stories of literacy

In Chapter 3, I argued that reading stories with children is important because stories help with language development. Although most of this book will focus on the uses of story and storytelling techniques in teaching and leadership, it is crucial we explore the importance of literacy first because without literate learners, our stories will be inaccessible. In this chapter we will unpack this tricky term 'literacy' and in Chapter 5 we will examine the component parts of 'reading comprehension'.

According to the National Literacy Trust's *Seldom Heard Voices: Adult Literacy in the UK* report,[1] citing a 2016 report from the OECD, "one in six (16.4%) adults in England are estimated to have very low literacy, which means they may struggle with longer texts and unfamiliar topics".

As noted by the OECD's International Survey of Adult Skills,[2] the UK is the only OECD country where young adults do not have better literacy skills than those nearing retirement. The National Literacy Trust provide the following statistics:[3]

- The average worker in the UK with very low literacy will earn approximately 7.1% less than if they had a basic level of literacy. This means that they would need to work an additional 1.5 years over their lifetime to make up for this disparity.

- A girl born in a ward with some of the greatest literacy challenges in the country will live 20.9 years shorter than a girl born in a ward with some of the fewest literacy challenges.[4]

But why are levels of literacy so poor?

One reason is this: vocabulary is critical to success in reading as well as academic achievement more generally. The size of a child's vocabulary in their early years of schooling (the number and variety of words that the young person knows) is a significant predictor of reading comprehension in later schooling and in life. Most children are experienced speakers of the language when they begin school but reading the language requires more complex, abstract vocabulary than that used in everyday conversation.

DOI: 10.4324/9781003465492-5

Children who have had stories read to them during the first years of their lives are exposed to a much broader and richer vocabulary than those contained in everyday conversations and, as such, arrive at school better prepared for reading.

Our understanding of a word grows with repeated exposure to it. Learning vocabulary takes place on a continuum, ranging from never having seen or heard a word before to having a deep knowledge of that word and its different meanings, as well as the ability to use that word confidently and accurately in both speaking and writing.

Acquiring vocabulary is incremental because words differ in many ways:

- They differ according to **syntax**: knowing what part of speech a particular word is can assist reading.

- They differ according to the **size** of their 'family': knowing one of a family of words will help the reader determine a number of others.

- Some words are polysemous, which means they can have multiple **meanings** (e.g. the word *scale* means to climb, a feature of a fish, a plant disease, a measuring instrument, the ratio of distance on a map to that on the ground, and so on).

Children who know multiple meanings of words are more prepared to read widely and across multiple contexts. If a learner knows the meaning of the word *happy* and knows the single letter-sounds that make up that word, then the word can be easily decoded and understood when read in a text. The words *happier* and *happiness* are also more likely to be read and understood. With only a few exposures, these words will be familiar enough to be recognised on sight and so a learner's reading vocabulary grows.

In short, vocabulary is complex but also vital to developing reading comprehension.

The Matthew Effect

Young people who develop reading skills early in their lives by reading frequently add to their vocabularies exponentially. This is sometimes called the 'Matthew Effect' after the following line in the Bible (Matthew 13:12): "The rich shall get richer and the poor shall get poorer." In the context of literacy, the Matthew Effect is that 'the word-rich get richer while the word-poor get poorer'.

In his book, also called *The Matthew Effect*,[5] Daniel Rigney argues that, although good readers acquire new skills rapidly and transition from learning to read to reading to learn, weak readers grow frustrated with the act of reading and try to avoid it.

Various research papers cite a significant word gap between rich and poor children.[6] The word-poor cannot catch up with the word-rich because to do so they'd need to be able to learn more words more quickly than the word-rich. A learner who does not know the meaning of the word *happy* will struggle over that and related words (e.g. *happiness, happier, happiest, unhappy*) in connected text, even if they can decode them, because transforming letters into words is useless if those words do not have a meaning.

If a learner continues to experience frustration when reading because they are word-poor, then they are likely to give up, denying themselves the opportunity to build vocabulary, fluency, and world knowledge.

Young people who do not acquire these skills easily will become increasingly disadvantaged over time. Vocabulary helps to build comprehension and is therefore a key tool for reading. Young people who lack vocabulary and prior knowledge (context) will have difficulty understanding the books they encounter in school, especially as those books become more difficult.

Building word power

So, the big question is: what can we do to help the word-poor become richer?

One answer is to **plan group work activities** which provide an opportunity for the word-poor to mingle with the word-rich to hear language being used by learners of their own age and in ways that they might not otherwise encounter.

Another answer is to **model higher-order reading skills** because, as the literate adults in the room, we teachers use these skills unconsciously all the time, so we need to make the implicit explicit. For example, we could model:

- Moving quickly through and across texts

- Locating key pieces of information

- Following the gist of articles

- Questioning a writer's facts or interpretation

- Linking one text with another

- Making judgements about whether one text is more reliable/more interesting than another

We can **promote the love of reading** for the sake of reading too, encouraging our learners to see reading as something other than a functional activity. It is the responsibility of every adult working in a school (not just teachers, and certainly not just English teachers) to show that reading because we like reading is one of the hallmarks of civilised adult life.

And another answer is to teach **reading behaviours**. I'll share four such behaviours with you shortly, but first another anecdote.

Inspiration
Telling my story

Libraries gave us power

I was invited to Finland a few years ago to work with schools and colleges in their capital city, Helsinki. Six months earlier, I'd travelled to Estonia for similar reasons. While I was in both countries, I was afforded the opportunity to analyse what they did in order to be ranked among the most literate nations on Earth.

After much analysis, I decided that there was really only one secret – and it was a secret hidden in plain sight: in Finland and Estonia, children love books. They read lots of them and they do so from an early age. Indeed, a study by John W. Miller that pitched Finland as the world's most literate nation did so based on what he called 'literate behaviours'.[7]

I once delivered training at a Muslim girls' school which referred to its library as 'the place of knowledge'. It stopped me in my tracks. The deputy head, noting my excitement, explained that many Islamic countries call their libraries 'dar al-'ilm', which translates as 'the house of knowledge'.

Public libraries – or 'houses of knowledge' – started to appear in major Islamic cities around the world in circa the ninth century. They were intended to promote the dissemination of secular knowledge. Islamic libraries are thought to have been the first to have implemented a catalogue of owned materials. In other words, the content of a bookshelf was recorded on paper and attached to the end of each shelf, and books were organised by name or nature.

Arab-Islamic people were strong advocates of public knowledge, and information was offered freely to every member of society rather than reserved for clerics and academics. Some 'houses of knowledge' were said to have permitted lenders to check out up to 200 items at any one time and the buildings were designed for readers' comfort.

The destruction of many libraries by Mongol invasions – and later through a succession of wars – signalled a decline of learning and, one might argue, a less liberal, less secular, less inclusive way of life.

I was rather taken with the fact the school I visited called its library a 'place of knowledge' (but then I'm also rather taken when schools call their libraries 'libraries' rather than the dry, prosaic alternative 'learning resource centre'). I was also impressed that they had made their 'place of knowledge' a central feature of the school building; it acted as the school's beating heart, pumping knowledge through its artery of corridors and into classrooms. The library's language and location signalled its importance as a hub in which to study and in which to learn.

Sadly, for the last decade or so, school libraries have been under threat from budget cuts. And they are not the only libraries to be endangered. Central and local library services have also been under increasing pressure due to repeated cuts in council funding since 2010.

Closing libraries is not the act of a civilised society.

In an article for *SecEd Magazine* in May 2023,[8] I talked about 'the home advantage' afforded to affluent, middle-class learners. I said that, increasingly, "learners are expected to complete work at home, whether homework, coursework, or revision [and] those who do not have a home life conducive to independent study are therefore placed at a disadvantage, compounded for those who do not have parents with the capacity to support them (in terms of time, ability, or the money to buy resources or indeed private tutoring)".

These young people rely on public services such as libraries to mitigate the disadvantages into which they were born. And yet, as I argued in the same article, "spending cuts have led to a steep decline in the number of libraries and to cuts to the opening hours of those that remain. The last decade or so has seen spending on libraries fall by a quarter and 773 libraries close – that's one fifth of libraries in the UK".

Libraries are more important than ever, and we must protect them.

Creating good readers

Into practice
Writing your story

Earlier, I said we can help the word-poor become richer by teaching reading behaviours. Broadly, there are four behaviours associated with good reading comprehension:

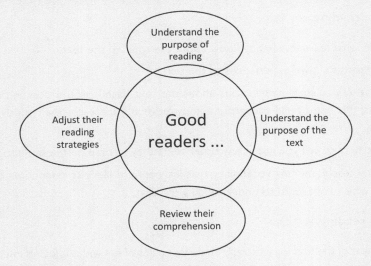

Firstly, *good readers understand the purpose of reading*, and so are able to adjust their reading style accordingly. In other words, they know why they are reading and how they should read. They can skim the contents page, chapter headings, and paragraph openings to get the gist of a text and to extract key information which enables them to interpret what a text means on the basis of their prior knowledge.

Secondly, *good readers understand the purpose of the text*: good readers are not only purposeful themselves, but they also understand that writers are purposeful. A writer may wish to provide very simple information (e.g. instructions for assembling a cabinet) or more complex information (e.g. a report on stem cell research). A writer may wish to persuade, inform, or entertain the reader. A writer may wish to present opinions as indisputable fact. Understanding a writer's purpose makes good readers aware of how particular literary devices are being used to influence their response.

Thirdly, *good readers review their comprehension*: good readers constantly review, analyse, and assess their comprehension in order to ensure there are no gaps in their understanding. They relate information in a text to their own experiences or prior knowledge and evaluate information to determine whether it confirms or contradicts what they already know. This is known as schema theory. Good readers ask questions as they read and search for the answers in the text.

And finally, *good readers adjust their reading strategies*: good readers are able to adjust their reading strategies, slowing their reading speed when sentences are long and complex, re-reading a section if they begin to lose meaning, and drawing inferences from surrounding text or using their letter-sound knowledge in order to help construct the meaning of unfamiliar words. Good readers can also pause to take notes which help them retain complex information.

To help the word-poor embed these four behaviours in their reading, you can do the following.

Before reading, you can:

- Explore what learners already know about the topic of the text.
- Relate learners' own experiences to the text.
- Ask learners to make predictions about the text based on the title and any illustrations; this helps build background knowledge and increases their motivation for reading.
- Ask learners to tell you about any other texts they've read on the same topic.
- Explicitly teach any new vocabulary that learners are likely to encounter, especially words which are crucial to understanding the text.

While reading, you can:

- Read most of the text – particularly important parts of it – without lots of interruptions so that learners can understand the plot and structure (following a sequence of events) and so that learners can attune to the written style. Asking questions before and after reading the text is more effective and less intrusive than questions asked during reading.
- Signpost the new vocabulary you taught before reading.
- Pause occasionally – where appropriate – to gauge learners' reactions: ask for comments, questions, and predictions.
- Teach learners strategies for regaining the meaning of a text when they begin to struggle or lose interest: e.g. re-read the sentence carefully and think about what might make sense; re-read the sentence before and after the one you're stuck on, looking for familiar words inside or around an unfamiliar word.
- Teach learners to monitor their understanding of the text by using post-it notes or page markers. Post-it notes could be used to indicate a connection between the text

and a prior experience or piece of knowledge, as well as between the text and another text; to identify information which surprised them; and to highlight something learners want to ask later.

After reading, you can:

- Teach learners how to identify the key words in a passage (the words that explain who, what, where, when, how, or why).

- Teach learners note-*making* skills – as opposed to note-*taking* – and other ways of summarising information such as graphic organisers (e.g. story maps, timelines, flow charts, plot profiles, etc.).

- Ask questions that help learners to identify a sequence of events.

- Teach learners to look out for cause-and-effect relationships.

- Ask learners to rewrite the text in a different form: for example, from a diary to a timeline, from a set of instructions to a flow chart, from a piece of descriptive writing to a drawing.

- Teach learners to use reference material such as a dictionary and thesaurus, a glossary and bibliography.

What have we learned?

In this chapter, we have discovered that:

Children who benefit from bedtime stories early in their lives get exposed to a broader and richer vocabulary than those children whose language exposure is limited to everyday spoken conversations. Accordingly, these children arrive at school better prepared for reading. Although vocabulary is complex, it is also crucial to developing reading comprehension.

Broadly speaking, good reading comprehension is built on four behaviours. Good readers:

1. Understand the purpose of reading

2. Understand the purpose of the text

3. Review their comprehension,

4. Adjust their reading strategies

What can we do?

To put the advice contained in this chapter into practice, it might be helpful to consider the following questions:

1. Is there a literacy gap in your school? Whose literacy is below expected standards and how do you know? What more can you do to address this deficit?

2. Do you use group work activities in your lessons to help the word-poor mingle with the word-rich?

3. Do you model higher-order reading skills in class?

4. Do you promote a love of reading? Do all your colleagues across the school? How?

5. Do you have a school library? Is it used? By whom, for what, and how often? What more could you do to encourage those with low levels of literacy and little to no access to books at home to access the library more?

6. Do all teachers in your school teach subject-specific reading behaviours?

Notes

1 https://literacytrust.org.uk/research-services/research-reports/seldom-heard-voices-adult-literacy-in-the-uk/

2 See: www.oecd.org/skills/piaac/ Also: www.oecd.org/skills/piaac/Country%20note%20-%20United%20Kingdom.pdf

3 https://literacytrust.org.uk/research-services/research-reports/seldom-heard-voices-adult-literacy-in-the-uk/

4 The sources for these statistics can be found in the following reports: www.probonoeconomics.com/paying-the-price-the-cost-of-very-poor-adult-literacy; https://literacytrust.org.uk/research-services/research-reports/literacy-and-life-expectancy/

5 Rigney, D (2010). The *Matthew Effect: How Advantage Begets Further Advantage*. Columbia University Press.

6 See Hart, B & Risley, T R (1995). *Meaningful Differences in the Everyday Experience of Young American Children*. Brookes. Also: Hart, B & Risley, T R (2003). The early catastrophe: The 30 million word gap by age 3. *American Educator*, 27(1), 4–9.

7 Miller, J W (2016). *World Literacy: How Countries Rank and Why It Matters*. Routledge.

8 www.sec-ed.co.uk/content/best-practice/working-class-students-in-pursuit-of-equity-in-education

5 The stories beyond comprehension

Articulate like an automaton

Inspiration
Telling my story

A few years ago, I discovered an app which collates reading material – newspaper articles and webpages, say – and converts them into audio so that I could listen to them on my daily dog walks. Text-to-speech technology allowed me to 'read' articles and research papers while on the move. But there was a problem …

Like all text-to-speech programs, the speaking voice on my app was somewhat stilted and robotic and was unable to detect nuance. Of course, it might be argued that most written texts lack nuance because it's difficult to discern – accurately and with any surety – the writer's mood and intended tone of voice. Short-form texts and transactional texts which are ephemeral, contemporaneous, and written hastily – such as text messages, social media posts, and emails – are particularly difficult to 'read' for 'voice'. It's difficult to identify sarcasm, for example, and often a tongue-in-cheek 'joke' is interpreted as rude or offensive. Try saying 'shut up' in as many tones of voice as possible. Say it as if you're furious. Now as if you're embarrassed. And scared. And irritated. Bored, even. Tired. And so on. Tone matters.

But with text-to-speech, this difficulty to discern tone is writ particularly large. What was lacking from the app's robotic voice was comprehension or, more accurately, fluency. The automated voice merely sounded out letters and letter combinations without any sense of meaning. The robot didn't know, for example, whether the word 'read' should be pronounced as 'red' or 'reed'. And it certainly didn't know if words should be read in a happy or sad tone. So, what is fluency and why is it important?

Fluent in the language of reading

Fluency is the ability to read text quickly and accurately, adopting the appropriate intonation. It requires some background knowledge about the text, as well as an ability to rapidly retrieve the requisite vocabulary. Fluency also requires a knowledge of syntax and grammar in order to predict the words that are likely to appear next. Let me illustrate.

DOI: 10.4324/9781003465492-6

Read the following sentence quickly and instinctively (i.e. without looking ahead):

He could lead if he would get the lead out.

How about this one:

The dump was so full that it had to refuse more refuse.

And:

The bandage was wound around the wound.

The ability to adapt one's vocabulary and intonation according to a text's syntax and grammar, and the ability to read ahead, helps with both speed and accuracy.

English is not easy, of course. Just think of the number of ways in which -ough can be pronounced:

A rough-coated, dough-faced, thoughtful ploughman strode through the streets of Scarborough; after falling into a slough, he coughed and hiccoughed.

Experienced readers integrate these processes so that reading becomes automatic, which allows their cognitive energy to be focused on the task of discerning meaning. A useful analogy would be learning to tie your shoelaces. When you first learn to tie your laces, because it is an unfamiliar task, you must dedicate all your attention to it, utilising your working memory. You must concentrate on how to tie your laces, what goes where and in what order, and so cannot concentrate on anything else at the same time. To do so would be to reach *cognitive overload* whereby thinking and doing fails. When you are first learning to tie your shoelaces, it is difficult – if not impossible – to do so while engaging in a conversation, for example. However, once you've mastered the art of lace tying – through repeated exposure to the task – you reach the point of *automaticity*, thus you can do it through habit without having to think about it. This frees up valuable space in your working memory to dedicate to other tasks, such as holding a conversation.

Unconvinced? Think about the first time you tried to drive a car. It felt difficult, didn't it? You had so much to remember and do. Controlling the pedals, the steering wheel, the indicator stalks – all while keeping a constant watch on the windscreen, rear-view mirror, and wing mirrors – was so difficult that it took all your working memory capacity, and you couldn't possibly do anything else at the same time. Now, however, you can drive and talk fluently to your passenger. In fact, and I'm not suggesting this is a good thing, you can drive so easily and habitually that I bet you sometimes arrive home and can't remember a single thing about the journey; you didn't think about it at all! Now that's automaticity!

Reading is just the same. Through repeated exposure to reading, to decoding words and their meanings, you come to do it automatically, which frees up cognitive capacity for you to read ahead, to think about syntax and grammar, and to discern meaning and tone, context and connotation, bias, and allusion. All of this enables you to truly understand a text. In other words, there is a strong correlation between fluency and reading comprehension; indeed, it is such a strong link that fluency and comprehension can be regarded as interdependent. After all, fluency only occurs when a reader understands the text; if reading is hesitant and disjointed, all sense of meaning is lost. It is impossible to be a fluent reader if you must keep stopping to work out what a word is. To be fluent you must move beyond the decoding stage to accurately read whole words.

A fluent reader has ready access to a vast bank of words which can be used in different contexts. The words to which a reader has immediate access are called their 'sight vocabulary'. Even complex words that originally had to be decoded – like 'originally' and 'decoded' rather than monosyllabic functional words like 'that' and 'had' – but which can now be recognised on sight become a part of the fluent reader's lexicon. But recognition is not enough to achieve fluency. As well as being in the reader's sight vocabulary, words must also be stored in their 're-ceptive vocabulary' – that is to say, words which the reader knows the meaning of. The larger the bank of words that are both recognised and understood on sight, then the broader the range of texts which are accessible. For this reason, developing sight vocabularies and receptive vocabularies is the most effective way of developing both fluency and reading comprehension.

Once children's sight and receptive vocabularies have been developed, they need to be exposed to texts that are appropriate to their age and reading ability so that they do not contain unfamiliar or technical words that are outside children's knowledge bases. This is why early readers need simple texts to help them develop both speed and confidence. Although it's sometimes tempting to give children 'harder books' as a way of challenging them, this is not always the best approach. Texts within a child's knowledge base provide them with opportu-nities to practise their vocabulary, develop appropriate expression, and build confidence and belief in themselves as readers.

Once they've developed accuracy, children need to develop speed, increasing the rate at which they can access texts. Reading speed is also strongly linked with reading comprehension. When a reader is both accurate and quick, word identification becomes automated and they no longer require cognitive energy or attention, thus freeing up precious space in the working memory for higher-order comprehension. Reading speed is not the same as reading fast. Peo-ple who read too quickly and therefore show no regard for punctuation, intonation, or com-prehension are not fluent readers. Reading speed is about being able to process texts quickly while understanding the text and taking account of punctuation and adopting an appropriate intonation. In short, improving children's reading speed is important but it must not be at the expense of comprehension. As a 'back of an envelope' calculation, the average reading speed in the primary phase is as follows:

- By the end of Year 1 = 60 words per minute

- By the end of Year 2 = 90/100 words per minute

- In Years 3 to 6 = 100–120 words per minute with fewer than 3 errors

After accuracy and speed, prosody – that is to say, reading with expression – is the third component of reading fluently. Prosody is more difficult to achieve than accuracy and speed because it involves developing stress, pitch, and rhythm. However, prosody is essential in rendering reading aloud meaningful. Poor prosody can cause confusion and has an impact on readers' interest and motivation to read. Good prosody, meanwhile, makes reading aloud come alive and reflects the author's message more accurately and more meaningfully. In sum:

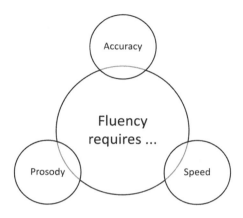

Modelling fluency

Into practice
Writing your story

One of the best ways for teachers to help learners develop fluency is to read aloud to them in an engaging and motivating way to model fluency for them. This might include:

- Doing all the voices when reading aloud, adding sound effects and dramatic pauses to heighten learners' engagement.

- Using 'fluency cards' which contain lines of single letters and common letter combinations because fluency is achieved through automatic recognition of words and parts of words, including letter sounds.

- Displaying high-frequency irregular words. Word walls – when they are referred to and used in quizzes – help build learners' automatic recognition of words.

- Giving direct instruction in how to read punctuation. Most learners, although they know how to punctuate their writing, have less idea how to read punctuation.

- Engaging in whole class reading of short pieces of dialogue. This is a low-risk activity – particularly when the teacher reads the passage first and then learners repeat it – which builds fluency in lower-ability readers.

- Repeatedly reading a text to provide the practice needed to develop accuracy, speed, and confidence. Pair learners up and ask the more fluent reader to model the appropriate rate and intonation for the less fluent reader, who then repeats the passage. Alternatively, ask both learners to read simultaneously. The more fluent reader in the pair is likely to start fractionally ahead of the less fluent reader, modelling accuracy, rate, and intonation, but as the less fluent reader gains in confidence, the two learners will blend together.

● Reading lots of poetry. Poetry tends to have a natural rhythm when it is read aloud.

● Reading aloud from a script, say a monologue or short scene. The focus is not on dramatic kinaesthetic performance but on interpreting the text using only the voice.

● Listening to audio books or asking older volunteers (parents, local people, sixth formers) to record their favourite stories to play to the class.

What have we learned?

In this chapter, we have discovered that:

The ability to read text quickly and accurately, adopting the appropriate intonation, is called *fluency*. It requires background knowledge about a text, as well as an ability to quickly retrieve the vocabulary that's needed to understand the text. It also requires a working knowledge of syntax and grammar so that the reader can predict what's likely to appear next. Reading aloud to learners in an engaging manner is one of the most effective means of developing their fluency.

What can we do?

To put the advice contained in this chapter into practice, it might be helpful to consider the following questions:

1. Do you explicitly teach accuracy, speed, and prosody to develop your learners' reading fluency and do so in a subject-specific way? When, and how? Does it work? How do you know? What more could you do to improve reading fluency?

2. Do you read aloud to the class and model appropriate intonation? Do you think aloud while so doing to model your thought processes?

3. Do you use fluency cards and/or display high-frequency irregular words? Do you give direct instruction on how to read punctuation?

*

So far, we've explored the stories we tell ourselves and those we tell our children, as well as considering the importance of storytelling to literacy. All of this brings me to the stories we tell our learners …

In Part 2, I'll explore ways of using story to improve our teaching.

PART 2
Teaching through storytelling

will reach the ambitious destinations we plan for them to reach but if we don't set them on a journey towards these destinations, we can be sure they won't.

The destination is what we want learners to know and do at the end — what knowledge, skills, and understanding we want them to acquire. These outcomes should not only be what's needed to pass exams and get qualifications, though this is undoubtedly important; rather, these outcomes should equip learners with the tools they need to be fully prepared for the next stage of their lives and to be independent and successful. The starting points tell us what learners already know and what they can already do, as well as what gaps exist in their prior knowledge and what misconceptions they bring with them which need addressing. The waypoints are the threshold concepts which mark progression, checkpoints through which learners must pass in order to possess the knowledge and skills required to move on to more challenging curriculum content. Think of waypoints as stepping stones or rather rungs on a ladder that lead learners upwards towards ever more complex concepts.

But, having mixed my metaphors, I'd now like to switch analogies. Rather than articulate the curriculum as a journey, I think it's better to compare the curriculum to a story — permit me another anecdote to explain why.

Inspiration
Telling my story

Taking 'the lead'

Having worked on a student newspaper while at university as a sports and features writer reporting on, among other things, Hull City home games (which involved a terrifying climb up the side of a crumbling stadium to a commentary box literally hanging from the rafters), I started as a part-time apprentice on my local paper. I spent my days manning a complaints line in a call centre and then walked across town to the newsroom to work evenings. Every day I was sworn at, belittled, and abused — and the complaints line was no better.

This was the mid-90s and the newsroom was always shrouded in a fog of cigar smoke, seasoned reporters reeked of alcohol from long lunches, and it wasn't so much what you knew as who you knew that dictated which journo got the biggest by-lines. I was an anonymous apprentice, somewhat shy and nervous around the big beasts, but eager to learn the trade. Although my tenure was short-lived and my by-line appeared on only a handful of sidebar pieces (garden fetes, charity walks, neighbourly disputes, etc.), I did learn something that stuck with me and proved useful when, some years later, I became an English teacher.

I learned a technique called the 'inverted pyramid structure', which dictates how to order a news report. The inverted pyramid — think of it as an upside-down triangle — acts as a funnel whereby the key facts are filtered into finer details the further into the report you read. The mouth of the funnel, its widest point, is at the top, which means the first sentence of a report should contain all the key facts of the matter. To be more specific, the opening sentence of a well-written news article should answer the following questions: Who? What? Where? When? The order can be altered for effect as so:

Mickey Mouse (the 'who?') died (the 'what?') at Disneyland Paris (the 'where?') yesterday (the 'when?').

Yesterday, Mickey Mouse died at Disneyland Paris.

At Disneyland Paris yesterday, Mickey Mouse died.[2]

Sometimes there are two *who's* in a story: the subject (the do-er) and the object (the done-to), thus:

Minnie Mouse (the subject) shot dead Mickey Mouse (the done-to) at Disneyland Paris yesterday.

But the point remains that the first sentence packs a punch and sets out the key facts of a story. This is called 'the lead'. Some hacks are accused of 'burying the lead', which means they fail to emphasise the most important part of a story or hide the real scoop among other distracting information. But I digress – well, sort of …

One of the reasons I think we should use storytelling techniques to organise our curriculum and structure lessons is to ensure we don't 'bury the lead' and distract learners from the curriculum content we need them to learn. 'The lead' is what we want learners to know and do at the end – be that the end of a lesson, sequence of lessons, topic, course, or at the end of schooling. It is our 'destination'.

The process of learning is the interaction between the sensory memory and the long-term memory. The sensory memory is made up of what we see – this is called our iconic memory; what we hear – this is called our echoic memory; and what we touch – our haptic memory. The long-term memory, meanwhile, is where new information is stored and from which it can be recalled when needed, but the information stored in long-term memory cannot be directly accessed. As such, the interaction that takes place between the sensory memory and the long-term memory occurs in the working memory, which is where we think and do. It is all too easy for learning to fail simply because we haven't gained learners' active attention (identified the lead) or because we have focused their attention on the wrong things (buried the lead). Identifying the lead is important because if learners don't think, they don't learn. I'll come back to 'the lead' shortly.

Hooking the fish

As I said in my story above, the inverted pyramid structure refers to news reports where readers require facts. Newspaper columns – thought pieces, comment pieces, investigative pieces, and long reads – run by different rules. Here, it's best to start with a 'hook'. A hook is an anecdote or idea which relates – perhaps directly or perhaps tangentially – to the content of the article; it adds colour and texture.

Using story in teaching requires both identifying 'the lead' and using 'hooks'.

For the past ten years, I've had a regular column in the education magazine *SecEd*. Many of my articles start with a hook – although it's a bone of contention with my editor that when I file an article over the word count (which is *every* article), the first thing to go is my carefully crafted, highly amusing hook! The hook brings a story to life; it makes it more relatable, more easily understood, and more personal.

For my article about dealing with low-level disruption in the classroom, I recalled the time I was stuck on a train with two intoxicated passengers:

Imagine, if you will, an intercity train from the 1970s. You know the type: a rust-bucket with well-worn seats in brown-and-orange hues. Now imagine that same train rattling through the Pennines half a century later, coughing diesel fumes.

Recently, I travelled on that train to visit a school. I was fortunate to find a seat and managed to squeeze my laptop onto the pull-down tray table and set to work. My productivity was short-lived. At the next station, two party-goers boarded. I shall call these passengers Sharon and Steve, for these were their names; monikers they repeatedly hollered at each other.

Sharon and Steve were three sheets to the wind and on their way to a karaoke bar. They made good use of their time aboard to practise their singing (a term I use quite loosely). They were harmless, just drunk and happy and loud. Truth be told, I was more jealous than annoyed. But they did break my concentration. Try as I might, Sharon and Steve's raucous behaviour made it impossible for me to work and so I stared at my screen for the next hour, not a single word written or read.

Which brings me to the subject of low-level disruption in the classroom. How many of our pupils are prevented from learning by the behaviour of their fellow class-mates? How many are unable to concentrate because the kid in the corner is acting the class-clown again? And, more importantly, what can we, as teachers, do about it?

Tackling low-level disruption in the classroom,
Matt Bromley, *SecEd*, November 2021[3]

And for my article exploring Robert Gagné's Nine Events of Instruction, as a hook I shared my experiences of learning to ice-skate:

I've started ice skating lessons. Think of me not as some pound-shop Christopher Dean in sequined Lycra, but as a middle-aged father talked into supporting his daughters. I am, by some margin, the oldest person on the ice. Most of the other skaters are young children. The coaches are half my age. The experience is a masterclass in being stranded far outside one's comfort zone.

I often talk to new teachers about the importance of learning to fall – facing your fears and doing it anyway. Well... My most spectacular fall occurred the night I had to drive from the arena to give a talk. I lost my footing while forward gliding at speed and fell backwards, cracking my head and back hard on the ice. Later, I hobbled onto the stage like an octogenarian.

The experience, though, has been enlightening. There's something about learning a new skill – where you are devoid of prior knowledge – that really focuses your attention on the process rather than the content. It has reminded me of Gagné's nine principles.

Nine principles of effective teaching, Matt Bromley, *SecEd*, July 2023[4]

The above hooks were intended to grab my readers' attention and to help them remember the content of my articles. Hooks in teaching act in the same way. Hooks stimulate learners' senses to help gain the active attention of their working memories. The more powerful, sensorily, a hook is – in other words, the more it appeals to the various senses – then the more evocative the memory will be and thus the more securely the information being imparted will be stored in, and be retrievable from, long-term memory.

In teaching, these hooks might take the following forms[5]:

1. **Instant immersion in questions:** Problems, challenges, situations, or stories that require learners' wits, not just knowledge.

2. **Thought provocations:** Anomalies, weird facts, counter-intuitive events or ideas, and mysteries that appeal to the gut, making the strange familiar and the familiar strange.

3. **Experiential shocks:** This type of activity can be characterised as an intellectual outward-bound experience in which students have to confront feelings, obstacles, and problems personally and as a group to accomplish a task.

4. **Personal connection:** Students often become more engaged when given opportunities to make a personal connection to the topic or to pursue a matter of interest.

5. **Differing points of view or multiple perspectives:** A deliberate shift of perspective can nudge students out of their comfort zone to stimulate wonderment and deeper thinking.

Using leads and hooks in teaching

I said I'd come back to the use of 'the lead'. To do that, let's go back to basics and ask, 'What is a story?'

The Cambridge Dictionary defines a story as "a description, either true or imagined, of a connected series of events".[6] Merriam-Webster, meanwhile, says it is "an account of incidents or events".[7] Story is narrative; it connects events in a chain to suggest causality or reason. Story, as I have already argued, brings order to chaos.

A story commonly has a beginning that sets up a conflict or expectation, a middle that complicates it, and an end that resolves it. The defining feature of stories, as distinct from other kinds of text which might be said to contain a narrative such as essays, historical records, scientific reports, and so on, is that stories orient our feelings about their contents.

I believe we should rethink the school curriculum not as set of objectives to be met, but as a good story to be told.

Curriculum as story

To structure the curriculum as a story to be told, we might:

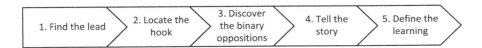

Step 1. Find the lead: What is the most important 'takeaway' from this subject/unit/topic? What knowledge, skills, and understanding do we need learners to acquire? Why does/ will this matter to learners?

Step 2. Locate the hook: What is the most interesting and engaging aspect of this subject/ unit/topic? What will pique learners' curiosity? What questions beg urgent answers and will make learners hungry for knowledge?

Step 3. Discover the binary oppositions: What powerful binary opposites best capture the importance of this subject/unit/topic? (Refer back to Chapter 2 for more on 'binary oppositions'.)

Step 4. Tell the story: What narrative best articulates the subject/unit/topic in story form? What is the beginning, where's the conflict? What's the middle, where's the complication? What's the end, where's the resolution?

Step 5. Define the learning: Has the subject/unit/topic been understood? What knowledge, skills and understanding have learners taken away? How does this relate to the real world? What's next for learners? How will this learning be consolidated and extended?

Story as lesson structure

As well as using storytelling techniques to organise the curriculum and structure lessons, they can also lend structure to the teaching strategies we employ in lessons. Here are two to consider: *Show don't tell* and *Flashback and flashforward*.

Show don't tell

Storytelling can also be used as a framework for teacher explanations and modelling – which can be an effective way to make complex or abstract concepts more accessible and relatable for learners. By framing our explanations as stories, we can help learners understand how different pieces of information fit together and how they relate to real-world situations.

I have long advocated a four-step sequence for introducing learners to new information. The four steps are:

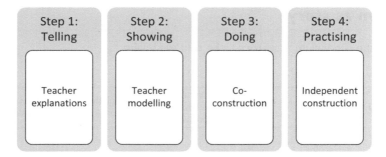

Telling – or teacher explanation – works best when the teacher presents new material to learners in small chunks and provides scaffolds and targeted support.

Showing – or teacher modelling – works best when the teacher models a new procedure by, among other strategies, thinking aloud, guiding learners' initial practice, and providing learners with cues.

Doing – or co-construction – works best when the teacher provides learners with 'fix-up' strategies – corrections and 'live' feedback.

Practising – or independent construction – works best when the teacher provides planned opportunities in class for extensive independent practice.

Of course, the process does not end here; rather, learners need to garner feedback on their independent practice and then act on that feedback in order to improve by increments. I'll come to feedback shortly, but let's focus now on the uses of story and storytelling for framing teacher explanations and modelling.

Teacher explanations remain the most efficient method of teaching, not to mention the least likely to lead to misconceptions among learners and a misunderstanding by the teacher of what learners can and cannot do.

The best teacher explanations make use of storytelling techniques such as metaphors and analogies because this enables the teacher to contextualise new information so that abstract ideas or hitherto alien concepts are made concrete, tangible, and real, and so that they are related to learners' own lives and experiences.

The best teacher explanations follow the storytelling maxim of 'show don't tell'. One way to do this is to utilise dual coding. In other words, teachers' verbal instructions, as well as any text-based explanations displayed on the board or in handouts, are paired with and complemented by visuals such as diagrams, charts, graphics, and moving images in order to show not tell.

And the best teacher explanations, like the best stories, are reciprocated. Thus, learners tell their own stories, explaining concepts back to the teacher as well as to each other. This works on the basis that only once you teach something have you truly learned it.

Once teachers have explained something, they should make effective and plentiful use of models – exemplars of both good and bad work, as well as exemplars from a range of different contexts – which show learners what a final product should look like and what makes such products work. Modelling *is* storytelling writ large.

Good models demonstrate what works as well as what doesn't. It is important to show learners what excellence looks like by sharing models of the very best work, giving them something to aspire to and an understanding of how to produce high-quality work of their own. But it is equally important to show learners models of ineffective work, work that isn't quite the best, so that learners can learn what not to do and how to avoid making the same mistakes themselves.

All the models that are shared should be dissected in front of learners, with the teacher demonstrating the dissection process. For example, if a model of a persuasive speech is shown on the board, the teacher should analyse it using text marking, pointing out and then annotating how it works, what makes it effective, breaking it apart to identify and discuss each of its component parts. Then the teacher should reconstruct the speech, explaining how the component parts hang together to create an effective argument, and how the whole becomes something much greater than the sum of its parts.

Here are some ways we can use storytelling as a framework for teacher explanations and modelling:

1. **Begin with a hook:** Hooks aren't just useful for units or topics; as I explored above, they can also be used at the start of a teacher explanation to grab learners' attention and pique their curiosity. The hook could be a surprising fact, a relevant anecdote, or a dramatic opening statement.

2. **Use analogies and metaphors:** Analogies and metaphors can be used to explain complex concepts in a way that's more relatable and understandable for learners. For example, a maths teacher might use a baking analogy to explain fractions, or a science teacher might use a sports analogy to explain the properties of motion.

3. **Create a narrative arc:** Teacher explanations, not just whole topics, can be structured as a narrative arc, with a clear beginning, middle, and end. This helps to create a sense of coherence and understanding for learners because they can see how each piece of information fits into the larger narrative.

4. **Dual code:** Visuals, such as images or videos, can be used to enhance the narrative and help learners to visualise the concepts being explained. This can make the explanation more engaging and memorable for learners.

5. **Use real-world examples:** Real-world examples can help to ground abstract concepts in sensory reality and make them more tangible for learners. This can be news stories, historical events, or personal anecdotes which illustrate how the concepts being explained apply to real-life situations.

Overall, using storytelling as a framework for teacher explanations and modelling can help make learning more engaging and effective for learners. Moreover, by framing explanations as narratives and incorporating analogies, metaphors, visuals, and real-world examples into teacher modelling, we can help learners to understand complex concepts in a way that is meaningful and relatable.

Flashback and flashforward

Stories don't have to be linear, told in chronological order. Indeed, some novels, such as Martin Amis's *Time's Arrow*, are told backwards; others move back and forth in time to conceal or reveal key information so that it has the most impact dramatically and emotionally. Two common storytelling techniques that play with a plot's timeline are 'flashback' and 'flashforward'.

As I'm sure you know, a flashback (sometimes called an analepsis) is an interjected scene that takes the narrative back in time from the timeframe of the main plot. Flashbacks are often used to recount events that happened before the story began and are used as a mechanism for providing backstory that can provide valuable insights into the reason for current events and into characters' motivations.

A flashforward (also called a prolepsis), meanwhile, is an interjected scene that takes the narrative forward in time from the current timeframe. Flashforwards are often used to show events that are expected or projected to occur at some point in the future. They may also reveal significant parts of the story that have not yet occurred.

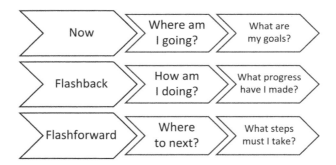

These storytelling techniques can be particularly useful when giving feedback to learners. Why? Because, in my opinion, the best feedback does not compare a learner with other learners in a class (which is, for the learner at least, an arbitrary and pointless comparison because the two learners are different people with different starting points, different interests and different abilities) but, rather, compares each learner with their earlier self by articulating the 'story arc' the learner is following.

Firstly, feedback reminds learners where they are going – their intended outcomes, which might be a goal or set of success criteria. Secondly, feedback shows learners where they've been – their starting points and the progress they've made thus far from those starting points. This might include observations on what they've done well and/or what they could have done better. Then, feedback – or more accurately 'feedforward' – provides actionable steps for learners to take in order for them to make further such progress.

Feedback is, therefore, twofold: it is *feeding back* on the progress made so far and *feeding forward* to what needs to be done next to make continued or expedited progress. Feedback thus makes use of the storytelling techniques of flashback and flashforward to inform a learner's narrative.

Further, research has found that narrative – or 'comment only' – feedback is more effective than giving learners assessment marks or a combination of marks and comments. Narrative feedback causes thinking and gives learners something to act upon and do. Therefore, feedback might best follow the structure of a story in that it has a beginning, middle, and end:.

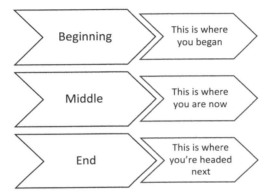

Keep it simple, stupid

Let's return to the nub of this chapter: how to use story and storytelling techniques to organise the curriculum and structure lessons.

When using story to structure a lesson, it's best to focus on one main concept at a time. This is called chunking. Chunking is when we combine information into meaningful units to utilise our limited working memory capacity. It might take the form of a mnemonic or other memory aid, or it might take the form of small steps of instruction. To illustrate, let's return to the subject of the article I cited earlier about Robert Gagné's Nine Events of Instruction.

In 1965, Gagné proposed a series of nine events which offer a useful way of thinking about chunking and sequencing learning.[8] The events are as follows:

1. **Gain learners' attention:** Gagné advised that teachers ensure learners are ready to learn by presenting a stimulus to capture their attention. In practice, this might mean stimulating learners with something novel or different.

2. **Objectives or learning intentions:** Once teachers have gained learners' attentions, Gagné advised they inform learners of the objectives or outcomes of the unit or lesson to help them understand what they are expected to learn and do, and why this matters.

3. **Recall of prior learning:** The third layer in Gagné's sequence is helping learners to make sense of new information by relating it to something they already know or something they have already experienced. Connecting the learning is about explicitly sharing learning goals, making clear what success looks like and how learners are going to achieve it. It is also about sharing the purpose of learning – making clear why learners need to achieve

the learning goals and of what use their learning will be to them in the future. And, finally, it is about sharing learners' starting points – understanding what prior knowledge and skills learners bring with them.

4. **Present the content:** The fourth event is to use strategies to present and cue lesson content to provide more effective instruction. Gagné advised teachers to organise and group content in meaningful ways and provide explanations after demonstrations.

5. **Provide learning guidance:** The fifth event is to advise learners about strategies to aid them in learning content and tell them about the available resources. In other words, help students learn how to learn.

6. **Elicit performance (practice):** Gagné said that learners should apply what they have learned to reinforce new skills and knowledge and to confirm correct understanding of course concepts. This may take two forms – joint practice, then independent practice.

7. **Provide feedback:** Gagné argued that teachers should provide timely feedback of learners' performance to assess and facilitate learning and to allow learners to identify gaps in understanding before it is too late.

8. **Assess performance:** Gagné argued that following feedback teachers need to test whether the expected learning outcomes have been achieved on previously stated course objectives.

9. **Enhance retention and transfer:** To end his sequence, Gagné argued that teachers need to help learners retain more information by providing them with opportunities to connect classroom concepts to potential real-world applications. This might be done by associating lesson concepts with prior (and future) concepts and by building upon prior (and preview future) learning to reinforce connections. It might be done by incorporating questions from previous tests in subsequent examinations to reinforce lesson information. It might be done by having learners convert information learned in one format into another format. And it might be done by clearly articulating lesson goals, using specific goals to guide instructional design, and aligning learning activities to lesson goals.

We might regard these nine steps as chapters of a novel or plot points on a narrative arc. They give shape and structure to learning and help learners understand the bigger picture.

The 4Cs of story

In his paper, 'The privileged status of story', cognitive scientist Daniel Willingham says that there are 'important cognitive consequences of the story format'.[9]

Psychologists refer to stories as 'psychologically privileged', meaning our minds treat stories differently to other types of material. "People find stories interesting, easy to understand, and easy to remember", Willingham says, and "to understand why these benefits accrue, it is necessary to understand the underlying format of stories."

Definitions of *story* vary, but a useful starting point, according to Willingham, is to consider how professional storytellers – that is, playwrights, screenwriters, and novelists – define *story*.

There is relative agreement, Willingham says, on the basic features of good stories – which are sometimes called 'The 4Cs':

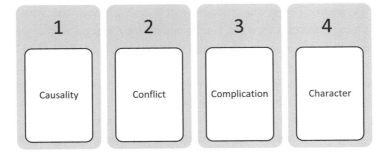

Below, I've paraphrased Willingham's description of each C:

1. **Causality:** Events in stories are related because one event causes or initiates another. For example, "The King died and then the Queen died" presents two events chronologically, but "The King died and the Queen died of grief" links the events with causal information.

2. **Conflict:** In every story, a central character has a goal and obstacles that prevent the goal from being met. "Scarlett O'Hara loved Ashley Wilkes, so she married him" has causality, but it's not much of a story. A story moves forward as the character takes action to remove the obstacle. In *Gone with the Wind*, the first obstacle Scarlett faces is that Ashley doesn't love her.

3. **Complications:** If a story were just a series of episodes in which the character hammers away at her goal, it would be dull. Rather, the character's efforts to remove the obstacle typically create complications – new problems that she must try to solve. When Scarlett learns that Ashley doesn't love her, she tries to make him jealous by agreeing to marry Charles Hamilton, an action that, indeed, poses new complications for her.

4. **Character:** Strong, interesting characters are essential to good stories, and screenwriters agree that the key to creating interesting characters is to allow the audience to observe them in action. F. Scott Fitzgerald went so far as to write "Action is character".[10] Rather than tell us that Scarlett O'Hara is popular and a coquette, the first time we meet her we observe two men fawning over her.

So, how can the 4Cs be used to organise the curriculum and structure lessons? Here's Willingham again to explain what this might look like in a history lesson:

> History is a natural story; it has the four Cs – causality, conflicts, complications, and character – built in ... There are ways to use the four Cs as the framework for developing lesson plans. For example, a typical lesson on the Spanish-American War emphasises President Cleveland's and then President McKinley's reluctance to do anything about the Cuban revolution against the Spanish, despite the considerable economic stake that

the U.S. had in the country. Successive events (the publishing of an insulting letter by the Spanish Minister and the sinking of the *Maine*), lead to a U.S. ultimatum that is rejected by the Spanish, whereupon the U.S. declares war. Considering the four Cs might lead to a different framework. The strong *character* in this drama is Spain, because it is Spain's actions that move the story forward. Thus, a teacher might begin with the background of how Spain first came to control Cuba and the failed revolt of 1868–1878. The central *conflict* of the story is how the Spanish should deal with the revolt: put it down or try to accommodate the Cubans. The first *complication* is the increasing involvement of the U.S. in this conflict, which offers a third option—allow the U.S. to mediate. At each step, the teacher would ensure that the *causal* link between one event and the next was clear to learners. Story format can inform the structuring of a lesson plan, even if the lesson does not include a story *per se*.

Story structure is important because it requires the reader to make inferences which causes thinking. Indeed, Sung-il Kim tested this very idea in a 1999 study when he had subjects read short passages and rate them for interest.[11] In some passages the penultimate sentence provided a reason for the final action taken, but other passages omitted the reason. Subjects found text more interesting if the reason for the ending was not explicitly in the passage.

Stories are also easier to comprehend than other forms of text. In one study by Arthur Graesser, Murray Singer, and Tom Trabasso, published in 1994,[12] the experimenters had their subjects read several different types of text. Willingham explains:

> Texts varied in the familiarity of their content and in their format; some were stories (e.g., one that is very familiar, Princess and the Pea, and one that is not, Bodisat) and some were expository texts (e.g., concerning earthquakes or harvester ants). Each text was read on a computer screen, one sentence at a time; subjects pressed the space bar when they were ready to read the next sentence, so the experimenters were able to measure reading time.

> The experimenters had analysed each sentence on a number of dimensions including number of words, grammatical complexity, number of propositions (a linguistic measure of ideas), position in the text, topic familiarity, and narrativity.

> The experimenters then calculated which of these text characteristics were associated with fast reading times, and which with slow. They found that most of these dimensions had some impact on reading time (e.g., subjects were somewhat slower to read sentences that had more words), but narrativity had the largest effect by far. Stories were read much faster than expository texts. The researchers take the faster reading speed to indicate greater ease of comprehension."

One reason stories are easy to comprehend is that we know the format, and that gives us a reasonable idea of what to expect. When an event is described in a story, we expect that the event will be causally related to a prior event in the story. The listener uses his or her knowledge of story structure to relate the present event to what has already happened.

A dead simple structure

I'm a big fan of crime fiction, particularly detective novels. I once travelled the length and breadth of New Zealand in a camper van armed only with a tattered edition of the *Complete Stories of Sherlock Holmes* (and clean underwear). And I'll never forget the day I borrowed a copy of Ian Rankin's *Fleshmarket Close* from the school staffroom's book swap shelf and got hooked on Detective Inspector John Rebus, later taking a trip to Edinburgh to have a pint of IPA in the Oxford Bar.

I like the detective novel because it is formulaic in the best sense of the term: there is a shape and pattern that must be obeyed: in the 'whodunnit', a murder mystery must be solved by the end of the book and there are hidden clues for the reader to unravel. In fact, detective novels often take the shape of something similar to Freytag's Pyramid.

Freytag's Pyramid, also known as the dramatic structure, is a model used to analyse and describe the plot of a story. The pyramid was named after German novelist Gustav Freytag, who first described this model in his book *Technique of the Drama* in 1863.[13]

As well as exploring the 4Cs, when I teach creative writing, I teach learners how to use Freytag's Pyramid to structure their narrative.

Freytag's pyramid

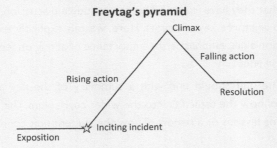

Freytag's Pyramid consists of five parts:

1. **Exposition:** This is the beginning of the story where the setting, characters, and background information are introduced.

2. **Rising action:** This is where the conflict of the story is introduced, and events begin to unfold, leading up to the climax.

3. **Climax:** This is the turning point of the story, where the conflict reaches its highest point, and the protagonist faces their greatest challenge.

4. **Falling action:** This is where the events following the climax begin to unfold and loose ends are tied up.

5. **Resolution:** This is the end of the story, where the conflict is resolved and the story concludes.

As well as providing a framework for crime fiction, Freytag's Pyramid can also be a useful tool for structuring learning in a way that engages learners and helps them retain information.

Pyramid planning

Into practice
Writing your story

Here are some ways to apply Freytag's Pyramid to lesson planning:

1. **Exposition:** Begin the unit by introducing the topic and providing background information. This can include teacher explanations which frontload key concepts and vocabulary as well as activate relevant prior knowledge, or it can be a video or research assignment that set the scene for the lesson.

2. **Rising action:** This is where the bulk of the unit takes place. Here we provide examples and engage learners in activities that build their understanding of the topic. This can include teacher modelling and 'thinking aloud', as well as co-construction, independent practice, and group work.

3. **Climax:** The climax of the unit should be a moment where learners apply their new knowledge to a challenge or problem. This can be a case study, a debate, or a hands-on project. This is where the unit reaches its peak, and learners are challenged to use what they have learned.

4. **Falling action:** After the climax, it's important to provide opportunities for learners to reflect on what they have learned. This can include a discussion, a journaling activity, or a quiz to reinforce key concepts. Here, we can explicitly teach metacognitive and self-regulation skills, emphasise the importance of acting on feedback to improve, and develop resilience.

5. **Resolution:** The unit should end with a summary of the key points and a clear understanding of how the topic fits into the wider curriculum. This can include a preview of upcoming lessons or a review of how the current unit connects to real-world applications.

Thus, by structuring learning according to Freytag's Pyramid, we can create a compelling narrative that engages learners and helps them retain information. This, in turn, can help learners stay focused and motivated, and it can also make our lessons more memorable and impactful.

What have we learned?

In this chapter, we have discovered that:

Stories are easy to understand and remember and can, therefore, be used to structure learning. Doing so helps provide continuity to the curriculum and connect lessons in a sequence. This, in turn, helps learners to remember more of what they learn. In practice, this means that we should consider the curriculum as a story to be told rather than a set of objectives to be learned. We can do this by finding the lead, locating the hook, discovering binary oppositions, and by telling the story.

Stories can also be used to frame teacher explanations and modelling. By framing our instructions as stories, we can help learners understand the bigger picture, how constituent parts fit together. We can also help learners understand how classroom learning relates to the wider world.

Storytelling techniques such as flashback and flashforward can be useful when giving feedback to learners because the best feedback does not compare a learner with other learners in a class but, rather, compares each learner with their earlier self by articulating the 'story arc' the learner is following – in short, it feeds back on the progress made to date and feeds forward on what needs to be learned next.

What can we do?

To put the advice contained in this chapter into practice, it might be helpful to consider the following questions:

1. Do you plan a sequential curriculum akin to a story plot? Do you share this 'narrative arc' with learners so that they know what they're learning and why this matters to them?

2. Are you clear about 'the lead' in every lesson? Do you share this, in some form, with learners?

3. Do you use 'hooks' to grab your learners' attention and to bring curriculum content to life, perhaps with an analogy? If so, do you make sure the analogy works by assessing learners' existing background knowledge?

4. Do you identify the 'binary oppositions' in your curriculum? And do you tell the story of your curriculum, finding the complication and resolution, for example by using the 4Cs or Freytag's Pyramid?

5. Do you build increasing independence by gradually relinquishing control to learners, perhaps in a 'I do, we do, you do' form?

Notes

1 Bromley, M (2023). *Intent Implementation Impact: How to Design and Deliver an Ambitious School Curriculum*. Spark Education Books.
2 Rest assured, the real Mickey is alive and well and living in a care home for retired fictional characters.
3 www.sec-ed.co.uk/content/best-practice/behaviour-tackling-low-level-disruption-in-the-classroom
4 www.sec-ed.co.uk/content/best-practice/nine-principles-of-effective-teaching
5 I adapted this list from *Understanding by Design* by Grant Wiggins & Jay McTighe (1998, Association for Supervision and Curriculum Development).
6 https://dictionary.cambridge.org/dictionary/english/story
7 www.merriam-webster.com/dictionary/story
8 Gagné, R M, Briggs, L J, & Wager, W W (1992). *Principles of Instructional Design* (4th ed.). Harcourt Brace Jovanovich College Publishers.
9 www.aft.org/periodical/american-educator/summer-2004/ask-cognitive-scientist

10 Written in the notes for his final novel, *The Last Tycoon* (1941).

11 Sung-il Kim (1999). Causal bridging inference: A cause of story interestingness. *British Journal of Psychology*, 90(1), 57–71. https://bpspsychub.onlinelibrary.wiley.com/doi/abs/10.1348/000712699161260

12 Graesser, A C, Singer, M, & Trabasso, T (1994). Constructing inferences during narrative text comprehension. *Psychological Review*, 101(3), 371–395.

13 Freytag, G (1863). *Technique of the Drama*. Various publishers.

7 Using story to aid learners' memorisation

Learning is the acquisition of knowledge, skills, and understanding and the application of that knowledge, skills, and understanding at a later time. Thus, learning is a long-term process. In order to learn something, at least in any meaningful sense, learners must retain information and be able to retrieve that information in the future. Memorising information is therefore essential. Story and storytelling provide an excellent means of aiding learners' memory. Why? Because stories are easy to remember.

In one study into the efficacy of story in aiding memorisation by Arthur Graesser and colleagues, published in 1994,[1] subjects listened to a set of stories and expository texts. Their memory was later tested. Story won the day: subjects remembered about 50% more from the stories than they did from the expository passages. Familiarity had some impact on memory, but the main effect was for the so-called *narrativity* of the passages.

For 'narrativity' read 'causality': the story format has psychological significance, which leads to better comprehension and better memory because we know what to expect in a story and these expectations are driven by a mental representation for story structure.

When we are exposed to new information, we process it and then attempt to connect it to existing information (in other words, we try to assimilate new knowledge with prior knowledge). The richer – sensorily and emotionally – the new information is, and the deeper the existing information is ingrained, the stronger we will encode the new information in our long-term memories.

In short, stories have 'stickability' because:

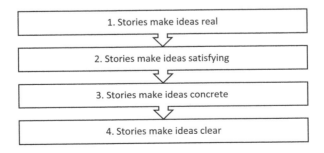

1. Stories make ideas real

2. Stories make ideas satisfying

3. Stories make ideas concrete

4. Stories make ideas clear

DOI: 10.4324/9781003465492-9

1. Stories make ideas real

Stories have stickability because they make ideas tangible through the use of analogy and metaphor. Metaphors are good at making ideas stick and aiding memory because they bring ideas to life; they draw connections between new knowledge and existing knowledge. For example, if you are trying to describe how electricity flows through a material, you'll need to explain the structure of atoms. You might use a metaphor which describes atoms as 'nature's building blocks' to help learners understand an atom's function. You will then need to explain how each atom is comprised of protons, which are positively charged, neutrons, which have no charge, and electrons, which are negatively charged. Then you would need to explain that, together, the protons and neutrons form the 'nucleus' of the atom, and that the electrons travel around this nucleus. You might then use a metaphor which compares this 'orbit' to the way the Earth travels around the sun. In each case, you are relating new information which learners are unlikely to be able to process, and therefore retain, with existing information (or prior knowledge) to help them imagine it, process it, and retain it.

2. Stories make ideas satisfying

Stories have stickability because they make information rewarding by first piquing learners' curiosity and then satisfying that curiosity. Unless learners know why facts are important, they are unlikely to retain them. Before teaching our learners facts, we can use story to pique learners' curiosity and make them realise why they need those facts. The secret to convincing learners that they need the information we intend to teach them is to start by highlighting the knowledge they are missing. Another technique is to start a lesson by asking learners to make a prediction.

3. Stories make ideas concrete

Stories have stickability because they make information concrete. Learners find it hard to care about or understand abstract concepts. Stories make ideas concrete by grounding them in sensory reality. The more sensory 'hooks' we use, the better the ideas will stick.

Take, for example, Jane Elliott's famous 'blue-eyed/brown-eyed' experiment with third grade learners the day after Martin Luther King had been assassinated in 1968. The purpose of the exercise was to teach her learners the effects of belonging to a minority. Firstly, Elliott had a class discussion about racism but said she "could see that [the learners] weren't internalising a thing". Instead, "they were doing what white people do … when white people sit down to discuss racism … [they experience] shared ignorance".[2]

Most of Elliott's learners were, like her, born and raised in a small town in Iowa, and were not normally exposed to Black people. She felt that simply talking about racism would not allow her all-White class to fully comprehend its meaning and effects. Accordingly, she divided the class into brown-eyed and blue-eyed children. She told the class that the blue-eyed children were the superior group, provided them with brown fabric collars, and asked the blue-eyed learners to wrap them around the necks of their brown-eyed peers as a method of easily identifying the minority group.

She gave the blue-eyed children extra privileges, such as second helpings at lunch, access to the new jungle gym, and five extra minutes at recess. The blue-eyed children sat in the front of the classroom, and the brown-eyed children were sent to sit in the back rows. The blue-eyed children were encouraged to play only with other blue-eyed children and to ignore those with brown eyes. Elliott often chastised the brown-eyed learners when they did not follow the exercise's rules.

At first, there was resistance among the learners in the minority group to the idea that blue-eyed children were better, but eventually those who were deemed 'superior' became arrogant, bossy, and otherwise unpleasant to their 'inferior' classmates. Their grades also improved, doing mathematical and reading tasks that had seemed outside their ability before. The 'inferior' classmates also transformed into timid and subservient children who even during recess isolated themselves, including those who had previously been dominant in the class. These children's academic performance suffered, even with tasks that had been simple before.

Once she had concluded the experiment, she asked the children to reflect by writing down what they had learned, and it became clear that her learners had come to deeply understand racism because Elliott had made it feel real; she had grounded an abstract concept in sensory reality and thus engaged her learners' emotions.

As I said earlier, if learners are made to care about something, they are made to feel something, and this is an important part of the learning process. In short, we should obey the storytelling maxim 'show don't tell' wherever possible. Telling learners something means we do all the work for them; showing them means they must work for themselves.

4. Stories make ideas clear

Stories have stickability because they make information clear. Although we are not naturally good thinkers and like to avoid challenging cognitive tasks if we can, we do enjoy problem-solving because it is fun and rewarding – and stories allow us to frame our key messages around a problem to be solved or an enquiry to be investigated and answered. After all, at the heart of every good story is a mystery, a question that begs an answer, a problem that demands a solution, a heart that needs mending.

Stories can also be used to explain and illustrate abstract ideas or concepts in a way that makes them accessible and attainable because they bring facts to life, making the abstract concrete. Storytelling is a means of meaning making; it breaks down communication barriers between experts and novices to create a bridge on which both can meet intellectually.

In a study by Fiona Banister and Charly Ryan conducted in 2001,[3] children remembered abstract science ideas more effectively when they were taught in a story format. Remembering isolated and disconnected facts and concepts is more difficult than recalling this type of content in a story because in a story the information is presented in a coherent and connected way.

*

In sum, stories are interesting, easy to remember, and easy to understand, and as such they are an ideal way to introduce learners to a new topic that will really 'stick'. But that's not all. Stories also allow us to introduce new material in a way that is both non-threatening and interesting. We might, for example, know of a story that complements the lesson's learning outcome in a way that's less taxing, more fun, and more interesting.

Biographies are a great way of making curriculum content more relatable on a human level. For example, biographies of scientists can read like whodunnits as a boffin follows clues to hunt down a solution to a scientific problem. Biographies of scientists and mathematicians can also act as role models because the protagonists invariably display passion and dedication. Biographies also enable learners to gain important personal perspectives on historical events, bringing history to life through the eyes of ordinary people.

The learning process

At the start of this chapter, I defined learning as the acquisition of knowledge, skills, and understanding and the application of that knowledge, skills, and understanding at a later time. Learning is a complex cognitive process and there is much we still don't know about it but, broadly speaking, I think it occurs in four stages:

Stage 1: Attention

Samuel Johnson is reported to have said that "the true art of memory is the art of attention". Thus, we need to think about how our lessons will gain and retain our learners' attention. To be attentive to a task, learners must be motivated by it and must believe that making an effort will pay off. There are two main types of attention: goal oriented and stimulus oriented. Goal-oriented attention is gained through motivation, curiosity, and other self-driven forces – in other words, we actively attend to something – and is retained through intent. Stimulus-oriented attention is gained through the sensory stimuli that surround us – in other words, our response to sights, sounds, and smells – and is retained subconsciously, thus overriding our goal-oriented attention. These goal-oriented and stimulus-oriented attention-grabbers operate at the same time and our ability to regulate them – to stay focused on our goal-directed attention and limit the influence of our stimulus-driven attention – is one of the keys to learning.

It's not difficult to see how story and storytelling can help us to gain the goal-oriented and stimulus-oriented attention of our learners. Stories pique and satisfy learners' curiosity and are structurally rewarding because they set up a problem which is then solved. And stories appeal to the senses because they add hue and texture, and a human connection.

Stage 2: Encoding

When we are exposed to new information, we process it and then attempt to connect it to existing information (in other words, we try to assimilate new knowledge with prior knowledge to provide a context within which to make sense of it). The richer – sensorily and emotionally – the new information is, and the deeper the existing information is engrained, the more strongly that new information will be encoded in our memories. We can infer from this that effective learning is the result of two things:

Firstly, learning is the result of multi-sensory and emotional experiences. The richer our sensory-emotional experience of new information, the more deeply we will encode it. For instance, if we are made to feel something, we are more likely to encode new information. Again, it is not difficult to see how powerful stories can be in achieving this. Good stories are designed to make us feel something. Biographies bring history to life and help us make personal connections. Making ideas concrete makes them more credible.

Secondly, learning is the result of contextualising information. When we have strong, vivid prior knowledge about a subject, we have easier access and greater insight into any new knowledge related to that subject that we acquire. In other words, when we have previous experience of something, we can encode new information about it more effectively and more richly. I'll return to this notion shortly when I circle back to schema theory but suffice to say stories are the best way of contextualising information because they provide background and meaning to information, and thus help bring the curriculum to life.

Stage 3: Storage

A memory is a neural connection. Thoughts and experiences build connections between the billions of neurons in our brains, establishing new networks and patterns. Neural connections fade away if they are neglected but can get stronger with repeated use because repetition leads to neural habits of thought. In other words, making associations strengthens our memories. The number of connections we make influences the number of times memories are revisited, which in turn influences the length of time we retain a memory. When we connect different pieces of information with each other, we retain them for longer because we retrieve them more often. It follows that the more often we connect what we are teaching today to what we taught previously, the better the information will be learnt. Equally, the more we connect what we're teaching today to contextual information, the better our learners will learn. Again, I will return to this shortly.

Stage 4: Retrieval

Being forgetful is a good thing. For example, I'm delighted I've been able to forget most of the things I said and did when I was behaving badly in my late teens and early twenties. After all, if I hadn't forgotten such things, I might not be able to look at myself in the mirror or, worse still, climb atop the moral high ground from where I can throw stones of piety at the unethical valley of youth below. Forgetting is good because it helps us to stay focused. If we were incapable of forgetting, we'd become overloaded with information and our brains would simply erupt like a volcano, hot molten brain-lava shooting from the tops of our heads. Perhaps.

For teachers, the act of forgetting means that, even if we are able to sustain our learners' attention, even if we are able to help our learners encode information more richly, and even if we are able to create opportunities for our learners to consolidate that information, they will still forget things. In fact, we forget about half of the information that enters our working memories every hour, and two-thirds of the information we process disappears every day. We mustn't beat ourselves up when learners can't remember everything we said in the previous lesson. It is natural and it is healthy. But there are things we can do as teachers to help our learners retrieve important information more easily.

One of those things is to plan learning in such a way as to allow interleaving. Interleaving means placing something between the layers of something else. In this context, it is the act of repeating information periodically but with spaces in between where other information is learnt. Interleaving is the opposite of cramming – rather than focusing on one topic for a long period of time and never returning to it again, interleaving focuses on each topic for a shorter period of time but returns to it several times in between studying other topics. Each time we return to information, we increase its storage strength and improve our ability to retrieve it. The more times we review and relearn information, the better able we are to retain it over time.

Repeatedly retrieving information from our long-term memories improves the strength with which such information is stored. The more we retrieve information, the stronger the memory becomes. If we retrieve a memory to connect prior knowledge to new information, the memory is strengthened even further. In practice, this means we should plan opportunities for our learners not only to revise information they have previously learnt but to reorganise that information by writing about it or talking about it. Our learners will forge new connections if they retrieve information from their long-term memories and re-encode it with new information. And the more connections our learners make between similar types of memories, the more easily they will be able to retrieve those memories later in much the same way as I can more easily find the book I want to read because I have organised my books in alphabetical order rather than hidden them individually around the house. At least that's what I tell visitors when they stand in astonishment at my bookcase.

Anyway, I said I'd come back to schema theory …

Making connections for comprehension

Schema theory is a cognitive theory that explains how people organise and understand information in their minds. A *schema* is a mental structure or framework that helps individuals organise and interpret information. Schemas are formed through experience and learning, and they influence how people perceive, think about, and remember information. Schemas can be activated automatically and unconsciously, which means they can influence our perceptions and behaviours without us realising it. For example, if someone has a schema for a 'restaurant', they might automatically think of certain things such as tables, chairs, menus, waiters, and food. This schema helps them quickly recognise and understand new restaurants they encounter.

Schemas can also be influenced by cultural and social factors, as well as individual differences. For instance, someone from a particular culture might have a different schema for a 'family' than someone from another culture.

never make it into the warehouse. If the boxes are unpacked but their barcodes are not scanned, though they may end up somewhere in the warehouse, we will not know where and so will struggle to find them later. The logistics process succeeds or fails in that holding bay. And learning is just the same.

Learners must unpack curriculum knowledge in the holding bay that is their working memories – in other words, information must be actively attended to, thought about, and processed. If learners do not actively think about something, it will not make it into their long-term memories. Learning must therefore be challenging – we need learners to think hard about information for it to be actively processed.

Then learners must ensure information is stowed in a known location of their long-term memories so that it can be retrieved later and used. If information is inaccessible, it will decay over time and eventually be lost. Learning must therefore involve making connections – developing ever more complex schemas. And learning must involve repeated retrieval – the activating of and adding to prior learning.

The analogy of the chocolate boxes helps to make the abstract process of learning – which is something we cannot see – more concrete and real. It helps to anchor the unfamiliar within a relatable context. It makes the intangible tangible.

What have we learned?

In this chapter, we have discovered that:

Story and storytelling have a psychological significance which improves comprehension and bolsters memory traces because we know what to expect in a story and possess a mental representation for story structure. In other words, stories have the 'stickability' factor because they make ideas concrete.

Stories also help develop learners' background knowledge and experience – or schema – because narratives give context and meaning to otherwise arbitrary information. With stories, learners are able to draw upon their prior knowledge and experience to help them understand new ideas.

What can we do?

To put the advice contained in this chapter into practice, it might be helpful to consider the following questions:

1. Do you use story and storytelling to make curriculum concepts tangible to your learners, perhaps through analogy? Do you make ideas concrete through exemplification, telling real-life stories?

2. Do you make connections between what you're teaching and learners' own lives, as well as with other aspects of your subject curriculum and the wider world?

Notes

1 Graesser, A C, Singer, M, & Trabasso, T (1994). Constructing inferences during narrative text comprehension. *Psychological Review*, 101(3): 371–395.
2 Various sources. See: https://thedailyomnivore.net/2012/12/11/jane-elliott/
3 Banister, F & Ryan, C (2001). Developing science concepts through story-telling. *School Science Review*, 83(302), 75–83. www.researchgate.net/profile/Charly-Ryan/publication/234691332_Developing_Science_Concepts_through_Story-Telling/links/5510101f0cf2ac2905afc3cb/Developing-Science-Concepts-through-Story-Telling.pdf
4 Keane, E & Zimmerman, S (1997). *Mosaic of Thought: Teaching Comprehension in a Reader's Workshop.* Heinemann.
5 Harvey, S & Goudvis, A (2000). *Strategies That Work: Teaching Comprehension to Enhance Understanding.* Stenhouse Publishers.

8 Using story to engage learners' curiosity and wonder

Storytelling can be a powerful tool for teaching because it can help to engage learners, make learning more enjoyable, and enhance their understanding of complex concepts. Using stories in the classroom can help make abstract concepts concrete and turn the theoretical into the tangible.

According to Jerome Bruner in his 1986 book *Actual Minds, Possible Worlds*,[1] "[Story] deals in human or human-like intention and action and the vicissitudes and consequences that mark their course. It strives to put its timeless miracles into the particulars of experience and to locate the experience in time and place."

Bruner argues that stories can help teachers reach learners in ways that we could not do with traditional, dry, and deductive strategies. Stories can bring disparate information to life in a meaningful and connected way; they can engage our thinking, emotions, and imagination all at once.

Because stories teach us about the human experience and are woven into the fabric of our lives, no school subject is beyond the world of human experience or the art of storytelling. Indeed, while stories have always been a feature of the English classroom, they should actually play a part in the teaching of every subject discipline.

We've already seen research that proves people find material presented in a story format more engaging than information presented in an expository text.

There are many ways in which stories can be used in the classroom to pique learners' curiosity and engage their interest, including by:

1. **Teaching story-based lessons:** We can use a story to illustrate – and make more real – key concepts and ideas which can help learners to visualise and thus remember information more effectively.

2. **Telling personal stories:** We can also use our own stories or those of our learners to illustrate important ideas or concepts. This can help to make information more relevant and relatable for our learners by 'talking to' their own lived experiences.

3. **Using role-playing and simulations:** Role-playing and simulations can be used to create a story-based learning experience that engages learners and helps them to develop important skills, such as critical thinking and problem-solving.

DOI: 10.4324/9781003465492-10

4. **Engaging in creative writing:** We can encourage learners to use narrative in their own creative writing, such as short stories or essays. This can help to develop their own story-telling skills and enhance their understanding of narrative structure and techniques.

5. **Using digital storytelling:** With the help of technology, we can create multimedia presentations that incorporate audio, video, and images to tell a story or illustrate a concept. This can help to engage learners and make learning more interactive and engaging.

According to a Harvard Business Publishing article by Vanessa Boris entitled 'What makes storytelling so effective for learning?' (2017),[2] "Telling stories is one of the most powerful means that [we] have to influence, teach, and inspire."

What makes storytelling so effective for learning, Boris says, is that:

[It] forges connections among people, and between people and ideas. Stories convey the culture, history, and values that unite people. When it comes to our countries, our communities, and our families, we understand intuitively that the stories we hold in common are an important part of the ties that bind. ... Good stories do more than create a sense of connection. They build familiarity and trust, and allow the listener to enter the story where they are, making them more open to learning. Good stories can contain multiple meanings so they're surprisingly economical in conveying complex ideas in graspable ways. And stories are more engaging than a dry recitation of data points or a discussion of abstract ideas.

Melanie Green, an associate professor of psychology at the University of Pennsylvania, writing for the Association of Psychological Science in 2004,[3] says that:

As [a teacher], you can capitalise on the inherent narrative structure of research as the quest for knowledge. [For example,] telling the story of how researchers became interested in a particular issue, without immediately providing the resolution, [can] motivate your class to think of their own approaches to solving the problem.

As Green also reminds us, characters are an important element of any story and stories can help make curriculum content concrete and memorable by putting a human face to it:

Learners may remember the peril of H. M., the patient who could not form new memories, long after they have forgotten other details of brain anatomy or memory research. If they remember the concrete elements of the story, they may then be able to reconstruct the abstract lessons illustrated by the story. Furthermore, listeners may identify with the protagonists of your stories, and thus might be better able to relate course material to their own lives. Making the material personally relevant can lead to increased thinking about the material and a greater ability to apply the new knowledge.

Coherence is another hallmark of a good story. Remembering a list of isolated concepts and definitions is difficult, but recalling the flow of a story is easy.

Stories can help create vivid mental images, a cue for recall. Because stories provide natural connections between events and concepts, mentioning one part of the story may help evoke other parts of the story, just as hearing one bar of a familiar tune may bring the entire song to mind.

Some learners may be intimidated by abstract concepts or may doubt their ability to master or understand new material. A story may provide a non-threatening way to ease learners into learning. A narrative opening may seem simple and straightforward, allowing learners to relax and grasp a concrete example before moving into more technical details of a theory or finding. Sometimes stories can even be about the learning process; tales of previous learners who struggled but then succeeded might serve as inspiration for current learners.

There is a wealth of sources for teachable stories – current events, history, television programmes, classic literature or drama, and personal experience (your own and others).

Some teachers find it useful to have a folder or notebook for teaching stories and make a habit of clipping relevant newspaper stories or making notes about events that are perfect illustrations of some concept that appears on the curriculum.

Textbooks may also be sources of stories; some books use stories to introduce or frame chapters, while others – like this book – intersperse narratives throughout.

The case study method is another useful means of introducing stories into the classroom. Cases typically set up a problem by giving background information about a situation, and they end with a current dilemma faced by an individual or organisation. They are often designed to illustrate a particular point or demonstrate certain analytic procedures. Learners are encouraged to generate possible solutions and consider the consequences of those solutions. This method encourages active learning and in essence puts learners in the role of writing the ending to the story.

Ultimately, though, the best way to pique learners' curiosity and wonder is to pose a big question – a mystery that demands a solution. Whether this takes the form of a case study, a personal anecdote, or an imagined story, the key is to captivate learners' attention by leaving an enquiry unanswered.

The big question

A well-crafted story typically revolves around a big question that captivates the reader's curiosity and drives forward the narrative. Earlier, I gave the example of detective fiction – the whodunnit – where our crime-fighting protagonist must work out who committed the murder. But a story's 'big question' can take various forms, such as:

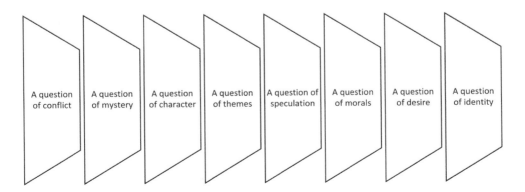

A question of conflict | A question of mystery | A question of character | A question of themes | A question of speculation | A question of morals | A question of desire | A question of identity

A question of conflict

A story might revolve around a central conflict or dilemma that poses a question with which the characters must grapple. The resolution of this question drives the plot.

A question of mystery

Stories that involve a puzzle (such as a murder mystery) inherently pose a question that the audience wants to see solved in the final act: whodunnit? The journey to uncover the truth and see justice served – and the trail of clues and misdirection we encounter along the way – keeps readers guessing and thus attentive.

A question of character

Characters often have personal questions to answer or internal struggles to wrestle with and overcome on their journeys of personal discovery. The questions and their answers provide an insight into the human condition and thus are universal – keeping readers engaged in the hope of learning something not just about the protagonist but also about themselves.

A question of themes

Many stories explore deeper themes or philosophical questions about life, morality, society, and more. These themes can create thought-provoking narratives that resonate with readers and reach beyond the page into their own lives.

A question of speculation

Science fiction and speculative fiction often raise questions by presenting alternative realities or 'what if' scenarios, challenging readers to consider the implications of these changes and confront their own beliefs and attitudes.

A question of morals

Stories that present characters with moral or ethical choices force readers to ponder what they would do in similar situations, prompting introspection and soul-searching that can lead to personal growth and greater self-awareness.

A question of desire

The protagonist's quest to achieve a goal or fulfil a desire raises the question of whether they will succeed and what challenges they will face along the way. Readers often see themselves reflected in these characters and so question their own journeys and intended destinations.

A question of identity

Stories that delve into a character's journey of self-discovery and identity often pose questions about who the character truly is and how they fit into the world which, in turn, forces readers to question their own identities and their worth.

*

Story questions create a sense of curiosity, anticipation, and emotional investment, encouraging audiences to stay engaged with the story to find answers. Whether the questions are explicitly stated or subtly woven into the narrative, they provide the framework around which the story unfolds, keeping readers hooked to the final page.

In sum, at the heart of every good story is a big question that's begging to be answered – and the classroom is no different. Questioning in the classroom is also about curiosity and wonder; educational questions pique learners' interests and pinpoint gaps in their existing knowledge which ache to be filled. Indeed, Socrates is said to have claimed that questioning is the only defensible form of teaching.[4]

Placing questions at the heart of story-based lessons is important because a *questioning classroom* leads to:

Increased learner engagement and curiosity: Asking questions taps into learners' natural curiosity and encourages active participation in the learning process. When learners are given the freedom to ask questions, they become more engaged and motivated to explore topics in depth.

The development of critical thinking skills: Questioning promotes critical thinking skills by requiring learners to analyse, evaluate, and synthesise information to arrive at meaningful answers.

A greater depth of understanding: Through asking questions, learners can delve deeper into subjects, uncovering underlying concepts, connections, and complexities that might otherwise remain unexplored.

Increased learner ownership of learning: When learners generate their own questions, they take ownership of their learning. This can lead to a sense of empowerment and increased self-directed learning.

The development of problem-solving skills: Questioning encourages learners to approach problems as challenges to be solved. They learn to develop strategies, seek solutions, and persist in the face of obstacles.

Lifelong learning: Cultivating a questioning mindset nurtures a habit of ongoing learning beyond the classroom. Individuals who are comfortable asking questions are more likely to seek out new information and continue learning throughout their lives.

Creating a questioning classroom is not easy, however. There are several challenges to overcome, including:

- **Balancing exploration with curriculum coverage:** While open questions encourage critical thinking, a degree of structure is often necessary to ensure learners cover essential content. Striking the right balance between exploration and curriculum requirements can be challenging. In a structured curriculum, there might be time constraints that limit the extent to which all questions can be explored fully. This can lead to a need for prioritisation. Ask yourself: how can I use questions to help me cover the curriculum rather than divert from it?

- **Varying levels of engagement:** Some learners might be more willing to ask and answer questions than others, potentially leaving certain individuals disengaged or hesitant to participate. Ask yourself: how can I engage quieter learners and those reluctant to take risks?

- **A lack of foundational knowledge:** In certain subjects, learners may lack the foundational knowledge required to formulate meaningful questions. In these cases, some guidance and initial instruction might be needed. Ask yourself: how can I assess and activate prior knowledge before engaging in questioning, and how can I fill gaps in prior knowledge where they exist without slowing learning down?

- **The need for direct instruction:** While encouraging independent thinking and questioning is important, direct instruction from teachers is still vital to ensure that learners are asking relevant and productive questions. Ask yourself: how can I manage the flow of information through teacher explanations and modelling, helping learners to become increasingly independent while harnessing the power of questions throughout the process?

Into practice
Writing your story

Some useful questioning strategies

What does a questioning classroom look like in practice? Here are some questioning techniques to consider embedding into the daily lives of your learners – we'll explore many more later:

Open questions: Pose open questions that encourage learners to think deeply and express their opinions. These questions often begin with words like 'why', 'how', or 'what if'. They allow for diverse responses and promote discussions.

Socratic questioning: Employ the Socratic method by asking a series of probing questions that guide learners towards discovering knowledge through classroom talk. This method fosters critical thinking and encourages learners to analyse concepts from various angles.

Question-response-evidence-explanation: Encourage learners to provide detailed responses by using the QREE framework. After answering a question, learners provide evidence from the text or their own experiences and then explain their reasoning.

Think-pair-share: Present a question to the class and have learners think about their responses individually before pairing up with a partner to discuss their ideas and then sharing their thoughts with the larger group. This strategy encourages collaboration and diverse perspectives.

Brainstorming questions: Start a lesson with a brainstorming session where learners generate questions related to the topic. This not only activates prior knowledge but also guides the direction of the lesson. Thinking of questions that need to be answered also piques learners' curiosity and thus fosters intrinsic motivation.

Entry and exit tickets: Use questions as entry or exit tickets. At the beginning of a class, ask a question related to the previous lesson to gauge understanding. At the end, ask a question to assess what learners have learned during the current class.

Reflective questions: Incorporate reflection into the learning process by asking questions that prompt learners to consider their learning experiences, challenges, and progress.

Problem-solving questions: Present real-world problems and ask learners how they would approach solving them. This strategy encourages application of knowledge and critical thinking skills.

The 'Harkness discussion method': Arrange classroom furniture in a circle and encourage learners to lead discussions by posing questions to their peers. This learner-led approach promotes active participation and peer-to-peer learning.

Bloom's Taxonomy: Utilise Bloom's Taxonomy to ask questions at different cognitive levels, from basic recall to complex analysis and evaluation. This helps scaffold learning and allows learners to engage with content on multiple levels. It's important to engage all learners in all levels of the Taxonomy and not use it as a means of differentiation.

Formative assessment: Use questions as a form of ongoing assessment to gauge learner understanding during a lesson. Adjust your teaching based on their responses to ensure everyone is on the same page.

Role reversal: Invite learners to take on the role of the teacher by allowing them to pose questions to their peers. This promotes leadership skills and a deeper understanding of the curriculum.

Visual aids and stimuli: Use visuals, videos, or real-world examples as stimuli to generate questions. This approach can make unfamiliar concepts more relatable and engaging and turn the abstract into the concrete.

Two types of question

The previous ideas are just some starter suggestions. We'll unpack many more of the questioning techniques that help embed story and storytelling techniques in the classroom later in this chapter. But first let's go back to basics. There are, broadly, two types of question at our disposal in the classroom:

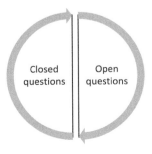

Closed questions   Open questions

Closed questions

Closed questions are a type of questioning that typically require short, specific answers. They can be valuable as a form of assessment in the classroom when used appropriately.

Here are some tips for using closed questions effectively for the purposes of assessment:

1. **Quick checks for understanding:** Closed questions can serve as quick checks to gauge learners' comprehension of basic concepts. They are especially useful for assessing factual knowledge, terminology, and basic recall.

2. **Identifying misconceptions:** By asking closed questions, you can identify any misconceptions that learners might have. If multiple learners provide the same incorrect answer, it's an indicator that a particular concept needs clarification.

3. **Focused assessment:** Closed questions allow you to assess specific learning intentions, making them particularly useful for assessing whether learners have mastered particular facts or skills.

4. **Objective marking:** Closed questions yield clear-cut, easily comparable answers. This can simplify the marking process and ensure consistency in evaluating learner responses.

5. **Practice and drill:** Closed questions are often used for practice and drilling, helping learners reinforce their understanding of foundational material.

6. **Building confidence:** Closed questions can help learners build confidence in their knowledge. Success in answering these questions can motivate them to engage more deeply with the subject matter.

As powerful as closed questions can be, it's important that we balance them with other assessment methods that encourage open-ended responses and critical thinking. This provides a more comprehensive picture of learners' understanding. It's also crucial to consider the context of an assessment: closed questions are more appropriate for assessing foundational knowledge or reviewing previously covered material rather than assessing complex, creative, or application-based concepts.

When using closed questions as a form of assessment, we need to provide feedback on incorrect answers to help learners understand their mistakes and learn from them. This can guide their future learning and improvement. Closed questions can be used in both formative and summative assessments. In formative assessments, they can guide instruction and help learners track their progress. In summative assessments, they can ensure that learners have grasped essential concepts.

When asking closed questions, we need to be clear and precise in our wording to avoid ambiguity or trick questions that might confuse learners.

Closed questions can take various formats, such as multiple-choice, true/false, fill-in-the-blank, or matching. We need to choose the format that best aligns with the learning objectives and the content being assessed.

Open questions

Open questions, meanwhile, are an excellent way to encourage deeper thinking, critical analysis, and meaningful engagement among learners in the classroom — and are great when used in tandem with story and storytelling techniques. Here's how you can use open questions to foster deeper thinking:

1. **Encourage critical thinking:** Open questions require learners to think critically and consider multiple perspectives before formulating their responses. This promotes a deeper understanding of the topic.

2. **Promote discussion:** Open questions often lead to rich discussions where learners share their thoughts, ideas, and interpretations. This collaborative environment encourages active participation and the exchange of diverse viewpoints.

3. **Explore complex concepts:** Open questions can help learners to explore complex or abstract concepts. Such questions encourage learners to delve into the nuances and intricacies of the subject matter.

4. **Pique learners' curiosity:** Open questions stimulate curiosity and make learners eager to explore and discover more about a topic. This intrinsic motivation that results can drive learners to seek out additional information beyond the classroom.

5. **Develop communication skills:** Responding to open questions helps learners develop their communication skills by articulating their thoughts clearly and persuasively.

6. **Connect to real-world applications:** Open questions can challenge learners to apply their knowledge to real-world scenarios. This bridges the gap between theoretical concepts and practical applications.

7. **Differentiate learning:** Open questions allow for diverse responses, catering to learners with varying levels of prior knowledge and different perspectives/lived experiences. This promotes a more inclusive classroom environment.

8. **Foster reflection:** Open questions can be used to encourage learners to reflect on their learning journeys by asking questions that prompt them to consider how their views and understanding have evolved over time.

9. **Build higher-order thinking skills:** Open questions align with higher-order thinking skills such as analysis, evaluation, and synthesis because learners must engage deeply with the content in order to provide thoughtful responses.

A chain of open questions that build upon one another can lead learners through a process of exploration and discovery. Learners can be asked open questions that present challenges or dilemmas and that elicit a discussion of pros and cons.

It's important, after asking an open question, to give learners ample time to process and formulate their thoughts before responding. This encourages more thoughtful and comprehensive answers.

By incorporating open questions into the classroom, you can create a classroom environment that values critical thinking, creativity, and exploration. These questions inspire learners to think beyond the surface, fostering a deeper and more meaningful understanding of the subject matter.

Critical thinking

Using questions to foster critical thinking in the classroom is a powerful strategy that encourages learners to analyse, evaluate, and synthesise information. Here's how you can effectively use questions to promote critical thinking:

1. **Ask big philosophical questions:** Pose questions that don't have a single correct answer and require learners to think deeply and explore different perspectives. These questions often start with words like 'why', 'how', and 'what if'.

2. **Challenge learners' assumptions:** Encourage learners to question their own assumptions and preconceived notions. Ask questions that prompt them to consider alternative viewpoints or solutions.

3. **Probe for evidence:** When learners present an argument or answer, ask follow-up questions that require them to provide evidence or examples to support their claims. This helps develop their analytical skills.

4. **Encourage analysis:** Ask questions that require learners to break down complex ideas into their constituent parts. For example, 'What are the key components of this theory? How do they interact?'

5. **Promote comparison and contrast:** Encourage learners to compare and contrast different concepts, theories, or approaches. This helps them identify similarities, differences, and underlying patterns and trends.

6. **Explore consequences:** Pose questions about the potential consequences of different decisions or actions. Encourage learners to think about the short-term and long-term effects.

7. **Apply concepts to real-world situations:** Present learners with real-world scenarios and ask them how they would apply their knowledge and critical thinking skills to solve problems.

8. **Encourage reflection:** After a discussion or activity, ask learners to reflect on what they've learned, how their thinking has evolved, and what questions they still have.

9. **Incorporate diverse perspectives:** Ask questions that encourage learners to consider perspectives from different cultural, historical, or social contexts. This broadens their understanding and critical thinking skills.

10. **Support collaborative problem-solving:** Pose questions that require learners to work together in groups to analyse a problem, discuss potential solutions, and justify their choices.

Another way to promote critical thinking is to foster a classroom culture where learners feel comfortable asking – and not just answering – questions. This promotes curiosity and helps them further develop their critical thinking skills.

Dialogic teaching

Another way to deepen learners' understanding, develop their critical thinking skills, and ensure active participation is to follow the Socratic method.

Socratic questioning is a form of dialogic teaching which is an approach to education that places a strong emphasis on interactive and collaborative dialogue between teachers and learners. Dialogic teaching focuses on creating a learning environment whereby learners actively engage in discussions, express their thoughts, ask questions, and work together to construct knowledge. The Socratic method intersects well with the storytelling approach to teaching too because it provides a means of exploring a narrative, peeling back page upon page to analyse a story's complexity.

Before we home in on the Socratic method, let's examine some key principles of dialogic teaching:

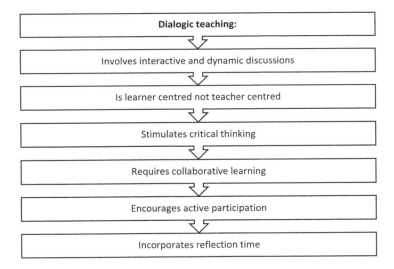

Firstly, in a dialogic teaching setting, classroom discussions are interactive and dynamic. Both teachers and learners contribute to conversations, sharing their ideas, perspectives, and experiences.

Secondly, dialogic teaching shifts the focus from a teacher-centred approach to a learner-centred one. Learners are encouraged to take ownership of their learning by participating actively in discussions and contributing their insights.

Thirdly, open questions that stimulate critical thinking are a central component of dialogic teaching. These questions prompt learners to analyse, evaluate, and synthesise information, fostering deeper understanding.

Fourthly, dialogic teaching requires collaborative learning whereby learners work together in small groups or as a class to explore topics, share their thoughts, and engage in problem-solving activities.

Fifthly, all learners are encouraged to actively participate in discussions. This includes quieter learners who might be less inclined to speak up in traditional teaching environments. But teachers also play a crucial role in guiding and facilitating discussions. Teachers need to use techniques like Socratic questioning to help learners clarify their thoughts, consider alternative viewpoints, and delve deeper into the subject matter.

Finally, dialogic teaching often incorporates opportunities for learners to reflect on their own learning, the learning process, and how their perspectives have evolved. In practice, this means encouraging a wide range of perspectives and experiences to enrich classroom discussions. Indeed, dialogic teaching values diverse viewpoints and encourages learners to consider different angles.

Dialogic teaching also encourages learners to think about their thinking and thus helps them to become increasingly metacognitive and self-regulated. This, in turn, helps them become more aware of their strengths and areas for improvement.

In dialogic teaching, knowledge is seen as something that is co-constructed through interactions between teachers and learners. Everyone contributes to building a collective understanding. Dialogic teaching aligns well with constructivist educational theories which emphasise the active role of learners in constructing their own knowledge. It also promotes a positive and inclusive classroom environment, where learners feel valued, respected, and confident in expressing their ideas.

Socratic questioning

Socratic questioning is a teaching technique inspired by the Socratic method of enquiry, which involves a series of open questions designed to promote critical thinking, deep understanding, and active engagement in discussions.

Socratic questioning encourages learners to explore complex ideas, analyse assumptions, and arrive at conclusions through thoughtful dialogue. Thus, Socratic questioning goes hand-in-hand with storytelling in the classroom.

Socratic questioning can be used to:

● Control a discussion.

● Explore more complex ideas.

● Uncover assumptions.

● Analyse concepts and ideas.

● Distinguish between what learners know and do not know.

Broadly, Socratic questioning performs two functions in the classroom:

1. To deeply probe learner thinking, to help learners begin to distinguish what they know or understand from what they do not know or understand.

2. To foster learners' abilities to ask Socratic questions and to help learners acquire the powerful tools of Socratic dialogue so that they can use these tools in everyday life (in questioning themselves and others).

Here's how Socratic questioning works in the classroom:

1. **The teacher poses thought-provoking questions.** They typically start with an open, thought-provoking question related to the topic of discussion. The question should stimulate curiosity and encourage learners to think critically.

2. **The teacher facilitates discussions** rather than gives a lecture. They avoid providing direct answers or explanations as the teacher. Instead, they guide the discussion by asking follow-up questions that encourage learners to think deeply and articulate their thoughts.

3. **The teacher engages with learner responses.** When learners respond to a question, the teacher acknowledges their answers but, rather than commenting on those answers or providing a 'correct' answer, they ask further probing questions to deepen learners' thinking. Here, the teacher's task is to encourage learners to elaborate, provide evidence, or consider alternative viewpoints.

4. **The teacher seeks clarification** by asking learners to refine their ideas, definitions, or assumptions. This helps learners develop a clearer understanding of the concepts being discussed.

5. **The teacher challenges learners' assumptions.** They pose questions that challenge learners' biases and preconceived notions and encourage learners to examine the underlying beliefs that influence their thinking.

6. **The teacher encourages learners to identify contradictions** or inconsistencies in their own or others' arguments, which prompts deeper analysis and encourages critical thinking.

7. **The teacher prompts learners to provide evidence**, examples, or real-world applications to support their ideas, which helps learners to connect theory to practice and develop a more robust understanding of the subject being debated. A part of this stage of the process is to encourage learners to respond to each other's ideas and build upon the discussion, thus fostering collaborative learning and the exploration of diverse perspectives.

Throughout this process, the teacher should aim to use a variety of question types. They should incorporate different types of Socratic questions, including clarifying questions, probing questions, hypothetical questions, and reflective questions – on which, more shortly. This creates a well-rounded dialogue that promotes comprehensive exploration. They should also prompt learners to reflect on their own thinking processes and the reasoning behind their answers. This cultivates metacognitive awareness and enhances their ability to think critically in the future.

Crucially, and perhaps most difficult to master, the teacher should also facilitate rather than dictate. They should guide the discussion and prompt deeper explorations. They should avoid dominating the conversation or steering it towards a predetermined answer. What's more, as the discussion progresses, the teacher should help learners to synthesise their ideas and arrive at conclusions. One way to do this is to summarise key points and encourage learners to reflect on what they've learned.

Into practice
Writing your story

Six Socratic questions

Socratic questioning is, by design, a formulaic approach and thus it's best to stick rigidly to the process — at least to begin with. To do this, it helps to follow a six-part structure as follows:

| 1. Conceptual clarification | 2. Probing assumptions | 3. Probing rationale | 4. Questioning perspectives | 5. Probing implications | 6. Questioning the question |

1. Conceptual clarification questions

The first type of Socratic question requires learners to clarify their thinking. These questions might be:

"Why do you say that?"

"What exactly does this mean?"

"Could you explain that further?"

"What do we already know about that?"

"Can you give me an example?"

"Are you saying … or …?"

"Can you rephrase that, please?"

2. Probing assumptions questions

The second type of Socratic question challenges learners about their pre-existing assumptions and makes them think about their hitherto unquestioned beliefs. This might include the following questions:

"Is that always the case?"

"Why do you think that assumption holds here?"

"Please explain why/how …?"

"How can you verify/disprove that assumption?"

There are three basic elements to a Socratic seminar:

1. Story

The story (which may be in the form of a book, an article, a short video or audio clip, or even a stimulus such as a painting, an object, or an artefact) should contain important and powerful ideas and values relevant to the topic being taught. The story should be pitched at the appropriate level for learners in the class in terms of its language and the complexity of its argument, and it should relate directly to the core concepts of the content being studied. It is beneficial if there is a certain degree of ambiguity in the text and, therefore, the potential for different interpretations because this makes for richer discussions. It helps if all learners have read the text in advance.

2. Classroom

Ideally, the classroom should be arranged so that learners can look at each other directly, as this promotes discussion and enables learners to display and respond to active listening cues such as body language. An agreed set of discussion *norms* or classroom rules should be displayed. More on this in a moment.

3. Questions

It is best for the teacher to prepare several questions in advance, in addition to the questions which learners may bring to class having read the text. The questions should be open-ended and reflect a genuine curiosity. There should be no right answer. At the end, it is useful to debrief learners and encourage them to reflect on how successful they feel the seminar has been.

Here are some sample questions which could serve as the key question or which could help learners to interpret the story:

- What is the main idea/underlying value in the story?
- What is the author's purpose or perspective?
- What does (a particular phrase) mean?
- What might be a good title for the story?
- What is the most important word/sentence/paragraph?

Here are some sample questions which could help move the discussion along:

- Who has a different perspective?
- Who has not yet had a chance to speak?
- Where do you find evidence for that in the story?

- Can you clarify what you mean by that?

- How does that relate to what (someone else) said?

- Is there something in the story that is unclear to you?

- Has anyone changed their mind?

Here are some sample questions which could help bring the discussion to a logical conclusion:

- How do the ideas in the story relate to our lives?

- What do they mean for us personally?

- Why is this material important?

- Is it right that …?

- Do you agree with the author?

And here are some sample questions for the final debriefing:

- Do you feel like you understand the story at a deeper level?

- How was the process for us?

- Did we adhere to our norms?

- Did you achieve your goals to participate?

- What was one thing you noticed about the seminar?

Creating the culture for questioning

Socratic questioning – like all forms of dialogic teaching – encourages learners to take an active role in their learning, develop analytical skills, and engage in meaningful discussions. It also supports a learner-centred classroom where curiosity, enquiry, and critical thinking are at the forefront of the learning process. But this requires a classroom culture that is conducive to discussion and debate.

Establishing clear rules and routines for classroom discussions is therefore crucial to creating a productive and respectful learning environment where learners feel comfortable expressing their thoughts and engaging in meaningful dialogue.

Here are some key rules and routines to consider implementing in your 'questioning classroom':

Rule 1: Be respectful

What does this mean in practice? We should encourage learners to:

- *Listen actively when others are speaking.*

- *Speak politely and avoid interrupting.*

- *Disagree respectfully and focus on ideas, not individuals. Use phrases like "I see your point, but I think …" or "Another way to look at it is …"*

Rule 2: Take turns

Encourage learners to:

- *Raise your hand to indicate you want to speak.*

- *Wait for the teacher to acknowledge you before speaking.*

- *Give others a chance to contribute before speaking again.*

Rule 3: Stay on task

Encourage learners to:

- *Keep the discussion focused on the topic at hand.*

- *Avoid going off on tangents or discussing unrelated matters.*

Rule 4: Develop others' ideas

Encourage learners to:

- *Respond to and expand upon their peers' contributions.*

- *Use phrases like "I agree with …" or "Adding to what [learner] said …"*

Rule 5: Provide supporting evidence

Encourage learners to:

- *Support your ideas with evidence from the text, class materials, or personal experiences.*

- *Use phrases like "In the text, it says …" or "I noticed that …"*

Rule 6: Take part

Encourage all learners to:

- *Participate willingly and without fear – take a risk and make a mistake.*

- *Share their thoughts before opening up to the whole class.*

Rule 7: Allow sufficient wait time

Encourage learners to:

- *Allow a few moments of silence after a question is asked before responding in order to afford time to think.*

- *Give thoughtful responses by taking time to process their thoughts before speaking.*

The teacher may need to guide and moderate discussions to ensure they stay on track and that all learners have opportunities to participate. To help, the teacher could ask follow-up questions to promote deeper thinking and guide the conversation. After a discussion, the teacher could ask learners to summarise the main points or ideas discussed and encourage learners to synthesise multiple viewpoints and draw conclusions.

The teacher also needs to hold learners accountable for adhering to the established rules and routines. To achieve this, they can praise and acknowledge learners who consistently contribute positively to discussions. They can also periodically revisit class rules and routines to ensure they are working effectively, and perhaps ask learners for their input on how discussions can be improved and adjusted.

Further, the teacher may need to create a comfortable and welcoming physical environment that encourages open dialogue. In particular, visual reminders of the rules can be displayed on walls in order to reinforce expectations.

As with all learning habits, it is important that the teacher models the behaviours they expect learners to adopt and use. For example, the teacher could model appropriate discussion, demonstrating active listening, respectful communication, and thoughtful contributions.

Some learners, particularly younger children, may need a graduated approach whereby they begin with smaller guided discussions, with a gradual increase in the complexity of debates as learners establish greater levels of autonomy over time.

Learner grouping

As well as establishing the right culture and articulating and reinforcing rules and expectations, it is important to consider how learners will be grouped for discussions in our questioning classrooms.

Grouping learners for classroom debates requires thoughtful consideration in order to ensure a balanced and productive learning experience. The choice of grouping is, of course, contextual: it depends on the learning objectives, the nature of the topic, and the dynamics of the class. But here are some grouping strategies you may wish to consider:

Heterogeneous groups: Create groups with a mix of abilities, learning styles, and perspectives. This approach promotes collaboration, as learners can learn from one another's diverse viewpoints and skills.

Homogeneous groups: Group learners with similar knowledge levels or skills. This strategy can be effective for targeted discussions or debates focused on specific concepts.

Mixed-ability pairs: Pair a high-performing learner with a learner who's struggling in the task at hand. This promotes peer support and helps learners learn from one another.

Interest-based groups: Group learners based on their interests or areas of expertise. This approach can enhance engagement and motivation, as learners are discussing topics that they're passionate about.

Random groups: Assign groups randomly to promote interaction among learners who might not usually work together. This can be particularly effective for fostering a sense of classroom community.

Assigned roles: Assign specific roles within each group, such as a facilitator, a timekeeper, a note-taker, and a spokesperson. This ensures that responsibilities are distributed and that discussions are well organised.

Pre-selected groups: Form groups in advance based on your observations of learner dynamics. This allows you to create balanced groups and anticipate potential challenges.

Choice-based groups: Allow learners to choose their group members based on shared interests or working relationships. This empowers learners and encourages collaboration. However, this approach is best left until learners are older and more experienced at holding class discussions.

Debating teams: For debates, consider using a format whereby learners are divided into two teams with assigned roles (e.g., speakers, researchers, rebuttalists, etc.). Alternatively, you can have learners choose their positions randomly to promote critical thinking and persuasive skills.

Rotation: Rotate group members periodically to ensure that learners collaborate with different classmates over time. This helps learners build a variety of interpersonal skills.

Flexible grouping: Adapt your grouping strategy based on the specific activity or learning objective. This approach allows you to tailor the grouping to the task at hand.

When deciding on a grouping strategy that suits the context, consider factors such as the goals of the discussion or debate, the size of the class, individual learner needs, and the classroom dynamics. Be prepared to adapt your approach based on feedback you observe and the progress made during the discussions. Ultimately, the goal is to create an environment that encourages active participation, collaboration, and critical thinking among all learners. Whatever works, works.

Eliciting responses to questions

Knowing who should answer a question is almost as important as the question itself. The general rule of thumb is this: avoid the 'hands-up' approach which invariably elicits responses from higher-performing and more garrulous learners, thus skewing the data and allowing quieter learners to hide in the shadows.

Targeting questions at specific learners rather than allowing hands-up responses can have several advantages in the classroom:

Firstly, it **increases the level of engagement**. Why? Because when questions are directed at specific learners, everyone in the class is more likely to stay attentive and engaged. Learners know that they might be called on, so they are more likely to actively participate in discussions.

Secondly, it **ensures more equitable participation**. Why? Because allowing hands-up responses can – indeed, often does – result in the same few learners volunteering while others remain quiet. Targeting questions ensures that a broader range of learners can contribute their thoughts and ideas. Further, it improves accountability because when learners know they might be called upon to answer a question, they are more likely to come prepared and be attentive to the material being discussed. This accountability can improve overall participation and learning outcomes.

Thirdly, it **improves learners' listening skills** because when learners know they might be called upon to answer, they need to actively listen to the question being posed to them or their peers. This can translate into better comprehension of the material. Further, being called upon to answer encourages learners to think on their feet and articulate their thoughts in real time. This, in turn, helps develop their communication skills and their ability to express ideas clearly and confidently.

Fourthly, it can **lead to more diverse perspectives** being shared. Why? Because targeted questioning allows the class to hear from a variety of learners, each with their unique viewpoints and insights. This enriches classroom discussions by bringing in diverse perspectives. By targeting questions, teachers can also assess learners' understanding of the material more effectively. This enables teachers to identify misconceptions and adjust their instruction accordingly.

Fifthly, it can **improve classroom dynamics** because directed questions create a classroom environment where every learner feels valued and included. Learners see that their contributions matter, fostering a positive and supportive atmosphere.

Ultimately, targeting questions promotes active participation rather than passive observation. Learners are more likely to be mentally engaged and ready to contribute when they know they might be called upon. It's important, however, to use targeted questioning in a way that is respectful and supportive. Teachers need to be sensitive to learners' comfort levels and readiness to respond. If they notice a learner struggling to answer, they should offer guidance or provide the learner with opportunities to think and respond at their own pace.

Teacher talk

One of the advantages of using story and storytelling techniques and of creating a 'questioning classroom' to explore stories is that it avoids too much 'teacher talk'.

Here are some other ways of reducing 'teacher talk' in order to create a questioning classroom:

Chunk information: Break down content into smaller chunks to prevent information overload. Provide opportunities for learners to process and discuss the information after each chunk.

Use visuals: Incorporate visuals, diagrams, videos, and interactive materials to convey information visually and engage multiple senses. Ensure you dual code – combining images with verbal commentary or explanations.

Incorporate active learning: Integrate active learning strategies such as group discussions, problem-solving activities, debates, and hands-on projects. These strategies keep learners engaged and encourage them to apply their learning.

Use 'think-pair-share': Ask a question, have learners think individually, pair up to discuss their thoughts, and then share with the class. This strategy encourages peer interaction and reduces the need for prolonged teacher lectures.

Provide guided practice: After introducing a concept, provide guided practice activities that allow learners to apply new information. This ensures active engagement and reinforcement of learning. While so doing, set time limits for teacher-led instruction. Use a timer to remind yourself to transition to more interactive activities. You could also leverage technology like interactive whiteboards, polling apps, and online discussion platforms. These tools can further facilitate engagement and active participation.

Use peer teaching: Design opportunities for learners to teach their peers about a specific topic or concept. This promotes active involvement and reinforces learning through teaching.

Questioning with purpose

While asking questions is a great way to encourage active participation and critical thinking, it's important to strike a balance and use questions purposefully. Asking too many questions without a clear purpose or without giving learners adequate time to respond can potentially have negative effects on the learning environment.

Here are some ways to ensure questions have purpose:

Quality over quantity: Focus on asking thoughtful and open questions that promote deeper understanding and encourage meaningful discussions.

Give time for thought: Allow learners sufficient time to process the question and formulate their responses before expecting an answer. Rushing through questions may hinder learners' ability to engage in higher-order thinking. Implement 'wait time' after asking a question to give learners a chance to think and formulate their responses. This encourages deeper thinking and more thoughtful answers.

Vary question types: Use a mix of question types, including factual, analytical, evaluative, and application-based questions. Varying the types of questions keeps learners engaged and addresses different levels of cognitive thinking.

Avoid rapid-fire questioning: Rapidly firing multiple questions without allowing for substantial responses can be overwhelming for learners and hinder their engagement. Instead, encourage learners to ask questions and lead discussions. This empowers learners to take ownership of their learning and contributes to a more dynamic classroom environment.

Use questions to guide exploration: Use questions to guide learners' exploration of a topic or concept. Allow them to engage in enquiry-based learning by investigating and seeking answers.

Reflect on timing: Consider when and where in the lesson you ask questions. Use questions strategically to introduce a topic, check understanding, or encourage reflection. Ensure that all learners have opportunities to respond to questions. Avoid relying solely on a small group of active participants.

Give feedback: Use questions to assess learner understanding, identify misconceptions, and provide timely feedback. Balance assessment-related questions with those that encourage exploration and critical thinking. While so doing, engage in a natural and authentic dialogue with learners rather than turning the classroom into an interrogation. Also, monitor learners' body language, participation, and reactions to gauge if they are engaged and responsive to your questions.

Timing questions right

As well as considering *what* questions to ask, we need to think carefully about *when* to ask questions.

The timing of questions in class can significantly impact learner engagement and understanding. Different moments during a lesson serve different purposes for questioning. It might help to consider the following 'trigger points' when timing your questions:

The beginning of the lesson: You could start the lesson with an open question related to the topic. This will activate learners' prior knowledge and set the scene for the upcoming discussion. Wording learning objectives as questions can be really powerful – particularly if they are 'how?' or 'why?' type questions which provoke deeper thinking and discussion.

During teacher explanations: You could ask questions as part of your direct instruction – explanations and modelling – in order to check for understanding. You could, for example, use questions to guide learners' attention to key concepts, definitions, or important details.

During guided practice and group work: You could also incorporate questions into group discussions, problem-solving activities, and hands-on projects. Questions can guide and scaffold learners' thinking as they engage with the material. During think-pair-share activities, you could ask a question, have learners think individually, pair up to discuss, and then share their thoughts with the class. This strategy encourages collaboration and provides time for deeper thinking before sharing with the whole group.

After presenting new content: You could pause after presenting new information and ask questions to reinforce understanding. You could use questions to encourage learners to summarise the content in their own words.

Before task transitions: You could ask a question before transitioning to a new topic or activity. This will help refocus learners' attention and prime them for the upcoming content.

During reflection and in plenaries: You could use questions to prompt learners to reflect on what they've learned. You could also end the lesson with a question that encourages learners to connect the new knowledge they've acquired to prior understanding.

... and all times in between: In addition to the above, you could space questions throughout the lesson to maintain a steady level of engagement. This will prevent periods of passive listening and keep learners actively involved and on their toes!

Remember, though, that the best time to ask questions depends on the specific lesson, learning intentions, and the dynamics of your class. As with all aspects of the classroom, context is all, and pragmatism is key! But the goal is to create a rhythm that keeps learners engaged and encourages them to think critically while also allowing time for reflection and application of the content.

More questioning strategies to deepen thinking

Into practice
Writing your story

Here, hidden, head

In 1993, Lorraine Graham and Bernice Wong developed the 3H strategy for developing learners' comprehension.[5] The 3 Hs in question are: Here, Hidden, and Head. Moving learners through the three stages takes them from literal to deductive questions.

- 'Here' questions are literal questions, the answers to which are apparent in the text. For example, 'What was the Stable Buck called in *Of Mice and Men*?

- 'Hidden' questions require learners to synthesise information from different parts of a text. For example, 'How did Curley's wife's life change when she got married?'

- 'Head' questions require learners to use their prior knowledge in order to predict or deduce. For example, 'Do you think George ever really believed he'd own his own ranch? Why do you think that?'

Collaboration questioning

I've mentioned several questioning strategies so far which require collaboration – passing questions from learner to learner can be a dynamic and effective way to promote discussion and deepen learners' understanding. Strategies like think-pair-share encourage all learners to engage with the material and respond to each other's perspectives.

Here are some other methods for passing questions around the classroom:

1. Question chains

How it works:

- Start by asking an open question related to the topic of discussion.
- After one learner responds, ask that learner to pose a follow-up question to another learner in the class.
- Encourage the recipient of the question to respond and then pass on a new question to another classmate.
- Continue this chain until most or all learners have had the opportunity to contribute.

2. Question cards

How it works:

- Prepare question cards with open questions related to the lesson.
- Distribute the cards randomly to learners.
- Instruct each learner to answer their question and then select another question from the stack to ask their peer.
- This method allows learners to engage in thoughtful discussions with a variety of questions.

3. Pass the parcel

How it works:

- Divide the class into small groups of three to four learners.
- Start a discussion by posing an initial question.
- After a few minutes, or when the music stops, instruct one learner from each group to 'pass' the conversation to another group by sharing their group's key insights or questions.
- This encourages learners to synthesise their group's discussion and share diverse perspectives.

4. Gallery technique

How it works:

- Post a series of questions on different positions around the classroom.
- Divide learners into small groups and assign each group to a starting position.
- Instruct learners to discuss and respond to the question at their assigned position.
- After a set time, have groups rotate to the next position and continue the discussion based on the new question.

5. Think-pair-share PLUS

How it works:

- Begin with an initial open question.
- Ask learners to individually write down their response to the question.
- Then have learners pair up and discuss their responses.
- Next, ask each pair to come up with a new question related to the topic and share it with another pair.
- Continue this process to create a chain of discussions and new questions.

6. Reflection journals

How it works:

- Distribute journals to learners and provide them with a prompt or question related to the topic.
- Have learners write their responses.
- Afterwards, ask them to exchange journals with a peer and respond to their class-mate's entry.

We will explore some more questioning techniques in Chapter 10.

What have we learned?

In this chapter, we have discovered that:

Using stories in the classroom can help learners grasp complex concepts because stories can turn abstract concepts into concrete ones. Stories can also help pique learners' curiosity by making ideas more personal and relatable.

Stories create vivid mental images which act as a useful cue for recall. Stories are also non-threatening and so can ease learners into challenging learning.

One effective way of piquing learners' curiosity is to ask a big question or present a mystery that begs a solution. This could take the form of a case study, a personal anecdote, or an imagined story. A story's 'big question' can take many forms, such as a question of conflict; a question of mystery; a question of character; a question of themes; a question of speculation; a question of morals; a question of desire; and a question of identity.

What can we do?

To put the advice contained in this chapter into practice, it might be helpful to consider the following questions:

1. Do you structure learning around a big question? Are questions at the heart of your lessons?

2. Do you use closed questions to check learners' understanding and diagnose next steps?

3. Do you use open questions to deepen learners' thinking, perhaps in the form of dialogic teaching strategies such as Socratic questions?

4. Do you use questions to help learners become more critical thinkers?

5. How do you use different types of learner grouping to change the dynamic and outcome of classroom discussions?

6. How do you strategically time questions to get the most from them?

Notes

1 Bruner, J S (1986). *Actual Minds, Possible Worlds*. Harvard University Press, p. 13.
2 www.harvardbusiness.org/what-makes-storytelling-so-effective-for-learning/
3 www.psychologicalscience.org/observer/storytelling-in-teaching
4 There is some debate about the provenance of this quote.
5 Graham, L & Wong, B L (1993). Comparing two modes of teaching a question-answering strategy for enhancing reading comprehension: Didactic and self-instructional training. *Journal of Learning Disabilities*, 26(4), 270–279. https://doi.org/10.1177/002221949302600407

Using story to relate curriculum content to the real world

Stories are 'psychologically privileged' because our minds treat stories differently to other types of material. Stories are how we process the world. Stories give us the 'why': they lend meaning and purpose to our very existence.

Everyone loves a good story. Even small children who have difficulty focusing will sit with rapt attention in the presence of a good storyteller. But, as we've already seen, stories are not just fun; rather, there are important cognitive consequences of the story format. People find stories interesting, easy to understand, and easy to remember. As I explained earlier, this is, in part, because stories turn abstract ideas into concrete reality; stories bring facts to life and flesh out ideas. Stories certainly help us to relate theory to the real world and give ideas a human face.

According to the Historical Association:[1]

Through stories we can carry [learners] to different worlds in space and time. When telling stories, we find a key to unlock children's imagination and make the past intelligible to them. For example, in [the Historical Association's] story of Victorian children working down the mines,[2] our modern children can identify with the heroine being scared of the dark, and so they enter her world.

Stories can be used to convey information, ideas, and technical language through engaging learners' imaginations. They can also be used to create a context, providing a mental map and a visualisation of a past situation. And, says the Historical Association, they can help learners to "understand human situations and the human condition, and thus connect the past to the present".

The Historical Association advises that when telling stories to relate the curriculum to the real world, we should build our descriptions, flesh out our characters and the context they lived in by considering: How did they think, look, feel, and act, and what motivated them?

I'd like to focus on the importance of talking to learners' lived experiences through story and storytelling techniques.

I've already discussed the importance of using story to make the abstract concrete, and using stories that reflect learners' lives certainly does this. For example, analogies that compare

DOI: 10.4324/9781003465492-11

something new and abstract to something familiar and concrete – something learners have already experienced and know – helps them to understand that new information. Analogies help learners to make connections and thus to forge schema.

But talking to lived experiences is about more than analogy.

It's important, if we are to engage learners and help them to understand our curriculum, that the stories we tell hold a mirror up to their own lives. We want them to see themselves and their experiences – not to mention their own thoughts and emotions – reflected at them.

In an article I wrote for *SecEd Magazine* on achieving equity in education,[3] I argued that educators "need to think more carefully – nationally and locally – about who decides what knowledge is taught, when, and why [and] think more carefully about how representative that knowledge is of our school communities, how effectively it talks to students' lived experiences and to their family traditions and cultures".

But this is not enough. I went on to say that "once we have selected knowledge that does reflect our school community, we need to select knowledge that celebrates diversity beyond our community so that we can broaden our students' horizons".

In short, we need to ensure that stories:

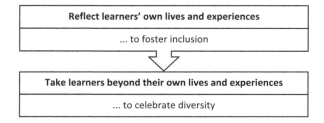

Stories: a mirror and a window

National Literacy Trust research on diversity in 2022 found that two in five (38.9%) children and young people think it's difficult to find books with characters or people like them, increasing to one in two (53.1%) children aged 8 to 11.[4] While just over one in three (34.9%) children and young people from White backgrounds say they struggle to see themselves in what they read, this increases to nearly one in two (45.2%) children and young people from Black ethnic backgrounds. More than two in five (42.5%) of those receiving free school meals report finding it difficult to see themselves in books compared with just over one in three (35.2%) of their peers who do not receive free school meals.

Crucially, the survey found that two in five (38.9%) children and young people agreed with the statement, 'Reading about characters that are like me makes me feel more confident about myself'. More children and young people who struggle to see themselves in books said they write about characters or people like themselves compared with those who do not find it difficult (35.0% vs. 23.4%). More also write about characters or people with similar experiences to them (37.8% vs. 24.7%). In addition, more children and young people who find it difficult to find books with characters or people like them said they choose to write about characters or people like themselves (35.0% vs. 23.4% of those who don't find it difficult).

The best schools reflect their local communities; they bring the community into their school and take learners out into that community. The best schools also look beyond their local communities and regard themselves as part of the national and international conversation. These schools teach learners how to be active members of their communities and how to be good citizens of the world. A school's success can, I think, be measured by the extent to which it prepares all the young people it serves for their next steps in life – do learners leave the school as well-rounded, cultured, inquisitive, caring, kind, resilient, knowledgeable human beings ready to make their own way in the world? And do schools, consequently, make the world a better place?

Stories are the secret to making the world a better place one learner at a time. Stories that are reflective of our own lives lend credence to those lives and make us feel included and – for want of a better word – 'normal' or accepted. Stories that are reflective of other lives different from our own help us to understand how other people live and lend empathy and compassion. In other words, stories should act as a mirror – reflecting learners' lives back at them so they feel included – and as a window, allowing learners to see other lives different from their own so they appreciate diversity.

Let us consider some examples of this in practice.

Taking our lead from the National Literacy Trust's research findings – though the notion of telling stories that talk to learners' lived experiences is, of course, universal – we might conclude that Black and ethnic minority learners are less likely to feel included in our curriculum than those from White British backgrounds. We might therefore consider *decolonising* our curriculum to ensure it is more representative of Black and ethnic minority voices. One way to do this is by ensuring that the school library is stocked with books showing diverse content from Black and ethnic minority authors; another way is to ensure the analogies, illustrations, and examples we use in class include stories by and about people with Black and ethnic minority backgrounds.

Selecting stories to promote inclusion

Into practice
Writing your story

BookTrust says that:

> Inclusive children's literature is vital. Children's books can act as mirrors, to reflect the readers' own lives, and also as windows, so readers can learn about, understand and appreciate the lives of others. They can shape how young readers from minority backgrounds see themselves as well as how readers from the more dominant culture see and understand diversity. The absence of an inclusive range of characters or creative role models in children's literature has the potential to deter children from minority backgrounds from reading and experiencing the associated benefits.[5]

BookTrust recommends the following books from Black authors:

All Because You Matter by Tami Charles
Reading age: 6+

You Are a Champion by Marcus Rashford and Carl Anka
Reading age: 8+

I Am Every Good Thing by Derrick Barnes
Reading age: 7+

Cane Warriors by Alex Wheatle
Reading age: 12+

Stand Up and Speak Out Against Racism by Yassmin Abdel-Magied
Reading age: 9+

Timelines from Black History: Leaders, Legends, Legacies, with an Introduction by Mireille Harper
Reading age: 9+

Baby Ruby Bawled by Malaika Rose Stanley
Reading age: 7+

My Hair by Hannah Lee
Reading age: 5+

Daddy Do My Hair: Kechi's Hair Goes Every Which Way by Tola Okogwu
Reading age: 5+

King of the Classroom by Derrick Barnes
Look Up! by Nathan Bryon
Reading age: 6+

Sulwe by Lupita Nyong'o
Reading age: 5+

Little Leaders: Bold Women in Black History by Vashti Harrison
Reading age: 7+

Run the Show Like CEO Oprah Winfrey by Caroline Moss

Reading age: 7+

Queer Heroes by Arabelle Sicardi
Reading age: 7+

The Undefeated by Kwame Alexander
Reading age: 8+

Windrush Child by Benjamin Zephaniah
Reading age: 9+

Clean Getaway by Nic Stone
Reading age: 9+

How High the Moon by Karyn Parsons
Reading age: 9+

High-Rise Mystery by Sharna Jackson
Reading age: 9+

Katherine Johnson: A Life Story by Leila Rasheed
Reading age: 9+

Ghost by Jason Reynolds
Reading age: 12+

Funky Chickens by Benjamin Zephaniah
Reading age: 9+

Peace Maker by Malorie Blackman
Reading age: 8+

Work It, Girl: Become a Leader Like Michelle Obama by Caroline Moss
Reading age: 8+

This Book Is Anti Racist: 20 Lessons on How to Wake Up, Take Action and Do the Work by Tiffany Jewell
Reading age: 9+

Noughts and Crosses by Malorie Blackman
Reading age: 12+

The problem of under-representation is cyclical: if young people do not see themselves reflected in the books they read at school then they are likely to conclude that the creative industries are not for them and thus fewer minorities enter the profession and fewer books are published by minority voices.

Indeed, BookTrust says that:

> The causes of under-representation of people of colour among children's book creators are complex, multifaceted and embedded in broader social inequalities. However, common barriers can be expressed as a negative cycle that not only prevents them from pursuing creative careers but can also hinder their careers once they have been published. This cycle begins with children not seeing themselves in books and not experiencing creative role models, with whom they identify, at a time when young people of colour might be considering their future professions. Even when a person of colour does make the decision to pursue a career in this precarious profession, they may face barriers when looking for an agent or publisher.[6]

Stories: making the classroom work for working-class learners

Again, taking a lead from the National Literacy Trust research, we might consider making our stories more representative of children on free school meals who are from working-class backgrounds. To be clear, not all children from working-class backgrounds live in poverty but all those who live in poverty are, by most definitions of social class, working class. And working-class children are underrepresented in the school curriculum and underachieve compared to their middle-class peers. Indeed, this was the subject of my 2023 book *The Working Classroom*.[7]

In that book, which I co-wrote with Andy Griffith, I argued that "so much of what schools do is classist". As I explained, "The stated aim of the national curriculum is to ensure that all students in England encounter the same content and material. The curriculum should provide students with 'an introduction to the essential knowledge that they need to be educated citizens'" but there are, I said, two problems with this:

Firstly, there's the problem of curriculum coverage: "One size doesn't fit all. Providing all students with the same curriculum further disadvantages those who are already disadvantaged." Yes, I explained, it is only right that we "offer the same ambitious curriculum to every student, irrespective of their background, additional and different needs, and starting points" but that's not enough; we should then offer more, not less – and crucially not the same – to working-class learners.

Secondly, and crucially for our present purposes, there's the problem of curriculum content: I argued that definitions of core knowledge are classist because they are "based on the notion that wealth and social status confer taste and discernment, and the selection of knowledge is made by those of a higher social standing rather than by a representative group of people from across the social strata". The same is true of the stories we tell in school – they are chosen by – and predominantly written by and about – middle-class people.

Schools are expected to teach learners 'the best that has been thought and said' but who decides what constitutes the 'best'? As I argued in *The Working Classroom*: "Notions of best are, by definition, subjective. Sadly, all too often, these choices are made by politicians from middle-class backgrounds." And yet every school's curriculum should celebrate working-class culture alongside culture from the dominant classes.

Stories by and about people from working-class backgrounds are integral to improving the educational and life chances of working-class learners. Stories from working-class backgrounds help to embed what Andy and I called the 'four knowledge domains' of disciplinary knowledge, personal knowledge, social knowledge, and cultural knowledge.

Disciplinary knowledge is the ability to speak, read, and write in ways that befit each subject discipline – for example, being able to speak, read, and write like a mathematician, a historian, an artist, a scientist, and so on. The development of disciplinary knowledge dominates the secondary school curriculum, and rightly so, because a lack of disciplinary knowledge holds back students from lower socioeconomic backgrounds.

Personal knowledge is about wisdom and wellbeing and encompasses the development of an empowering self-concept through the story you tell yourself about who you are and who you might become. In practice, it involves:

- Developing metacognitive knowledge and self-regulation skills, which are thought to be key ingredients of academic success.

- Learning about emotions (such as anxiety, anger, and sadness) and understanding the reasons for their existence and the best way to process them.

- Understanding notions of 'self' and the power of the stories you tell yourself about who you are, the beliefs you hold, and how you can alter your own personal stories or scripts.

- Realising personal strengths and interests that can unlock future career and leisure paths.

As I explained in Chapter 2, key to understanding self is understanding 'story'. The stories we tell ourselves derive in large part from our conditioning, perceptions, and lived experiences. Understanding our own stories can help us choose a better script to live by. When people realise that they can change their narrative, especially when the current one is self-defeating, and do so, extraordinary things can happen.

Cultural knowledge is about two things: Firstly, acknowledging that the dominant class uses their knowledge of culture as a tool to exclude others, it involves learning about so-called 'high art' and art created by the working classes. Secondly, it is accepting that no matter your social class, anyone can enjoy any form of art or culture – people should enjoy what they enjoy and not allow others to decide that a particular form of culture isn't for them.

Finally, *social knowledge* refers to the way in which society is organised and in whose interests it operates. The development of students' social knowledge inevitably involves raising their political awareness. Stories such as political biographies, historical records, and fiction such as George Orwell's *Animal Farm* are key to this.

More stories to promote inclusion

Into practice
Writing your story

Here, from *The Working Classroom*, are some books – in chronological order – we could include in our curriculum to make it more representative of working-class voices. Remember the importance of presenting learners with age-appropriate texts though – both in terms of subject matter and language requirements:

Elizabeth Gaskell – *North and South* (1854); Charles Dickens – *Great Expectations* (1861); George Eliot – *Middlemarch* (1871); Émile Zola – *Germinal* (1885); Thomas Hardy – *Jude the Obscure* (1895); W. H. Davies – *The Autobiography of a Super-Tramp* (1908); E. M. Forster – *Howard's End* (1910); D. H. Lawrence – *Sons and Lovers* (1913); Robert Tressell – *The Ragged Trousered Philanthropists* (1914); George Orwell – *Down and Out in Paris and London* (1933), *The Road to Wigan Pier* (1937), *Nineteen Eighty-Four* (1949), and *The Collected Essays, Journalism and Letters, Volume 1* (1920–1940); Alan Sillitoe – *The Loneliness of the Long-Distance Runner* (1959); Mikhail Bulgakov – *The Master and Margarita* (1967); Alan Garner – *Red Shift* (1973); Sue Townsend – *The Queen and I* (1992); Barry Unsworth – *Sacred Hunger* (1992) and *The Quality of Mercy* (2011); Roddy Doyle – *Paddy Clarke Ha Ha Ha* (1993); Irvine Welsh – *Trainspotting* (1993); James Kelman – *How Late It Was, How Late* (1994); Andrea Ashworth – *Once in a House on Fire* (1998); Zadie Smith – *White Teeth* (2000); Stuart Maconie – *The People's Songs* (2013); and Douglas Stuart – *Shuggie Bain* (2020).

And, because stories are not confined to books, here are some TV programmes and films – again in chronological order – we could use too. Again, remember the importance of choosing age-appropriate content:

Films: *An Inspector Calls* (1954), *The Admirable Crichton* (1957), *A Taste of Honey* (1961), *Kes* (1969), *Trading Places* (1983), *Brassed Off* (1996), *Billy Elliot* (2000), *I, Daniel Blake* (2016), *Parasite* (2019), *Us* (2019), and *Life and Death in a Warehouse* (2022).

TV shows: *The Century of the Self* (2002) written by Adam Curtis, *Shameless* written by Paul Abbott (2004–2013), *Black Mirror* (2011–) written by Charlie Brooker, *Broken* (2017) written by Jimmy McGovern, and *Anne* (2022) written by Kevin Sampson.

The universal

Storytelling is universal: we all tell stories and stories are integral to our recollections of the past and to our plans for the future; stories carry our hopes and our fears. The stories we hear when we're young teach us how to feel and how to talk; through stories we inherit our morals and values, our truths and beliefs. Harold Rosen, in a postscript to *And None of It Was Nonsense* by Betty Rosen (1988), argues that narrative "is nothing if not a supreme means of rendering otherwise chaotic, shapeless events into a coherent whole, saturated with meaning".[8]

Rosen says that stories do not offer single meanings; rather, they form interlocking sets of meanings, and listening to a story is a search for these meanings through the meanings we already possess. In retelling, we both repeat the words of others and change them. As I explained in Chapter 2, we even change our own personal stories, carrying forward some of the old, but shifting, however slightly, the meanings of the story. We are, Rosen says, incorrigible re-workers of our own and other people's stories.[9]

When selecting stories to bring the real world to life and to talk to learners' lived experiences, we might ask:

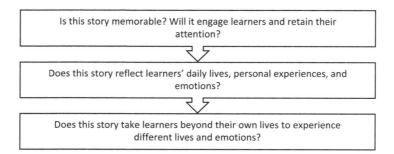

> Is this story memorable? Will it engage learners and retain their attention?

> Does this story reflect learners' daily lives, personal experiences, and emotions?

> Does this story take learners beyond their own lives to experience different lives and emotions?

Celebrating diversity through stories

Into practice
Writing your story

On the last point – telling stories that take learners beyond their own lives and experiences – I think it is helpful to encourage learners to imagine living the different lives they read about and to put themselves in characters' shoes to empathise with their feelings. Asking probing questions can help here.

To encourage learners to empathise with people who are different from them, we might ask the following questions as we read stories:

1. How do you think the character feels in this situation? Can you relate to any personal experiences or emotions that are similar?

2. If you were in the character's shoes, how would you react or make decisions differently? Why?

3. Can you identify any challenges or obstacles the character faces that you've encountered or can imagine facing in your own life?

4. What do you think the character's motivations are? Can you empathise with their reasons for their actions or choices?

5. How might the character's background or upbringing influence their behaviour and choices in the story? How does this compare to your own background?

6. If you were a friend or family member of the character, how would you support or advise them in their situation?

7. Have you ever felt misunderstood or judged, like the character might in this story? How did it make you feel, and how did you handle it?

8. Can you think of a time when you had to step into someone else's shoes to understand their perspective or feelings, just like we're doing with this character?

9. What lessons or insights can you take away from the character's experiences in the story that might help you in your own life or interactions with others?

10. How does your empathy for the character change as the story progresses? Are there moments when you feel more connected or less connected to them, and why?

11. Are there any supporting characters in the story who show empathy or lack of empathy towards the main character? How does this impact the main character, and what can we learn from it?

12. How might the character's background, culture, or experiences influence their beliefs and values? How do these factors shape their actions and decisions in the story?

13. What do you think the character needs most at this point in the story? How would you like to see their situation improve, and why?

14. Can you see any similarities between the character's experiences and real-world issues or challenges that people face today? How does this make you feel, and what actions or solutions can you propose?

15. If you could offer the character advice or support, what would you say or do to help them navigate their situation or emotions?

To help learners understand the different lives and experiences they encounter in stories, we might ask the following questions as we read:

1. What aspects of the character's life in the story are different from your own experiences and background?

2. How does the character's cultural background or upbringing influence their beliefs, traditions, and values?

3. Can you identify any challenges or advantages the character faces due to their socioeconomic status, race, ethnicity, or gender?

4. What can you learn from the character's experiences about the customs, traditions, or practices of their culture or community?

5. How does the setting of the story impact the characters' lives and choices? How is it different from your own environment?

6. Are there any cultural or historical events mentioned in the story that you are unfamiliar with? How do these events affect the characters?

7. What stereotypes or biases, if any, do you notice in the story, and how do these impact the characters' lives?

8. How do characters from different backgrounds interact with one another in the story? What conflicts or misunderstandings arise, and how are they resolved?

9. Can you relate to the character's struggles or aspirations, even if their background is different from yours? How can you connect on a human level?

10. How do the characters' different lives shape their goals, dreams, and ambitions? How do these differ from your own?

11. Are there any moments in the story where characters learn from each other's differences or grow through their interactions? What can we learn from these moments?

12. What lessons or insights can you take away from the characters' diverse experiences that might broaden your own perspective or understanding of the world?

13. If you were to step into the shoes of one of the characters with a different background, how do you think you would react to the challenges and opportunities they face?

14. How does the author use language, dialogue, and descriptions to convey the uniqueness of each character's life and experiences?

15. How do the characters' different lives contribute to the overall theme or message of the story? What is the author trying to convey about diversity and understanding?

Stories of the past

One area of the curriculum that would particularly benefit from having texts that tell diverse stories is history – the subject contains the word 'story' after all! Story and storytelling can be effective ways of introducing and extending historical knowledge. While 'history' may contain the word 'story', it's important to remember that history is not merely about recounting past events; rather, it is concerned with processes. Historians undertake investigations: they hypothesise and then attempt to justify their interpretations by reference to available data. In balancing historical knowledge and the process of investigating that knowledge, history can be said to encompass 'knowing-what' as well as 'knowing-how'.

Story and storytelling can be particularly useful in history in lending learners an understanding of chronology. Stories enable learners to place events and people within a historical framework or context. Even very young children can follow the chronological order of events in stories – the plot. Story and storytelling can also help in history to teach learners about change and causation. After listening to a story set in the past, we can ask learners questions which encourage them to identify all the changes that have taken place since the timeframe of the story. They can then make comparisons by considering the similarities and differences between the story's timeframe and now, or between the story's timeframe and the timeframe of another historical story they have read. By reading stories from different historical periods, learners can begin to develop knowledge of those periods and to understand why certain events occurred and why people acted as they did at certain times.

It's worth noting here that stories set in the past do not have to be true. Rather, they have to be authentic. We could, for example, tell a story about the life of a typical solider in the First World War to give a sense of what daily existence would have been like on the front line.

Stories are not just about people; they're also about place. Indeed, in many good stories the setting is itself a character, so integral is it to the plot. Thus, stories have an essential role to play not just in history teaching but in geography too. They enable us to teach learners about where people live and thus can help enhance geographical knowledge and understanding as well as promote geographical skills. Stories enable children to visit many different places.

What have we learned?

In this chapter, we have discovered that:

Our minds regard stories differently to other materials and thus they can be used to transmit ideas by engaging the imagination. What's more, stories can help create context.

The best stories reflect learners' lives, histories, and cultures, and so can be used to make the curriculum more representative of our school community and talk to learners' lived experiences. Stories don't just mirror learners' lives; they celebrate diversity beyond their lived experiences to lend empathy and understanding, tolerance and compassion.

We all tell stories, and stories are integral to our retelling of the past as well as to future plans. The stories we hear when we're young teach us how to feel and how to talk; through stories we inherit our morals and values, our truths and beliefs.

What can we do?

To put the advice contained in this chapter into practice, it might be helpful to consider the following questions:

1. Are you considered in your choice of curriculum content and in the examples you use to illustrate that content, making sure you represent all your learners and talk to their lived experiences?

2. To what extent do you achieve inclusion in your classroom? Do all learners feel a part of the curriculum and do they all routinely get involved in classroom discussions and activities?

3. Do you take learners beyond their own experiences and celebrate other cultures and traditions? Do you promote diversity and ensure learners are respectful of others?

4. Do you use stories to foster empathy, encouraging learners to put themselves in other people's shoes?

Notes

1 www.history.org.uk/primary/module/3657/primary-teaching-methods/3667/story-telling
2 www.history.org.uk/primary/resource/3769
3 www.sec-ed.co.uk/content/best-practice/working-class-students-in-pursuit-of-equity-in-education

4 https://literacytrust.org.uk/research-services/research-reports/seeing-yourself-in-what-you-read-diversity-and-children-and-young-peoples-reading-in-2022/

5 www.booktrust.org.uk/what-we-do/programmes-and-campaigns/booktrust-represents/support-for-schools/

6 www.booktrust.org.uk/globalassets/resources/represents/booktrust_diversityreport_execsummary_april2019.pdf

7 Bromley, M. & Griffith, A. (2023). *The Working Classroom: How to Make Secondary Schools Work Better for Working-Class Students.* Crown House Publishing, pp. 41–43.

8 Rosen, B (1988). *And None of It Was Nonsense: The Power of Storytelling.* Heinemann, p. 164

9 Rosen, B (1988), p. 170.

10 Using story to help foster inclusion

Bernstein's *code theory* is a sociolinguistic theory developed by Basil Bernstein, a British sociologist and linguist. The theory posits that there are two types of language codes used by individuals and groups within a society: the elaborated code and the restricted code.

The elaborated code is a more complex and diverse language code used by those in positions of power and privilege, such as the educated middle and upper classes. It is characterised by a wide range of vocabulary, complex sentence structures, and the ability to use language to express abstract concepts.

The restricted code, by contrast, is a simpler language code used by those in positions of less power and privilege, such as working-class or rural communities. It is characterised by a limited vocabulary, simple sentence structures, and a focus on shared experiences and assumptions.

Bernstein argued that the use of these different language codes can have a significant impact on social mobility and educational achievement. He believed that those who are raised using the elaborated code have an advantage in education and employment, as they are more able to navigate the complex language and social expectations of the dominant culture. Conversely, those raised using the restricted code may struggle to adapt to these expectations and may be at a disadvantage in terms of social mobility.

In sum, Bernstein's code theory highlights the important role that language and communication play in shaping social structures and power dynamics within a society.

In my 2023 book *Intent Implementation Impact*,[1] I argued that language was crucial to success because learners gain access to, comprehend, and demonstrate their understanding of the curriculum through their use of language. I cited American research that shows children in richer families experience 45 million words, while those in working-class families and those in families on welfare experience just 20 and 13 million, respectively. Literacy is a particular issue for disadvantaged learners. Ninety per cent of words will only be experienced in books. It's important to read because that's where we develop vocabulary. As such, I argued that a crucial – though not only – means of closing the attainment gap and providing equal access to our curriculum, and thus fostering inclusion is to develop learners' language and literacy skills.

DOI: 10.4324/9781003465492-12

The causes of disadvantage are complex and myriad; the causes will be different for each child and each child is very complex. As Paul Black and Dylan William explain in their 2018 article 'Classroom assessment and pedagogy':[2]

> Children from working class families, who are only familiar with the restricted code of their everyday language, may find it difficult to engage with the elaborated code that is required by the learning discourse of the classroom and which those from middle class families experience in their home lives.

Children born into families who read books, newspapers, and magazines; visit museums, art galleries, zoos, and stately homes and gardens; take regular holidays; watch the nightly news and documentaries; and talk – around the dinner table, on weekend walks, in the car – about current affairs and about what they're reading or doing or watching – develop *cultural capital*. These children acquire, unknowingly perhaps, an awareness of the world around them, an understanding of how life works, and – crucially – a language with which to explain it all. Cultural capital provides a solid foundation on which they can build further knowledge, skills, and understanding.

The unlucky ones – those children not born and brought up in such knowledge-rich environments, who therefore do not develop this foundation of cultural capital – don't do as well in school or later life because new knowledge and skills have nothing to 'stick' to or build upon. Educational disadvantage is an accident of birth. It is not about ability, innate or otherwise. But, unfortunately, a child's birth is often their destiny.

The poor shall get poorer

As I explained in Chapter 4, the Matthew Effect posits that disadvantaged learners shall get more disadvantaged because they do not possess the foundational knowledge they need to access and understand the curriculum. It is not that these young people are less able, but that they don't have the same amount of knowledge about the world as their more fortunate peers with which to make sense of new information and experiences. Put simply, the more you know, the easier it is to know more and so the culturally rich will always stay ahead of the impoverished, and the gap between rich and poor will continue to grow as children travel through our education system.

The best course of action to foster inclusion, therefore, is to help disadvantaged learners to build their cultural capital and, once again, stories are a means of doing this. By reading stories, we can help our learners to develop the language skills they need to access and understand the school curriculum, and then to achieve at school and in later life. Stories open a door to future success.

We know that one tangible form that cultural capital takes is a learner's vocabulary. The size of a learner's vocabulary in their early years of schooling (the number and variety of words that the young person knows) is a significant predictor of academic attainment in later schooling and of success in life. Most children are experienced speakers of the language when they begin school but reading the language requires more complex, abstract vocabulary than that used in everyday conversation. Young people who develop reading skills early in their lives by reading frequently add to their vocabularies exponentially.

To build cultural capital and therefore foster inclusion, we can plan group work activities which provide an opportunity for the word-poor to mingle with the word-rich and hear language being used by learners of their own age and in ways that they might not otherwise encounter. We can also give disadvantaged learners equal access to a knowledge-rich diet and provide cultural experiences in addition to, not in place of, the school curriculum. We can provide additional intervention classes for the disadvantaged (taking place outside the taught timetable to avoid withdrawing learners from classes) in which we teach and model higher-order reading skills because, as the literate adults in the room, we teachers use these skills subconsciously all the time so we need to make the implicit explicit. And we can support community projects such as reading mentor schemes, helping improve parents' literacy levels and encouraging parents and members of the community to engage with education. But, above all, we can ensure that stories and storytelling techniques are fully embedded across the curriculum.

Returning to Bernstein, using story is one way of 'levelling the playing field' for learners from working-class backgrounds who cannot easily or expediently access the elaborated code of academia. In other words, stories can make our curriculum more accessible to all and thus help us to achieve inclusion.

As we've seen, the use of stories in teaching can help make abstract concepts more accessible and relatable to learners, particularly those who may not have had the same experiences or cultural background as their teachers or peers. By connecting these abstract concepts to concrete examples and personal experiences, teachers can help to make learning more engaging and meaningful for learners and mitigate the disadvantages faced by those who do not have access to the elaborated code. Stories also have a familiar language which makes them easy to follow and which helps learners to make meaningful inferences whenever unfamiliar words are used.

But that's not all …

Stories don't just help learners to avoid using an elaborated code by simplifying the curriculum into more accessible narratives. Rather, they help learners to learn and use that elaborated code.

Indeed, by exposing disadvantaged learners to a wider range of vocabulary, sentence structures, and abstract concepts, teachers can help to bridge the gap between their existing restricted code and the more elaborated code of academic and professional settings. And Bernstein's code theory suggests that the use of complex narratives and language structures can be particularly beneficial for learners from disadvantaged backgrounds.

Story can therefore be a powerful tool for promoting greater linguistic and cultural diversity in the classroom, and for helping to 'level the playing field' for learners from disadvantaged backgrounds. By incorporating a range of language codes and narrative structures into our teaching, we can help provide learners with the skills and knowledge they need to succeed in today's complex and diverse society.

Language and literacy

Stories empower. Stories give us a voice and help us participate meaningfully and assertively in decisions that affect our own lives. Stories breed self-confidence. Stories enable people to read the world and to write their future.

In 1922, in his book *English for the English*,[3] George Sampson said: "Every teacher is a teacher *of* English because every teacher is a teacher *in* English". In other words, English is not the sole responsibility of English teachers; rather, English is the language of learning in every curriculum subject and thus must be actively taught by teachers of every curriculum subject. The same could be said of stories and storytelling. Stories are all our responsibility. Indeed, stories are the best means of teaching language and literacy.

Stories can help learners to communicate more effectively, and effective communication is one way of being included – it helps learners become part of the conversation, to understand the information they're being fed, and to impart information of their own.

According to the Newbolt Report of 1921,[4] it is "impossible to teach English grammar for the simple reason that no-one knows exactly what it is". It is certainly possible to define 'grammar' in myriad ways but, for our present purposes, let's agree that it is a combination of:

- **Syntax** – which is the study of sentence structure, an analysis of main and subordinate clauses, of simple, compound, and complex sentences, of subjects, verbs, and objects, and so on.

- **Morphology** – which is the study of word structure, an analysis of stem (or root) words, of prefixes and suffixes, inflections for tense, number, and person, and so on.

- **Semantics** – which is the study of meaning, an analysis of the things, people, and events we refer to when we're talking, as well as how meanings – both literal (denotation) and implied (connotation) – are conveyed, and how words can mask their true meaning (for example, through the use of euphemism).

Grammar teaching, therefore, should include the linguistic structure of words, sentences, and whole texts, and should cover:

- The word classes (or parts of speech) and their grammatical functions.

- The structure of phrases and clauses and how they can be combined (by coordination and subordination) to make complex sentences.

- Paragraph structure and how to form different types of paragraph.

- The structure of whole texts, including cohesion, and the conventions of openings and conclusions in different types of writing.

- The use of appropriate grammatical terminology in order to reflect on the meaning and clarity of both spoken and written language.

So, if that's what grammar is, why is it important that we teach it and – crucially – do so in every curriculum subject?

According to the now-defunct National Literacy Strategy, the only explicit justification for teaching grammar is its contribution to writing skills. While this is undoubtedly important, I'd go further and argue that grammar teaching also promotes learners' understanding and helps them to know, notice, discuss, and explore language features. Grammar teaching may also provide a tool for learning other languages.

And the best way to teach grammar? Through stories and storytelling, of course!

Teaching grammar is not the same as teaching English. Grammar – and disciplinary literacy more generally – is about helping learners to access the whole curriculum. Disciplinary literacy is about helping learners to read subject information and it is about helping learners to write so that they can assimilate this subject information and then demonstrate their learning.

Literacy supports learning because learners need vocabulary, expression, and organisational control to cope with the cognitive demands of all subjects. Writing helps learners to sustain and order thought, and literacy skills lead to improved self-esteem, motivation, and behaviour; literacy skills allow learners to be independent.

A teacher of, say, science, has a responsibility to help learners learn about science, but they also have a responsibility to help them speak, listen, read, and write like a scientist. In practice, this means that science teachers must possess some specialist knowledge of – for example – the conventions of scientific report-writing and of the ways scientists themselves write about science. It means they must develop an analytical self-awareness which enables them to identify how they speak, listen, read, and write about science so that those skills can be made explicit for their learners. But, perhaps more importantly, it means using stories and storytelling techniques as a vehicle for teaching language and literacy, modelling through story how scientists read and write, express complex theories and ideas, and report the findings of experiments.

Strategies to improve learners' literacy

Into practice
Writing your story

To improve learners' language and literacy skills, we can:

- Involve all teachers and demonstrate how they are all engaged in using language and literacy skills to promote learning in their subject.

- Identify the particular needs of all learners in reading, writing, speaking, and listening.

- Make strong links between school and home.

- Plan for the longer term, emphasising the integral relationship between language for learning and effective teaching in all subjects.

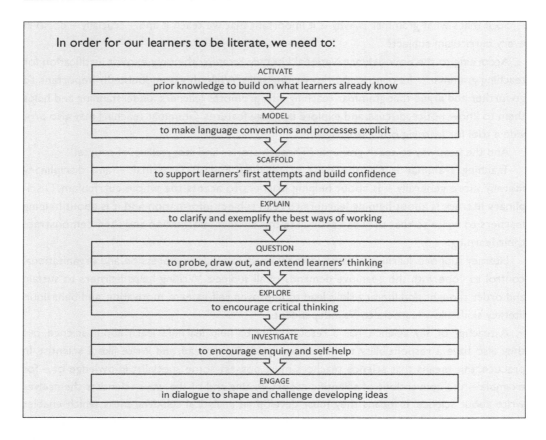

In order for our learners to be literate, we need to:

ACTIVATE
prior knowledge to build on what learners already know

MODEL
to make language conventions and processes explicit

SCAFFOLD
to support learners' first attempts and build confidence

EXPLAIN
to clarify and exemplify the best ways of working

QUESTION
to probe, draw out, and extend learners' thinking

EXPLORE
to encourage critical thinking

INVESTIGATE
to encourage enquiry and self-help

ENGAGE
in dialogue to shape and challenge developing ideas

Using stories to teach reading

To use stories as a means of improving our learners' language and literacy skills, we must first teach them how to read. Reading is about developing the ability to:

- Decode increasingly complex and challenging words across the curriculum.

- Read for meaning (using reading strategies such as prediction, skimming, scanning, inference, summarising, etc).

- Understand a writer's craft (analysing the effect of features of form, structure, and language).

- Read and engage with a wide variety of texts.

- Research for a wide range of purposes.

One of the key aspects of teaching reading skills is the use of subject-specific vocabulary. For learners to understand and be able to use with accuracy words with which they are unfamiliar, we need to introduce those words in a careful sequence. For example, we might begin by reading aloud a sentence in which the new word appears. Then we might show learners that word written down and ask them to say it aloud before asking them to repeat it several times. Next, we might debate possible meanings with the class and point out any parts of the word which might help with meaning, for example a prefix or Greek or Latin root. After this, we might re-read the sentence to see if there are any contextual clues and explicitly explain the meaning of the word through simple definition and the use of synonyms. We might provide several examples of the word being used in context, emphasising the word, and ask questions to determine whether learners have understood the word. We might also provide some sentences for learners to judge whether the word is used correctly and get learners to write their own sentences using the word. And, once the word has been introduced and reinforced in the lesson, we might explicitly use the word during the next few days to reinforce its meaning. One of the advantages of this sequence is that it ensures learners are exposed to new vocabulary several times and get to see, hear, and use new words in context.

Into practice
Writing your story

Here's a useful process to consider:

Show the word written down
Say the word out loud
Define the word
Exemplify the word
Explore the word's morphology
Explore the word's etymology
Show the word in several contexts

As well as teaching reading and explicitly introducing learners to new words, we can use stories to help develop our learners' fluency. I talked about fluency earlier so won't do so again in any detail here. Suffice to say, once new subject-specific words have been introduced, we want to help learners to read these words quickly and accurately, adopting the appropriate intonation. This is called fluency, and it requires a background knowledge of words and a text, as well as a rapid retrieval of the requisite vocabulary. Fluency also requires a knowledge of syntax and grammar to predict the words that are likely to appear next.

The ability to adapt one's vocabulary and intonation according to a text's syntax and grammar, and the ability to read ahead, assists with both speed and accuracy. Experienced readers integrate these processes so that reading becomes automatic – done without thinking – which allows their cognitive energy to be focused on the task of discerning meaning. Remember my analogy of learning to tie your shoelaces.

As I explained earlier, there is a strong correlation between fluency and reading comprehension – indeed, it is such a strong link that fluency and comprehension can be regarded as interdependent. After all, fluency only occurs when a reader understands the text; if reading is hesitant and disjointed, meaning is lost. It is impossible to be a fluent reader if you must stop to work out what a word is. To be fluent you must move beyond the decoding stage to accurately read whole words. Therefore, one of the first skills we need to teach through stories is accuracy. Developing learners' sight vocabularies and receptive vocabularies are the most effective ways of developing both fluency and reading comprehension. And stories are the best way to achieve this. Stories expose learners to new words but do so in context and with meaning.

Using stories to teach writing

Stories are not only a means of teaching reading, but they can also help teach learners how to write. Writing is about developing the ability to:

● Generate, plan, and draft ideas for composition.

● Select, shape, and construct language for expression and effect in composition.

● Proofread and redraft written work, drawing on conventions and structures.

● Use accurate grammar, punctuation, and spelling.

Stories can provide a model to follow and can also be used as a vehicle for explicitly exploring writing skills.

Writing has traditionally been one of the weakest areas of language and literacy teaching because, all too often, teachers assume that imparting knowledge – making sure learners know stuff – is enough. In reality, of course, the most common and effective means by which most knowledge is demonstrated and assessed – whether that be in exams or through controlled assessments and coursework, class and homework – is through learners' writing. Writing, therefore, needs to be taught by every teacher who uses writing as a means of demonstrating and assessing learning. This is not a case of asking teachers to do anything technical; it's simply about helping learners to write like a designer, or artist, or musician, or historian, or mathematician, or scientist, and so on.

Stories are a great way of teaching writing because the quality of learners' writing is usually better when it emerges from reading other people's writing. That doesn't mean simply displaying a good model of a text on the board, however. Rather, it involves:

● **Modelling:** sharing information about a text.

● **Joint construction:** working with learners to create a text collaboratively.

- **Independent construction:** learners constructing a text independently of others, albeit with support.

- **Active instruction** of vocabulary and sentence structures.

However, a word of warning: we can't teach writing simply by showing model texts, even if we annotate them to show what makes them work. Instead, we teach writing by writing. It's important, therefore, that learners write their own stories. If we simply read good stories in class, we are in danger of giving learners the mistaken impression that writing is a product rather than a process. Learners need to see that writing is something that involves making decisions and, for that matter, making mistakes. Learners need to see their teacher – and that means their teachers in all subjects – writing.

Into practice
Writing your story

We might model the writing process by:

Contemplating the *what* and the *how* of a text: what is its purpose and who is its audience? The answers to those questions will affect how the text is written in terms of both its language and its presentation.

Examining the conventions of a text: again, this is in terms of both language (formality, style, sentence structure, etc.) and presentation (paragraphs, sequence, bullet points, images, etc.).

Demonstrating how the text might be written – this is twofold:

Firstly, **planning**: this involves learners observing the teacher as they think aloud, explaining their decisions. For example, thinking aloud might sound like this: 'I need to write this like a historian would write it. It will need to be in the third person, so "he/she" and "they" not "I". It will need to be formal not colloquial but not too stuffy either; it must be accessible to a wide audience.'

Secondly, **drafting**: this involves writing a text while providing a running commentary, explaining the decisions that are made and how words are selected and rejected.

To help learners write their own texts that are appropriate to their audience and purpose, we might then use a sequence such as this:

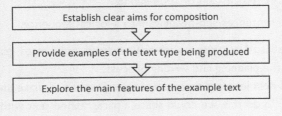

APT: A most suitable strategy

In establishing aims, we could use the mnemonic APT which stands for:

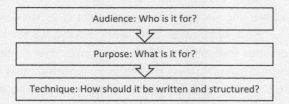

Under *audience*, we want learners to consider whether their audience is general or targeted and, if the latter, what characteristics they possess. For example, do they have technical prior knowledge about the topic of the text we're writing? What level of education will they have? How old will they be? Where will they live? What occupation will they have? Will they be a particular gender? And so on.

Under *purpose*, we want learners to consider what type of text they are writing, formal or informal, fiction or non-fiction, informative or descriptive, and so on.

And under *technique*, we want learners to consider the structure and presentational features required of their text, as well as language features. In terms of structure, should their writing be chronological or non-chronological, should it be written in paragraphs or bullets, should the paragraphs be long or short, how will ideas be linked together, and will there be a logic to the order and organisation of the text? In terms of language, what types of sentence should be included, both regarding purpose (inquisitive, exclamative, declarative, imperative) and syntax (simple, compound, complex)? And what kinds of words should be used, formal or colloquial, standard English or dialect/slang, active or passive, simple or complex, and so on? We also want to consider tense and narrative viewpoint.

Once we've explored APT, we could scaffold learners' initial attempts at composition – for example, using writing frames, lists of key words, stem sentences etc. We might then help learners to sequence and structure information, ideas, and events effectively. We could teach the main features of different text types (e.g. instructions are chronological) and we could make explicit a sequence for planning, which might include:

1. Write initial thoughts and ideas on sticky notes or cards.

2. Identify key words or phrases which need to be included.

3. Draft the topic sentences and/or sub-headings.

4. Organise these sentences/sub-headings into a logical sequence.

We could also use visual organisers such as flowcharts, mind maps, graphs, and tables in order to support the planning and writing process.

We might then help learners to construct paragraphs and make links within and between paragraphs. To do this, we could share a paragraphed text with learners and ask

have acquired. For example, in the case of explicit and implicit meanings, the early stages were as follows:

1. I can define the words explicit and implicit.

2. I can identify an explicit and implicit meaning in a non-fiction text.

3. I can identify both explicit and implicit meanings in a range of different text types.

4. I can explain why a writer has implied rather than explicitly stated something.

5. I can comment on the effect of both explicit and implicit meanings on the reader.

6. I can analyse writers' use of explicit and implicit meanings.

The benefit of this approach was twofold: firstly, these 'can do' statements proved a meaningful means of assessing what learners knew and could do rather than assessing something more arbitrary or abstract; secondly, these threshold concepts embodied retrieval practice because learners had to return to Step 1 in order to complete Step 2, and so on.

Then I worked hard to understand my learners' starting points – what they already knew and could do, and what they did not yet know and could not yet do, as well as what misconceptions or misunderstandings they brought to the classroom. I used this knowledge to fill gaps in prior knowledge, including in my learners' vocabularies, and to ensure that the pace and pitch of my teaching was suitably challenging. I also ensured that I knew about my learners' lived experiences so that I could teach new abstract information within the context of learners' existing concrete knowledge. This ensured, among other things, that my stories and analogies 'landed'.

I then used a small stimulus to explore myriad concepts. The key here was to reduce the source text to afford time to focus on meaning. And this is where stories play another crucial role because I spent several lessons teaching a single sentence from a story – the opening line of George Orwell's *Nineteen Eighty-Four*, which is as follows:

It was a bright cold day in April, and the clocks were striking thirteen.

Firstly, I used that solitary sentence as a form of retrieval practice to activate my learners' prior knowledge of the word classes, tense and number, syntax, inference, pathetic fallacy, allusion, and much more besides. The key was to show learners that simply feature spotting (such as identifying the line as a compound sentence) was fruitless; the magic is in being able to say *why* a writer made that stylistic choice and what impact it has on us as readers.

Once we'd explored the sentence, I gave learners an essay question and they used the planning technique I'd taught them to set out how they'd answer it.

My teaching followed a four-part sequence which afforded learners increasing independence. I started with teacher explanations, arming learners with the knowledge – technical terminology, techniques, etc. – they needed to complete a task. For example, in the case of writing about the impact of a text on them as a reader I signposted the use of the first person 'I' to ensure their response was personal not generic. Then I engaged in teacher modelling in which I produced examples of excellence 'live' in the classroom while thinking aloud to make my expertise visible. For example, I wrote an embedded quotation and deconstructed each element, making visible why I made the choice of quotation I did, how I embedded it, and how and why I punctuated it the way I did. Next, the class and I produced models together, or rather we added to my initial model. I targeted questions at learners and drip-fed technical terminology into the discussion while they contributed sentences to our analysis. And finally, learners completed the same task by themselves so that they could engage the cognitive processes required from start to finish.

The essay question I set my learners was this:

How does the opening line of George Orwell's _Nineteen Eighty-Four_ create a sense of foreboding?

We converted the question into the first line of our semi-colon list:

The opening line of George Orwell's _Nineteen Eighty-Four_ creates a sense of foreboding because:

And then we began constructing our list, exploring each feature in turn:

The opening line of George Orwell's _Nineteen Eighty-Four_ creates a sense of foreboding because: The use of a compound sentence suggests time is an important aspect of the novel's setting, and that we are about to enter a future that is unfamiliar to us; the use of the plural _clocks_ suggests Orwell's world is one of order and control; the use of pathetic fallacy suggests Orwell's world is an unpleasant one without any privacy or comfort; the word _thirteen_ is regarded as unlucky and its use suggests something bad is going to happen to our protagonist; the clocks all striking thirteen at once invokes a militaristic tone and a sense that the past has been erased.

I then reminded learners about the structure of each paragraph that followed – one paragraph tackling each of the above items in our list. And I shared a self-assessment checklist to help learners evaluate the effectiveness of their paragraphs:

1. Does my paragraph start with a one-sentence POINT linked to the introduction?
2. Do I support my point with EVIDENCE in the form of a quotation?
3. Is my quotation relevant to the point?
4. Is my quotation as short as possible?
5. Is my quotation embedded into my sentence and punctuated accurately?
6. Do I EXPLAIN the quote?

7. Do I explain the EXPLICIT meaning of the quote?

8. Do I explain the IMPLICIT meaning of the quote?

9. Do I comment on the language and/or structure of the quote?

10. Do I comment on the context, such as the use of allusion or references to the historical/cultural context?

11. Do I explore the writer's intentions?

12. Do I comment on the effect of the text on me as the reader using the first person?

Key to my success was selecting a story of sufficient quality to allow us to dissect it so carefully and slowly. Story allowed me to teach several transferable language features within a domain-specific way, anchored in meaning and context. Story made the intangible, tangible. Story made the unknown, familiar. And story made the abstract, concrete.

What have we learned?

In this chapter, we have discovered that:

Stories can help learners to develop the language and literacy skills needed for them to access and understand the school curriculum.

Stories are easy to follow, which helps learners make meaningful inferences whenever unfamiliar words are used. Thus, stories can help simplify the curriculum into more accessible narratives. But they also expose disadvantaged learners to a wider range of vocabulary, sentence structures, and abstract concepts, which helps bridge the gap between their existing restricted code and the more elaborated code of academic and professional settings.

To use stories as a means of improving our learners' language and literacy skills, we must first teach them how to read, which involves developing the ability to decode increasingly complex and challenging words, as well as read for meaning and understand a writer's craft.

Stories can also help teach learners how to write, which involves developing the ability to generate, plan, and draft ideas for composition, and then shape and construct language for expression and effect in composition.

What can we do?

To put the advice contained in this chapter into practice, it might be helpful to consider the following questions:

1. Do you use story and storytelling as a vehicle for teaching key vocabulary and to help learners acquire an elaborated code?

2. Do you use story and storytelling to teach literacy skills, including disciplinary literacy?

3. Do you use story to teach reading and writing in domain-specific ways?

Notes

1 Bromley, M (2023) *Intent Implementation Impact: How to Design and Deliver an Ambitious School Curriculum.* Spark Education Books UK.

2 Black, P & Wiliam, D (2018). Classroom assessment and pedagogy *Assessment in Education: Principles, Policy & Practice,* 25(6), 551–575, p. 570.

3 Sampson, G (1922). *English for the English: A Chapter on National Education.* Cambridge University Press, p. 25.

4 Newbolt, H (1921). *The Teaching of English in England.* HM Stationary Office, London, pp. 289–290.

Using story to prepare learners for future success

Using story to deliver the school curriculum is helpful not just in terms of boosting learning and academic outcomes but also as a preparation for later life, including the world of work. In this chapter, we will explore three ways of using story to prepare learners for future success:

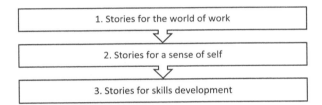

1. Stories for the world of work

2. Stories for a sense of self

3. Stories for skills development

1. Stories for the world of work

Stories are used in business all the time and, thus, being exposed to story and storytelling at school can give learners a head start in their future careers.

As we discovered in Chapter 8, according to Vanessa Boris of Harvard Business Publishing,[1] stories are important in the business world. Boris says that "an organisation's stories, and the stories its leaders tell, help solidify relationships in a way that factual statements encapsulated in bullet points or numbers don't [because they] build familiarity and trust and allow the listener to enter the story where they are, making them more open to learning".

Boris proffers the example of a company meeting:

At Company A, the leader presents the financial results for the quarter. At Company B, the leader tells a rich story about what went into the "win" that put the quarter over the top. Company A employees come away from the meeting knowing that they made their numbers. Company B employees learned about an effective strategy in which sales, marketing, and product development came together to secure a major deal. Employees now have new knowledge, new thinking, to draw on. They've been influenced. They've learned.

DOI: 10.4324/9781003465492-13

Kendall Haven, author of *Story Proof and Story Smart*, considers storytelling a serious business for, well, business: "Your goal in every communication is to influence your target audience (change their current attitudes, belief, knowledge, and behaviour). Information alone rarely changes any of these. Research confirms that well-designed stories are the most effective vehicle for exerting influence."[2]

Stories matter in the world of healthcare, too.

Clare Patey, Director of Empathy Museum and Cathy Irvin, Director of Communications at the Health Foundation, argue that:

> In health care, stories are … a useful tool in engaging people with quality improvement work. Telling the story of one patient's experience of care can memorably illustrate improvements or problems in a care pathway. Statistics and data have an important place in monitoring and understanding services and facilitating improvement, but the right story can also have the power to motivate and change minds.[3]

As Patey goes on to say:

> Stories have a transformative power to allow us to see the world in a different way than we do if we just encounter it on our own. Stories are an entry point to understanding a different experience of the world. This aspect of storytelling – presenting a different perspective of the world – is important when it comes to connecting with each other. It gives us an opportunity to learn from another person's experience and it can shape, strengthen or challenge our opinions and values. When a story catches our attention and engages us, we are more likely to absorb the message and meaning within it than if the same message was presented simply in facts and figures.

We will explore the role stories can play in leadership in the next part of this book.

2. Stories for a sense of self

Another aspect of preparing learners for future success is helping them to understand themselves and their place in the world.

Paul Hannam, author of *Significance*,[4] believes that "your life story is an unseen force that greatly influences your daily experience. Moment to moment, you are largely unconscious of its impact".

Your life story is your unique take on the 'good' and 'bad' experiences you've had, the choices you've made, and the significance of the different people you've met along the way. However, as Hannam also says, "Our predicament is that we don't experience reality, we experience our interpretation of reality." In essence, we are unreliable writers of our own story.

Teaching learners about story can improve their self-perception *and* help them develop a habit of questioning their own perceptions, beliefs, and ways of thinking.

Story can also help learners improve their perception of other people. Listening to stories from those with different experiences to our own enables us to develop empathy.

Coming from a disadvantaged background can make you feel out of place. Limited life experiences, such as eating in a restaurant, going on a foreign holiday, visiting the countryside, going to a museum or art gallery, and so on, can lead to a belief that you don't belong. Learners need to know that they have the power to make their story the best possible version of themselves. This doesn't mean creating a fake story in which they project themselves in a way that makes others like them more or which denies their roots – that's our conditioned self. Rather, it's about creating a story that makes them happy and content, one where they live by their values – this is the authentic self. We need to help our learners tell the story of their authentic selves and be proud of who they are and where they come from, as well as unafraid to encounter new people and places, make new memories, and tell new stories.

3. Stories for skills development

A third aspect of preparing learners for future success through story and storytelling is to equip them with an armoury of life skills. This is the aspect I'd like to focus on in the remainder of this chapter. To do so, permit me another anecdote.

Inspiration
Telling my story

Long live the king

The day the Queen died I was at a military training college speaking to a hundred cadets about life skills. As you might expect, I began with a story ...

I told the cadets that I didn't believe in conspiracy theories, but that Abraham Lincoln and John F. Kennedy have always made my spine tingle. After all, they had an awful lot in common.

Abraham Lincoln was elected to Congress in 1846; John F. Kennedy was elected to Congress in 1946. Abraham Lincoln was elected president in 1860; John F. Kennedy was elected president in 1960. The names Lincoln and Kennedy each contain seven letters. Both men were particularly concerned with civil rights. Both their wives lost children while living in the White House. Both presidents were shot on a Friday. Both were shot in the head. Lincoln's secretary, Kennedy, warned him not to go to the theatre; Kennedy's secretary, Lincoln, warned him not to go to Dallas. Both were assassinated by Southerners. Both were succeeded by Southerners. Both successors were named Johnson: Andrew Johnson, who succeeded Lincoln, was born in 1808; Lyndon Johnson, who succeeded Kennedy, was born in 1908. Both assassins were known by three names which comprised 15 letters. John Wilkes Booth was born in 1839. Lee Harvey Oswald was born in 1939. Having assassinated Lincoln, Booth ran from the theatre and was caught in a warehouse. Having assassinated Kennedy, Oswald ran from a warehouse and was caught in a theatre. Both Booth and Oswald were assassinated before their trials.

Spooky, eh? I don't know about you, but the hairs on the back of my neck are standing up just retelling that story. But, as I say, I don't believe in conspiracy theories.

I do, however, believe in coincidence. So, what's the difference? When you think about it, coincidences aren't spooky at all; they are in fact perfectly rational because they express a simple, logical pattern of cause and effect. Take, for example, academic achievement.

A decade or so ago, when I was a headteacher, I interviewed 50 learners in Years 11 and 13 who had achieved high grades in their GCSE and A level exams. I found something spooky – a series of apparent coincidences.

For example, all the learners I interviewed had an attendance of more than 95% per cent; 90% of them had a perfect attendance record. All the learners I interviewed told me they used their planners regularly and considered themselves to be well organised. As a result, they all completed their homework on time and without fail. All the learners I interviewed told me they always asked for help from their teachers when they got stuck. They didn't regard doing so as a sign of weakness but rather a sign of strength. Admitting they didn't know something and asking questions meant they learned something new and increased their intelligence.

Most of the learners I interviewed were involved in clubs, sports, or hobbies at lunchtime, after school, and/or at weekends. Though not all were sporting, they did all have get-up-and-go attitudes. They didn't spend every evening and weekend watching television or glued to their mobile phones. They were sociable and, to unwind, they read books. Lots of books. In fact, the school library confirmed that my cohort of 50 high achievers were among the biggest borrowers in school.

All the learners I interviewed believed that doing well in school would increase their chances of getting higher-paid and more interesting jobs later in life. Many of them had a clear idea about the kind of job they wanted to do and knew what was needed to get it. They had researched the entry requirements and had then mapped out the necessary school, college, and/or university paths. They had connected what they were doing in school with achieving their future ambitions. School work and good exam results had a purpose; they were means to an important end. In other words, they had written the story of their own futures – they had a clear narrative that gave purpose to their lives and learning.

Was it spooky that nearly all these high-achieving learners had done the same things? Or was it a simple case of cause and effect: *because* these learners shared these traits, they went on to succeed? I believe it was the latter: it was because these learners had attended school, were well organised, completed work on time, and had an end goal in mind that they had achieved excellent grades in their final exams. The cause was diligent study and determination – writing their own story; the effect was high achievement.

I began with this story – a mix of historical record and personal anecdote – as a 'hook' to engage a large group of potentially unruly military cadets but also to provide context and purpose to what followed. I argued that the young people I had interviewed could teach the students in front of me a valuable lesson – that the recipe for success is to:

- Have good attendance and punctuality.
- Be organised and complete all work on time.
- Be willing to ask for help when you're stuck.
- Have something to aim for and be ambitious.
- Map out your career path and be determined to succeed.

In short, I told the students gathered before me to write the story of their own futures and recount them every day.

I then went on to explore the second of these ingredients in more detail: personal organisation.

Get organised

Personal organisation is one way to help learners prepare for future success and – to my mind – it consists of study skills, research skills, and independent learning skills. At the heart of all these skills? You've guessed it: stories and storytelling.

According to Peter C. Brown, Henry L. Roediger, and Mark A. McDaniel in *Make It Stick*,[5] the following study skills are proven to be particularly helpful for learners:

1. Self-quizzing

Self-quizzing is about retrieving knowledge and skills from memory and is far more effective than simply re-reading. When learners read a text or study notes, we might encourage them to pause periodically to ask themselves questions – without looking in the text – such as:

- What are the key ideas?
- What terms or ideas are new to me? How would I define them?
- How do the ideas in this text relate to what I already know?

To help, we might usefully set aside a little time each week for learners to quiz themselves on the current week's work and on the material that we covered in previous weeks. Once they have self-quizzed, we might encourage learners to check their answers and make sure they've got an accurate understanding of what they know and what they don't know. Learners need to know that making mistakes will not set them back so long as they check their answers later and correct any errors.

We might also space out learners' retrieval practice, which means studying information more than once and leaving increasingly large gaps between practice sessions. Initially, new material should be revisited within a day or so and then not again for several days or a week. When learners are feeling surer of certain material, they should quiz themselves on it once a month. They should also interleave the study of two or more topics so that alternating between them requires them to continually refresh their memories of each topic.

2. Elaboration

Elaboration is the process of finding additional layers of meaning in new material. It involves relating new material to what learners already know, explaining it to somebody else or explaining how it relates to the wider world. An effective form of elaboration is to use a metaphor or image for the new material.

3. Generation

Generation is when learners attempt to answer a question or solve a problem before being shown the answer or the solution. The act of filling in a missing word (a cloze test) results in a stronger memory of the text than simply reading it. Before reading new texts in class, we might ask learners to explain the key ideas they expect to find and how they expect these ideas will relate to their prior knowledge.

4. Reflection

Reflection involves taking a moment to review what has been learned. Learners might ask themselves questions such as:

- What went well? What could have gone better?
- What other knowledge or experience does it remind me of?
- What might I need to learn to achieve better mastery?
- What strategies could I use next time to getter better results?

5. Calibration

Calibration is achieved when learners adjust their judgement to reflect reality – in other words, they become certain that their sense of what they know and can do is accurate. Often when we revise information, we look at a question and convince ourselves that we know the answer and then move on to the next question without trying to actually answer the previous one. But if we do not write down an answer, we may create the illusion of knowing when in fact we would find it difficult to give a response. We therefore need to teach learners to remove the illusion of knowing and answer all the questions, even if they think they know the answer and that it is too easy.

Other study skills to teach our learners:

1. Formulate helpful questions while reading a text.

2. Find terms they can't recall or don't know while reading a text – then learn them.

3. Copy key terms from a text – and their definitions – into a notebook.

4. Take regular practice tests.

5. Reorganise class material into a study guide.

6. Copy out key concepts and regularly test themselves on them.

7. Space out revision and practice activities.

Routines to help learners study

Into practice
Writing your story

Here are some tips for teachers to help learners study better:

Create desirable difficulties ...

... by using tests frequently. Design study tools that make use of retrieval practice, generation, and elaboration.

Activate prior learning ...

... space, interleave, and vary the topics covered in class so that learners frequently have to *reload* what they already know about each topic in order to determine how new material relates to, or indeed differs from, prior knowledge.

Plan for free recall ...

... whereby learners spend 10 minutes at the end of each lesson filling a blank piece of paper with everything they can remember from that lesson.

Set a weekly retrieval homework ...

... whereby learners create summary sheets on which they record the previous week's learning in text, annotated illustrations, or a graphical organiser to stimulate retrieval and reflection and to capture the previous week's learning before it is lost.

Explain how learning works ...

... to help learners understand that creating some kinds of difficulties during the learning process helps to strengthen learning and memory because when learning is easy it is often superficial and soon forgotten.

More questioning techniques

Earlier, I said I would return to questioning techniques and now is a good time to do just that because we can use questions to help learners prepare for future success. Let's start by exploring questions that promote progress.

Questioning to promote progress

Asking questions of increasing complexity in the classroom is a strategic way to scaffold learning *and* promote the gradual mastery of a topic. This approach helps learners build upon their existing knowledge and encourages them to engage in deeper levels of thinking.

Here's one way we can structure questions to increase complexity:

1. **Start with recall and factual questions:** Begin with questions that assess learners' basic recall of facts, key terms, and information. These questions help establish a foundation of knowledge and ensure everyone is on the same page.

2. **Move to comprehension and application:** Once learners have a grasp of the foundational facts/concepts, progress to questions that require them to comprehend and *apply* this information. Ask questions that prompt learners to explain concepts, interpret information, or apply knowledge to new scenarios.

3. **Introduce analysis and comparison:** Transition to questions that require learners to analyse information, relationships, and patterns. Encourage them to compare and contrast concepts, identify cause-and-effect relationships, and analyse data.

4. **Pose evaluation and synthesis questions:** Challenge learners with questions that involve the evaluation and synthesis of information. Ask them to critically assess ideas, arguments, or solutions. Have them synthesise multiple pieces of information to form new insights.

5. **Encourage reflection and prediction:** Include questions that prompt learners to reflect on their learning journey and predict potential outcomes. Ask for their opinions, personal connections, and predictions based on their understanding.

6. **Use 'what if' and hypothetical questions:** Incorporate hypothetical scenarios to encourage learners to think beyond the immediate context. Ask questions that start with 'what if' to explore alternative possibilities and encourage creative thinking.

7. **Interleave multiple concepts:** Create questions that interleave concepts from different parts of the curriculum. This challenges learners to synthesise information from various sources and demonstrate a holistic understanding. It also helps the development of schema and aids transferability.

8. **Offer feedback and encourage redrafting:** Provide feedback on learners' responses to complex questions. Encourage them to refine their answers based on your feedback and deeper reflection. Redrafting or improving by increments should be the default position.

Questioning as a form of retrieval practice

Questions can also play a crucial role in retrieval practice, a powerful learning strategy that involves actively recalling information from memory and that helps learners become increasingly independent and thus also prepares them for future success. Retrieval practice strengthens long-term retention, promotes deeper understanding, and enhances learners' ability to apply knowledge. Questions can serve as prompts for retrieval practice, guiding learners to recall information they've previously learned.

Here's how questions can be used as a form of retrieval practice:

Firstly, **questions can be used to prompt recall**. Questions act as triggers that prompt learners to retrieve information they've learned. When learners actively recall information, they reinforce their memory traces and make the information more accessible in the future.

Secondly, **questions can promote active engagement**. Answering questions requires learners to actively engage with the material rather than passively reviewing notes or texts. This active engagement enhances learning and strengthens memory retention.

Thirdly, **questions can be spaced and interleaved**. Retrieval practice often involves spacing out practice sessions over time. By revisiting information at intervals, learners strengthen their memory over the long term. Interleaving, meanwhile, involves mixing different topics or concepts during practice. Interleaving enhances learning by encouraging learners to discriminate between different ideas.

Fourthly, **the act of attempting to answer questions simulates a form of testing**. Research shows that being tested on material leads to better retention compared to passive study methods.

Fifthly, **when learners answer questions, they gain insights into what they know and what they need to review further**. Incorrect answers provide valuable feedback that guides future study efforts and helps identify areas for improvement. This helps learners to become increasingly metacognitive and self-regulated as learners. The process of retrieving information strengthens the connections between neurons in the brain, making it easier to retrieve that information in the future. This effect, known as the testing effect or retrieval practice effect, boosts long-term retention. What's more, retrieval practice enhances learners' ability to transfer knowledge to new contexts. When they practise retrieving information in different scenarios, they become better equipped to apply that knowledge flexibly.

Finally, **questions are an efficient self-study technique**. Retrieval practice is a more efficient study technique compared to more passive methods like reading and re-reading study notes. Spending focused time on active recall leads to more enduring learning outcomes. Using a variety of question types, including multiple-choice, short answer, and essay questions, can further engage different cognitive processes, which helps learners practise retrieving information in diverse ways.

Questioning techniques to combine with story and storytelling

Into practice
Writing your story

Hot seating

Hot seating is a role-playing technique which can be used to deepen learners' understanding of characters, historical figures, or concepts contained within stories. It works by immersing learners in the perspective of the subject being studied. It's an engaging way to encourage critical thinking, empathy, and active participation.

Here's how hot seating works in practice:

Step 1: Choose a character, historical figure, or concept relevant to your curriculum. This could be a literary character, a historical figure, a scientist, or even an abstract concept.

Step 2: Assign specific roles to learners. One learner will take on the role of the chosen character or concept, becoming the 'hot seater', while other learners will take on the roles of interviewers.

Step 3: Instruct the interviewers to prepare a list of thoughtful and relevant questions they would like to ask the hot seater. These questions can delve into the character's motivations, experiences, thoughts, and feelings.

Step 4: Have the hot seater take on the persona of the character or concept. The interviewers take turns asking questions, engaging in a role-playing conversation with the hot seater.

Step 5: The hot seater responds to the questions as if they were the chosen character or concept. Encourage the hot seater to think deeply and respond authentically based on what they know about the subject.

Hot seating prompts learners to step into the shoes of the character or concept, fostering empathy and a deeper understanding of their perspectives and motivations. The process also encourages critical thinking as learners analyse and synthesise information to respond effectively. After the hot-seating session, facilitate a discussion where learners reflect on the experience. Discuss how their understanding of the character or concept evolved and what insights they gained.

You could then extend the activity by having learners switch roles, allowing different learners to take on the hot-seater role. Consider introducing additional elements, such as incorporating historical context or setting the scenario in a different time period. Hot seating is particularly effective in English literature when exploring characters' motivations and perspectives, in history lessons when studying historical figures' actions and decisions, and in science lessons when discussing the viewpoints of scientists or concepts, though it can of course be utilised to good effect in any subject discipline because it's a versatile technique that engages learners' creativity, empathy, and critical thinking skills while making the subject matter come alive in a memorable way.

Think-pair-share

Think-pair-share is a cooperative learning strategy that encourages active participation, collaboration, and deeper thinking in the classroom. It involves a structured process where learners first think about a question or prompt individually, then discuss their thoughts with a partner, and finally share their ideas with the whole class. It can work well with stories because it allows learners to deepen their response to a story and to formulate different responses as well as appreciate and empathise with other learners' responses.

Here's how think-pair-share works:

Step 1: Think. The teacher poses a question, prompt, or topic related to the lesson. Learners are given a few moments (typically 1–2 minutes) to think quietly and independently about their response to the question.

Step 2: Pair. After the thinking period, learners are paired up with a partner. Partners take turns sharing their thoughts with each other, discussing their individual responses to the question. During this phase, learners actively listen to their partner's ideas, ask clarifying questions, and engage in a dialogue.

Step 3: Share. Once partners have had a chance to discuss their thoughts, the teacher opens the discussion to the whole class. Learners are invited to share key points from their partner discussions or their own thoughts. The teacher guides the class discussion, summarising ideas, asking follow-up questions, and encouraging participation.

There are several benefits of using this technique, including:

- **Engagement:** Think-Pair-Share promotes active engagement as all learners are actively thinking, discussing, and sharing their ideas.
- **Reflection:** The initial thinking phase allows learners to reflect on the question and organise their thoughts before discussing.
- **Peer interaction:** The pair-sharing phase encourages peer interaction and the exchange of diverse perspectives.
- **Enhanced participation:** Even quieter learners are more likely to share their thoughts with a partner before speaking to the whole class.
- **Deeper understanding:** Discussing ideas with a partner often leads to deeper understanding as learners explain and challenge each other's viewpoints.
- **Confidence building:** Learners gain confidence in their ideas through the partner-sharing phase, making them more comfortable sharing with the whole class.
- **Time efficiency:** Think-Pair-Share allows for individual reflection and in-depth discussions in a relatively short amount of time.

There are also several variations on the theme if you wish to shake things up:

Think-write-pair-share: Instead of just thinking, learners can write down their responses before pairing up. This provides a written record and encourages more thoughtful responses.

Think-triple-share: After pairing, learners form groups of three to share their discussions, promoting further collaboration and diverse perspectives.

You can also use a variety of question types, including factual, analytical, and open-ended questions, in order to encourage different levels of thinking.

Here's the answer, what's the question?

'Here's the answer, what's the question?' is an engaging and creative teaching strategy that flips the traditional approach of asking questions first and seeking answers second. With this approach, learners are presented with an answer or a piece of information, and their task is to come up with relevant questions that could lead to that answer. This works well when combined with story because it piques learners' interest and thus increases their level of engagement and motivation – they want to explore the story in order to find answers and close their knowledge gaps.

This technique encourages critical thinking, problem-solving, and the exploration of multiple angles of a topic.

Here's how it works in the classroom:

Step 1: Present the answer. Start by providing learners with a specific answer, fact, or piece of information. This answer should be interesting, thought-provoking, or even surprising. For example, give the answer 'gravity'.

Step 2: Task learners with generating questions. Instruct learners to work individually or in small groups to brainstorm a list of possible questions that could lead to the given answer. Encourage them to think creatively and consider various aspects related to the answer.

Step 3: Discussion and sharing. Have learners share their generated questions with the class. Engage in a discussion about the different types of questions and approaches learners took to arrive at the given answer. For example, learners may share some of the following possible questions for which the answer is 'gravity': What force keeps objects grounded on Earth? What phenomenon causes an apple to fall from a tree? What is responsible for the moon orbiting around our planet? How do planets maintain their orbits around the sun? Why do objects of different masses fall at the same rate in a vacuum? Each question can lead to a fascinating discussion.

Step 4: Reveal the original question. After learners have shared their questions, reveal the original question that led to the provided answer. Discuss the effectiveness of different questions in eliciting the answer and the thought processes involved. For example, reveal the original question as 'What force causes objects to fall towards the Earth's surface?'

This strategy encourages learners to approach learning from a different angle and helps them realise the importance of asking thoughtful and relevant questions to deepen their understanding. It's an engaging and effective way to stimulate curiosity and promote active engagement in the classroom.

There are several benefits of using this strategy, including:

- **Critical thinking:** Learners engage in higher-order thinking as they analyse the answer and reverse-engineer questions to reach that answer.

- **Creativity:** This approach encourages creative thinking, as learners must explore various angles and possibilities to come up with relevant questions.

- **Active participation:** Learners actively participate in generating questions, fostering engagement and a sense of ownership over the learning process.

- **Deeper understanding:** By considering multiple questions that lead to the answer, learners gain a deeper understanding of the content and its implications.

- **Diverse perspectives:** Different learners may generate different questions based on their background knowledge and perspectives, leading to rich discussions.

Cold-calling and show-calling

Cold-calling and show-calling are classroom management techniques that encourage learner engagement, active participation, and accountability during discussions. They involve calling on learners without prior notice to answer questions or contribute to the conversation. Both techniques aim to create a dynamic learning environment where all learners are involved and prepared to participate. Let's look at each.

In *cold-calling*, the teacher selects a learner at random to answer a question or contribute to the discussion. Here's how it works:

Step 1: Random selection. The teacher uses a random selection method to choose a learner to respond.

Step 2: Question pose. The teacher poses a question to the selected learner.

Step 3: Response. The learner must answer the question on the spot.

Cold-calling can be used for factual questions, higher-order thinking questions, or to encourage engagement from all learners in the class.

Cold-calling is effective because it encourages all learners to pay attention and be prepared to contribute, it reduces reliance on a small group of vocal learners, it promotes critical thinking and quick-thinking skills, it provides immediate feedback on learners' understanding, and it creates an inclusive classroom environment.

To make it work, it's important to foster a safe and respectful environment to ensure learners feel comfortable when called upon, to use a variety of question types and difficulty levels to accommodate different learners, and to balance cold-calling with other participation methods to avoid overwhelming learners.

Show-calling, meanwhile, is a variation of cold-calling where the teacher selects a learner and asks them to 'show' their answer or work to the class. This technique is often used in lessons that involve problem-solving. Here's how it works:

Step 1: Selection. The teacher randomly selects a learner.

Step 2: Question or problem. The teacher presents a question, problem, or scenario.

Step 3: Show work. The selected learner explains their thought process, solution, or approach to the class.

Step 4: Discussion. The class may engage in discussion, ask clarifying questions, and provide feedback on the presented solution.

The benefits of show-calling are that it encourages learners to articulate their thought processes, it provides insights into problem-solving strategies and approaches, it fosters peer learning through discussion and feedback, and it builds confidence in explaining concepts to peers.

To make it work, it's important to ensure that the focus remains on the process and approach, not just the correct answer, to create a supportive environment where learners feel comfortable sharing their thought processes and to give learners the opportunity to ask questions or seek clarifications from their peers.

Hinge questions

Hinge questions, also known as 'pivot questions' or 'checkpoint questions', are carefully selected questions strategically placed within a lesson to gauge learners' understanding and inform the teacher's instructional decisions. These questions serve as a 'hinge' point where the teacher assesses whether learners are ready to move on or if further clarification and instruction are needed.

Here's how hinge questions work in the classroom:

Step 1: Choose key concepts. Identify the key concepts, ideas, or skills you want to assess within the lesson. Hinge questions are typically focused on these essential elements.

Step 2: Formulate the question. Create a single, well-crafted question that targets the identified key concept. The question should be clear, concise, and focused on assessing understanding, not just recall.

Step 3: Strategic placement. Determine the appropriate moment in the lesson to introduce the hinge question. This is usually after you've taught the key concept but before moving on to the next section.

Step 4: Learner response. Ask all learners to respond to the hinge question individually and independently. This could involve writing down an answer, using a classroom response system (clickers), or raising their hand.

Step 5: Assess and analyse. Collect and assess the learners' responses to the hinge question. Analyse the data to identify patterns and trends in understanding.

Step 6: Instructional decision. Based on the learners' responses, make an instructional decision: If most learners have a solid understanding, you can proceed to the next part of the lesson. If many learners struggle to answer correctly, consider providing additional explanations, examples, or activities to address misconceptions.

Step 7: Feedback and discussion. Depending on the results, provide feedback to the learners. If necessary, engage the class in a brief discussion to clarify concepts or address common misconceptions.

Step 8: Adjustment and adaptation. Use the insights from the hinge question to adapt your teaching approach in real time. Modify the pace, level of detail, or activities based on the learners' needs.

There are several benefits of this approach. For example, hinge questions:

- Allow you to assess learners' understanding during the lesson itself, providing timely insights.
- Allow you to adjust your teaching strategies based on the real-time feedback from learners' responses.
- Allow you to identify areas of misunderstanding or confusion and address them immediately.
- Allow you to make informed decisions about whether to move forward or revisit certain concepts.
- Keep learners engaged and attentive with the anticipation of being asked a hinge question.
- Serve as formative assessment tools, guiding instructional planning.

To make hinge questions work, it's important to keep the question concise and focused on the core concept you want to assess; to ensure that the question requires critical thinking and understanding, not just factual recall; to use a variety of question formats, including multiple-choice, open-ended, and application-based questions; and to be prepared to adapt your teaching plan based on the results of the hinge question.

Exit tickets

Exit tickets are another form of formative assessment that we can use to gather feedback and insights from learners at the end of a lesson or topic and which can guide future learning, expedite progress, and thus help prepare learners for future success.

Exit tickets provide a quick snapshot of learners' understanding, opinions, and reflections on the material covered. Exit tickets are a valuable tool for gauging the effectiveness of our teaching, identifying areas that need further clarification, and tailoring future lessons to address learners' needs.

Here's how exit tickets work in the classroom:

Step 1: Plan the exit ticket. Determine the specific focus of the exit ticket. What aspect of the lesson or topic do you want to assess? Decide on the format of the exit ticket, such as a question, prompt, or task.

Step 2: Distribute the exit ticket. Towards the end of the lesson, distribute the exit ticket to learners. This can be in the form of a printed paper, a digital platform, or a simple index card.

Step 3: Pose the question or prompt. Pose a question, prompt, or task related to the content of the lesson. The question should be clear and concise, and it should align with the learning objectives.

Step 4: Set a time limit. Provide a specific time limit for learners to respond to the exit ticket. The time can range from a few minutes to around 5–10 minutes, depending on the complexity of the question.

Step 5: Collect the exit tickets. Collect the exit tickets from learners once they've completed their responses.

Step 6: Analyse and reflect. Review the responses from the exit tickets to gather insights into learners' understanding, misconceptions, and opinions. Look for common themes, patterns, and areas that need further clarification.

Step 7: Adapt instruction. Use the information from the exit tickets to adapt your instruction for future lessons. Address any misconceptions or areas of confusion that emerged from the responses.

Step 8: Provide feedback. If applicable, provide individual or collective feedback to the class based on the exit ticket responses. Clarify concepts, reinforce key points, and offer guidance for improvement.

Step 9: Reflect on teaching. Reflect on the effectiveness of your teaching strategies based on the exit ticket feedback. Consider how you can enhance future lessons to better meet learners' needs.

There are various types of exit ticket questions or prompts, including:

- **Content understanding:** Here, you ask questions that assess learners' understanding of the main concepts covered in the lesson.

- **Reflection:** Here, you prompt learners to reflect on what they learned, what was challenging, and what they found interesting.

- **Application:** Here, you pose a scenario or problem that requires learners to apply the newly learned concepts.

- **Opinions:** Here, you ask for learners' opinions on a topic, encouraging critical thinking and discussion.

- **Confusion clarification:** Here, you invite learners to identify any concepts they found confusing, allowing you to address these areas in future lessons.

Exit tickets are a flexible and efficient way to gain valuable insights into your learners' learning experiences and adjust your teaching strategies accordingly. They promote on-going assessment, learner reflection, and responsive instruction and thus help prepare learners for the next stage of their learning and lives.

Multiple-choice questions

Multiple-choice questions are a common type of assessment tool used to assess learners' knowledge, comprehension, and application of concepts. They aid reading comprehension and can assess reading comprehension as we tell stories in class. Multiple-choice questions present learners with a question and a set of possible answers, from which they must select the correct option.

Here's how multiple-choice questions work in the classroom:

Step 1: Design the question. Create a clear and concise question that addresses the learning objective or concept you want to assess. Ensure that the question is not ambiguous and has a single correct answer.

Step 2: Provide options. Present a set of answer choices, including the correct answer (known as the 'key' or 'correct response') and several distractors (incorrect options).

Step 3: Avoid tricky language. Craft answer choices that are plausible and avoid using overly complex or misleading language that could confuse learners.

Step 4: Use a variety of distractors. Distractors should be reasonable and reflect common misconceptions or errors learners might make. Vary the distractors to challenge learners' understanding and make the question more effective.

Step 5: Set clear instructions. Clearly specify how many answer choices learners should select (e.g. 'Select the best answer', 'Choose all that apply', etc.).

Step 6: Administer the question. Present the multiple-choice question to learners using a written assessment, a digital tool, or an interactive presentation.

Step 7: Learner selection. Learners review the question and the answer choices and choose the response they believe is correct.

Step 8: Assess responses. Evaluate learners' responses to determine whether they selected the correct answer or one of the distractors. Discuss misconceptions and the reasons for incorrect answers. Use the outcome to determine next steps – do you need to re-teach or recap content, or can you move on?

There are several benefits of using this strategy. For example, multiple-choice questions:

● Allow you to assess a wide range of content in a relatively short amount of time.

● Offer objective grading since answers are either correct or incorrect, reducing grading subjectivity.

- Can cover a variety of concepts within a single assessment.
- Are commonly used in standardised tests, helping learners become familiar with this format.
- Lead to instant feedback – especially when using digital platforms – which allows learners to learn from their mistakes immediately.

To make the strategy work, it's important to design questions that challenge higher-order thinking by requiring analysis, application, or evaluation; ensure that the question and answer choices are clear, avoiding double negatives or confusing wording; create balanced options and avoid leading learners to the correct answer through wording; analyse the common misconceptions or errors that could lead learners to select particular distractors; consider providing explanations for correct and incorrect responses to enhance the learning experience; and combine multiple-choice questions with other assessment formats to assess different skills and knowledge depths.

When using multiple-choice questions, aim to create questions that truly assess learners' understanding and encourage critical thinking. These questions can be a valuable tool for checking comprehension and providing insight into the effectiveness of your teaching.

Flashcards

Flashcards are a versatile and effective tool for helping learners memorise information in the classroom and for capturing key ideas from the stories we tell in class. They are particularly useful for learning vocabulary, key terms, formulas, names, historical dates and plotlines, themes and ideas, and other factual knowledge.

Here's how you can use flashcards to support learner memorisation:

Create clear and concise flashcards. Write down the term, concept, or information on one side of the flashcard. On the other side, write a clear and concise definition, explanation, or relevant details.

Use visual aids. Incorporate images, diagrams, or symbols on the flashcards to enhance visual memory. Associating visual cues with information can aid retention.

Organise content. Group related flashcards together based on themes, topics, or units. This organisation helps learners make connections and see patterns.

Practise regularly. Encourage learners to review flashcards consistently, ideally daily. Spaced repetition, where learners review cards at increasing intervals, enhances retention.

Variety of review methods. Use different techniques to review, such as self-quizzing, partner quizzes, or online flashcard apps.

Interactive learning. Turn flashcard review into a game or competition to make it more engaging. Use flashcards for interactive activities like matching games.

Self-monitoring. Have learners mark each flashcard with a self-assessment label, like 'mastered', 'need review', or 'struggling'. This helps them identify which concepts need more focus.

Incorporate mnemonics. Use mnemonic devices, acronyms, or memory aids to help learners remember complex information.

Include context. When applicable, provide examples or context on the back of the flashcards to deepen understanding.

Peer learning. Encourage learners to quiz each other or explain the concepts on the flashcards to a partner.

Personalise flashcards. Allow learners to create their own flashcards based on what they find most challenging to remember.

Digital flashcards. Use online flashcard platforms or apps to create digital flashcards that learners can access on their devices.

Regular review sessions. Dedicate short review sessions in class or as part of homework where learners go through their flashcards.

Celebrate progress. Recognise and celebrate learners' progress as they demonstrate mastery of flashcard content.

Using flashcards as a regular study tool can help learners internalise information through active recall and repetition. Flashcards are particularly effective for rote memorisation but can also support understanding when used creatively. Encourage learners to experiment with different flashcard techniques and find what works best for them.

Self-quizzing

Questions are not solely in the domain of the teacher. If we are to prepare learners for future success, it's important we teach learners how to ask questions too. They can ask questions in class which their peers answer, and they can ask themselves questions as a form of self-quizzing. As I said earlier, teaching learners effective study skills, including self-quizzing, is crucial for promoting independent learning and fostering academic success.

Here are some ways to help you teach learners self-quizzing and other valuable study skills:

Explain the benefits. Begin by explaining why self-quizzing and other study skills are important. Help learners understand that active engagement with the material enhances retention and comprehension.

Model and demonstrate. Show learners how to use self-quizzing techniques effectively. Demonstrate the process by quizzing yourself on content or asking learners to quiz you.

Provide guided practice. Start with guided practice sessions where you lead learners through the process of creating and using self-quizzes. Gradually shift the responsibility to learners as they become more confident.

Teach question generation. Teach learners how to create their own quiz questions based on the material they're studying. Encourage them to develop a variety of question types, including factual, application-based, and critical thinking questions.

Use retrieval practice. Explain the concept of retrieval practice, where actively recalling information from memory strengthens learning. Show learners how self-quizzing aligns with this effective study strategy.

Emphasise active engagement. Encourage learners to actively engage with their study materials rather than passively reading or highlighting. Self-quizzing, summarising, and teaching the material to someone else are effective active learning techniques.

Discuss effective study techniques. Introduce various study techniques, such as spaced repetition, summarisation, concept mapping, and mnemonic devices. Discuss when and how to use each technique based on the content being studied.

Provide structured resources. Offer templates or guidelines for creating flashcards, study guides, or self-quiz sheets. These resources can help learners structure their study sessions effectively.

Encourage self-monitoring. Teach learners to evaluate their learning progress through self-assessment and reflection. Encourage them to identify areas where they need further practice or clarification.

Offer timely feedback. Provide feedback on the quality of learners' self-quizzes and study materials. Help them refine their techniques for more effective studying.

Set realistic goals. Guide learners in setting achievable study goals, whether it's mastering a specific number of flashcards or completing a certain amount of self-quizzing.

Promote self-regulation. Teach learners how to manage their study time, break tasks into manageable chunks, and avoid cramming.

Celebrate success. Recognise and celebrate learners' efforts and progress in developing effective study skills. Positive reinforcement motivates them to continue using these techniques.

Reflect and adjust. Regularly discuss with learners how their study strategies are working for them and encourage them to make adjustments based on their experiences.

Teaching study skills like self-quizzing empowers learners to become active and self-directed learners. By equipping them with effective strategies, you're setting them up for success not only in your classroom but also in their future academic pursuits.

What have we learned?

In this chapter, we have discovered that:

Stories can help learners to prepare for their later life, including the world of work. We can tell stories for the world of work, as well as stories that help create a sense of self.

What can we do?

To put the advice contained in this chapter into practice, it might be helpful to consider the following questions:

1. Do you tell stories that help prepare learners for their future, including in the world of work?

2. Do you tell stories that help learners develop a greater sense of self, understanding themselves and their place in the world? Do you use story to help disadvantaged learners realise their potential and be their authentic selves?

3. Do you use story and storytelling to teach essential study skills?

Notes

1 www.harvardbusiness.org/what-makes-storytelling-so-effective-for-learning/
2 www.kendallhaven.com/contact
3 www.health.org.uk/newsletter-feature/power-of-storytelling
4 Hannam, P (2020). *Significance*. Bright Future Publishing, p. 26.
5 Brown, P C, McDaniel, M A, & Roediger, H L (2014). *Make it Stick: The Science of Successful Learning*. Belknap Press.

PART 3
Leading through storytelling

12 Using story to consult, communicate, and collaborate

The wisdom of crowds

Here's an interesting story for you …

On 5 June 1968, an American submarine called the *USS Scorpion* was declared lost and its 99 crew presumed dead. An immediate search was initiated but without success because – with a potential search area stretching out thousands of square miles – it was quite simply like finding a needle in a haystack. Accordingly, the *USS Scorpion* was struck from the Naval Vessel Register on 30 June.

Later that year, however, another search led by Dr John Craven – the chief scientist of the US Navy's Special Projects Division – employed rather different methods to try and find the vessel. Dr Craven polled a wide array of specialists in various fields for their thoughts on where the submarine might be. Their guesses were then pooled into a single average guess. This method draws on the Bayesian theory, which was first deployed during the search for a hydrogen bomb lost off the coast of Palomares, Spain, in January 1966.

Not one of the experts' guesses was right but the average of all their guesses was surprisingly accurate and led the recovery team to within just 183 metres of the lost submarine – in 3,000 metres of water about 740 kilometres southwest of the Azores Islands.

I believe in the Bayesian method of school leadership …

I have been a teacher and school leader for a quarter of a century and yet – let me whisper this – I have a confession: I do not possess a panacea; I do not have an elixir, a pill which once popped will proffer great teaching every time. But nor should I: it is not the job of a school leader to provide all the right answers; it is their job to ask all the right questions.

School leaders should not expect any one of their colleagues to know the secret to great teaching either. They will have their own thoughts about what works and what does not – and about what great teaching is and is not – but no single opinion will take a school to within 200 yards of excellence. However – like Dr Craven's team of experts – together, school leaders and their colleagues *can* find the answers. In short – and let this

DOI: 10.4324/9781003465492-15

be our motto – we are better together. Schools may not be democracies, but neither are they dictatorships relying on the single vision of the headteacher. They are communities and succeed through collaboration, not competition.

This is why we need to consult, communicate, and collaborate with our school colleagues – because, together, we can make a big difference to our learners' life chances. And story and storytelling techniques can play an important role in this process.

Consult, communicate, collaborate ...

As we've seen, stories have the power to engage emotions, convey complex information, and create a shared understanding among diverse groups. Thus, stories possess a power that bare facts and statistics do not have, and stories can weave magic into our interactions with colleagues and parents, and help create cohesion and a shared purpose, bonding the whole school community together in common cause.

In particular, stories and storytelling techniques can help school leaders to **consult with stakeholders** in the following ways:

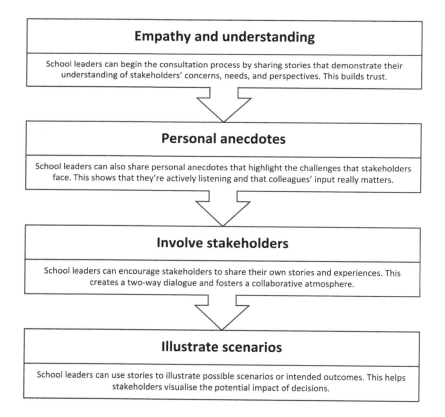

Empathy and understanding
School leaders can begin the consultation process by sharing stories that demonstrate their understanding of stakeholders' concerns, needs, and perspectives. This builds trust.

Personal anecdotes
School leaders can also share personal anecdotes that highlight the challenges that stakeholders face. This shows that they're actively listening and that colleagues' input really matters.

Involve stakeholders
School leaders can encourage stakeholders to share their own stories and experiences. This creates a two-way dialogue and fosters a collaborative atmosphere.

Illustrate scenarios
School leaders can use stories to illustrate possible scenarios or intended outcomes. This helps stakeholders visualise the potential impact of decisions.

Stories and storytelling techniques can help school leaders to **communicate with stakeholders** in the following ways:

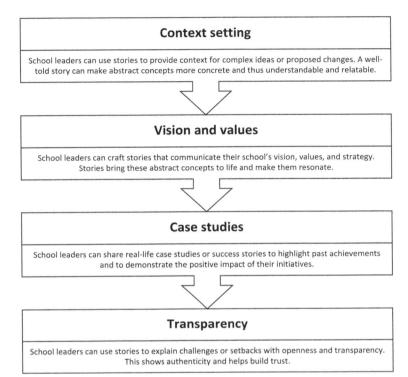

Context setting

School leaders can use stories to provide context for complex ideas or proposed changes. A well-told story can make abstract concepts more concrete and thus understandable and relatable.

Vision and values

School leaders can craft stories that communicate their school's vision, values, and strategy. Stories bring these abstract concepts to life and make them resonate.

Case studies

School leaders can share real-life case studies or success stories to highlight past achievements and to demonstrate the positive impact of their initiatives.

Transparency

School leaders can use stories to explain challenges or setbacks with openness and transparency. This shows authenticity and helps build trust.

Finally, stories and storytelling techniques can help school leaders to **collaborate with stakeholders** in the following ways:

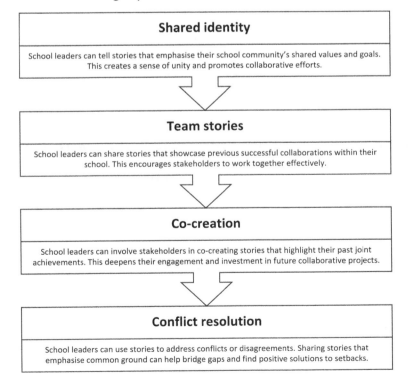

Shared identity

School leaders can tell stories that emphasise their school community's shared values and goals. This creates a sense of unity and promotes collaborative efforts.

Team stories

School leaders can share stories that showcase previous successful collaborations within their school. This encourages stakeholders to work together effectively.

Co-creation

School leaders can involve stakeholders in co-creating stories that highlight their past joint achievements. This deepens their engagement and investment in future collaborative projects.

Conflict resolution

School leaders can use stories to address conflicts or disagreements. Sharing stories that emphasise common ground can help bridge gaps and find positive solutions to setbacks.

Put simply, stories help to celebrate past success and highlight future promise. But while it might be simple, it's certainly not easy. Thus, to make storytelling work as an aid to consultation, communication, and collaboration, school leaders need to:

- **Be authentic:** Leaders should use personal experiences or real-life examples to make their stories authentic and relatable.

- **Engage the emotions:** Leaders should ensure their stories include emotions and sensory details to make them emotionally engaging.

- **Keep stories simple:** Leaders need to avoid complexity and jargon. They should keep their stories simple and focused on a key message.

- **Know their audience:** Leaders need to tailor their stories to the interests and concerns of their stakeholders and institutional setting.

- **Use variety:** Leaders should experiment with different types of stories – personal anecdotes, case studies, testimonials, etc.

- **Practice active listening:** Leaders need to listen actively to stakeholders' own stories as well as use stakeholders' input to inform their storytelling.

- **Include diversity:** Leaders need to highlight diverse perspectives and experiences through their stories to promote inclusivity.

- **Practice:** Leaders need to practise their storytelling skills to improve their delivery and impact.

By using storytelling to consult, communicate, and collaborate with stakeholders, leaders can create a more engaged, informed, and invested community. Stories have the power to inspire action, build relationships, and drive positive change.

Let's home in on two types of stakeholder by way of exemplification: governors and parents.

Consulting, communicating, and collaborating with governors

The relationship between school leaders and the governing body is vital if a school is to thrive. School leaders need to understand the role of the governing body, and governors need to appreciate what they are and are not permitted to do. A simple rule of thumb when demarcating roles and responsibilities is this:

- Governors are concerned with strategy direction and oversight.

- School leaders are concerned with leadership and management.

But school governance is an odd thing: the distinction between school leaders and governors can easily become blurred; it is not always clear where the real power lies and where support and challenge cross into direction and command. Some governing bodies are passive and trust school leaders to run the school how they see fit, relying on the local authority and the inspectorate to provide the appropriate checks and balances. Other governing bodies are active and hold school leaders firmly to account; they scrutinise every decision and pore over performance data and the school budget with keen eyes.

My own view is this: governors are akin to a board of non-executive directors in a company – they work for the school and should be champions of it, speaking highly of the school within the local community and protecting its best interests; governors are not independent arbiters or representatives of community interests or constituents. It is true that governing bodies exist to provide strategic direction and to be the accountable body. It is also true, therefore, that they need to be able to support and challenge school leaders' decisions. And to do this, they need to be kept informed and they need to understand the direction in which the school is headed. They need to know that the information with which they are supplied is honest and accurate. But governors' challenges should not extend to public criticisms of the school.

It is not uncommon for a chair of governors and headteacher to disagree over key decisions and for there to be a robust, often bitter, dispute. This is not entirely unhealthy because a head-teacher needs challenge, and if their decisions cannot be justified to the chair of governors then it is possible that they are bad decisions. Good or bad, decisions are always better when subject to scrutiny. Equally, a headteacher should be able to question the governing body's de-cisions and/or perceptions and make them see the reality of a situation. It is the headteacher, not governors, who is *on the ground* every day and has the better understanding of what works and what does not. It is the headteacher, not governors, who knows staff best and has a duty of care towards them. But disagreements between a headteacher and a chair of governors should be kept private – private from the community and private from other school staff – because it is important for morale that governors and school leaders are seen to have one voice, are seen to be working in unison. Public disagreements or disparaging remarks by governors can be damaging not only to the school's reputation but also to staff morale – which, in turn, could hamper performance and therefore be a self-fulfilling prophecy. It is equally important that the headteacher respects their governing body and involves governors in key decision-making. It is also important that they keep the governing body informed on a regular basis.

It is important that school leaders and governors support and respect each other and empathise with each other's roles. School leaders should never forget that (in most cases) governors are unpaid volunteers who dedicate a lot of their own time to helping the school, and they do so because they genuinely care about the school and about the young people in its care. Equally, governors should never forget that school leaders are paid to take difficult decisions and are appointed on the basis that they have demonstrated the capacity and ability to lead a school. Accordingly, they should be afforded the time and space required to lead the school effectively. If they are not afforded this time and space, then they cannot be held to account for the consequences of their actions or for the performance of their school. This del-icate balance is best struck through clarity of procedures and policies. Systems and structures need to be in place to make everyone's roles clear and to ensure everyone performs those roles effectively or are appropriately challenged if they fall short of what is expected of them.

School leaders should develop good working relationships with governors, especially the chairs of the various governors' committees through which important information can be fed.

Link governors should also act as conduits of information, and as such they need to develop effective working relationships with their link leaders, relationships based on mutual respect and trust. Link governors for some areas may need to make regular contact and be voracious in challenging their link leader about their decisions and actions; other link governors – secure in the improvements made by their link leader and by that person's knowledge, skills, and experience – can step back and need only provide support when it is asked for.

Also, school leaders should provide key briefing documents to governors in order to assist them in making important strategic decisions: this can best be achieved by leaders providing high-quality summaries or headline data (not long, detailed reports) and a set of reasoned options for governors to debate and decide upon. These documents should be distributed in advance of decision-making meetings to allow thoughtful consideration and to avoid protracted discussions.

The key to an effective working relationship between school leaders and the governing body is for both parties to be open and honest and to keep the other informed. There is nothing to be gained by keeping secrets or being duplicitous. Both parties should also remember that they are on the same side and should find ways of working together for the benefit of the school.

Using stories and storytelling techniques can be a powerful way for school leaders to improve their communication and collaboration with governors. Stories can engage, inform, and inspire people, and thus they are a valuable tool for sharing information and building relationships with governors.

Here are some suggestions of how school leaders can leverage stories and storytelling techniques to enhance their interactions with school governors:

Share school success stories:

Leaders can use anecdotes and narratives to highlight successful initiatives, learner achievements, or positive changes within the school. These stories can demonstrate the impact of decisions and policies, making it easier for governors to understand the outcomes and the value of their involvement.

Create a narrative for the school:

Leaders can develop a compelling narrative that encapsulates the school's history, vision, and values. This overarching story can help governors connect with the school's identity and purpose and place current priorities within a wider context. Such narratives also help to articulate the improvement journey to governors by creating a golden thread from the past to the present and into the future.

Personalise data:

Instead of presenting dry data and statistics, which some governors may struggle to interpret and understand, leaders can incorporate them into stories. For example, leaders could explain how an improvement in progress and outcomes positively impacted a specific learner or cohort, making the data more relatable and understandable. This is a good strategy to employ with inspectors too.

Use metaphors and analogies:

As we've seen, metaphors and analogies can simplify complex concepts and make them more accessible — particularly to the layperson. For example, leaders could compare the school's budget to managing a household budget in order to help governors grasp financial matters.

Narrate challenges and their solutions:

When discussing challenges that the school is facing, leaders can narrate the journey in order to identify these issues and the strategies being developed to overcome them. Storytelling can make problem-solving processes more transparent and engaging.

Leverage visual storytelling techniques:

Leaders can incorporate visual aids such as charts, graphs, and infographics into their stories. Visual storytelling can help convey information quickly and effectively.

Use personal stories:

Leaders can share their own experiences as a school leader to humanise their role and build rapport with governors. Personal stories can make leaders more relatable and authentic.

Invite feedback through stories:

Leaders can encourage governors to share their own stories and experiences related to the school. This can foster open communication and collaboration.

Use stories in governing body meetings and reports:

Leaders can integrate storytelling into formal meetings and written reports in order to support key points, rather than relying solely on dry data and soulless analysis.

Celebrate milestones and achievements:

Leaders can use storytelling to celebrate significant achievements, whether they're related to learners, staff, or the school community. This helps create a feeling of pride and a sense of shared success.

By integrating storytelling into their consultation, communication, and collaboration strategies, school leaders can make information more engaging, foster deeper connections with governors, and create a shared vision for their school's future. Effective storytelling can also help bridge the gap between school leaders and governing bodies, leading to more productive and collaborative relationships.

Consulting, communicating, and collaborating with parents

I have heard it said that parents are a school's customers. I disagree with this analogy. The relationship between a school and parents is much more complex than that which exists between a company and its customers. Yes, a school provides a service to its parents, but that service is one of the most important services imaginable: that of securing a good future for their children. Indeed, what could be more important — other than a child's health — than a child's education? But schools are not beholden to parents; they do not exist to serve parents. Often a school knows better than a parent what is in the best interests of the child (and I am speaking as a father). Often a school must challenge and question a parent's behaviour or beliefs. Often a school has to say difficult and unpopular things or refer a parent to the police or social services.

The relationship between schools and parents – however we wish to describe or define it – should be built on mutual trust and respect but this can often be hard-fought. The best starting point for school leaders when forging this relationship is to consider how their school is going to engage with parents. And, unsurprisingly, stories are the answer.

Parental engagement is of great import in all sorts of ways:

- It is associated with higher academic achievement.

- It can lead to increased rates of learner attendance.

- It can have a positive effect on learners' attitudes to learning.

- It can have a positive effect on learners' behaviour.

Getting a school's communications policy right can lead to an increased level of interest among learners in their work, increased parent satisfaction with their child's teachers, and higher rates of teacher satisfaction.

So, what should your school's parental engagement policy look like and what part can story and storytelling play in this?

Firstly, a parental engagement policy should set out what the school expects parents to do. For example:

We encourage parents to:

✔ *Be supportive.*

✔ *Be informed.*

✔ *Maintain a direct involvement in their child's progress.*

✔ *Understand what the school is trying to achieve for their child.*

✔ *Take a positive position – contribute to initiatives.*

✔ *Visit school and be informed about issues, including through consultation evenings.*

✔ *Support events that promote the school efforts.*

✔ *Be aware of and support any home/school agreements.*

A parental engagement policy should also outline how the school intends to communicate with parents and how it will consult with parents on key decisions. It may be useful to start with a statement of intent such as this:

Our school, to be effective, must acknowledge, appreciate, and respond to the views of parents. It needs to take informed decisions following consultation processes.

A school communicates with parents in a variety of ways including:

- Parents' consultation evenings

- Open evenings and events

- Parents' workshops and forums

- Parents' associations or committees

- Formal surveys and market research

- Regular newsletters

- The school website

- Online reporting and the parents' portal

- Text messages and emails

- Social media and direct messaging

- Phone calls and video calls

- Face-to-face meetings on and off site

A school needs a clear strategy for communicating effectively and expediently in each of these circumstances.

It's also important for school leaders to remember the following four cornerstones of effective parental engagement:

1. **Communication needs to start early and continue throughout a learner's journey through school.** The parents of learners moving from nursery to primary school, or from primary to secondary, will not want to receive information halfway through the summer holiday at which point it will be deemed too late. Schools need to engage with parents early and clearly set out their expectations and requirements.

2. **Communication needs to be a two-way process.** As well as a school staying in touch with parents, parents need a means of keeping in contact with the school. One way to do this is to create a frequently asked questions page, as well as a question-and-answer facility and a parents' forum on the school's website. This will need to be monitored carefully, of course, or perhaps pass through a 'gatekeeper' so that comments are vetted before being made 'live'. For it to be regarded worthwhile, the school will also need to communicate its response to parental comments and suggestions, perhaps through a *You Said, We Did* page.

3. **Communications need to be appropriately timed, relevant, and useful.** One way to do this is to utilise the experience and expertise of learners and their parents. For example, the parents of current Reception or Year 7 learners will be able to share their thoughts on what information they needed when they went through the transition process with their child not so long ago, as well as when they needed it most, while current Reception

learners will be able to offer their advice about how to prepare for primary school by sharing their advice on how to get ready for the first day of school, and current Year 7 learners will be able to offer their advice on how to prepare for secondary school by providing a reading list for the summer.

4. **Communications should take many forms and embrace new and emerging technologies.** The use of technologies such as email, text messages, websites, electronic portfolios, and online assessment and reporting tools have made communication between parents and teachers more timely, efficient, productive, and satisfying.

School leaders can enhance their consultation, communication, and collaboration with parents by effectively using stories and storytelling techniques. Storytelling can help school leaders build trust, engage parents, and create a strong partnership between the school and families. Here are some strategies for incorporating storytelling into leaders' interactions with parents:

Narrate school progress:

Leaders can use narratives to explain their school's progress, achievements, and challenges over time. By telling the school's story, leaders can convey a sense of continuous improvement and dedication to providing quality education.

Connect with the school's history:

Leaders can share stories about their school's history, its founding, and the values and traditions it upholds. This helps parents connect with the school's identity and heritage.

Personalise data and outcomes:

When presenting data and statistics, leaders can use stories to provide some helpful and instructive context. For example, they can explain how improvements in test or exam scores or attendance rates have positively impacted learners' lives and educational experiences.

Invite parents' stories:

Leaders can encourage parents to share their own stories and experiences related to the school. This can help leaders better understand parents' concerns, expectations, and aspirations for their children's education. Stories can also be used to showcase the positive impact of parental involvement in the school community by highlighting instances where parents have made a real and positive difference.

Provide a vision through stories:

When discussing future plans and initiatives, leaders can present them as a narrative journey by describing the school's current state, the desired future state, and the steps needed to get there. Storytelling can also be used to celebrate significant school milestones and achievements. This can instil a sense of pride and community among parents.

Use stories in parent–teacher meetings:

Storytelling can be incorporated into parent–teacher forums, parent information evenings, open evenings, and other events where parents are present. Leaders can share stories that illustrate their key messages and goals.

Use stories in the school newsletter or other communications:

Leaders can regularly share success stories through a school newsletter, website, or other digital platforms. These can serve as a repository of stories and updates for parents to access at their convenience.

By incorporating storytelling into consultation, communication, and collaboration strategies, school leaders can connect with parents on a more emotional level, build greater mutual understanding, and foster a stronger sense of community. Effective storytelling helps to bridge the gap between school staff and parents, promoting collaboration for the benefit of the learners.

Hard-to-reach parents

Even when a school has an established, embedded, and effective parental engagement strategy and uses story and storytelling techniques to good effect, some parents are likely to remain hard to reach and it's often these parents which a school needs to engage with the most. So why do some parents find it difficult to talk to their child's school?

Sometimes it's because they lead busy, complicated lives and schools don't often present themselves as being high on their to-do list. Also, school operating hours tend to clash with parents' working lives. Other times, it's because a parent had a difficult experience of school as a youngster or with other institutions as an adult and remains reluctant to enter a school building or talk with teachers. They may be daunted and even afraid. In both these cases, a school may need to consider alternative approaches, such as engaging with parents by telephone in the evenings and weekends, or meeting with them at another – neutral – location nearby, perhaps even using a 'go-between' such as another parent who is known to be engaged and reliable.

We also need to be mindful that some parents will have poor levels of literacy and so will need to be communicated with more sensitively so that they do not misunderstand the nature and purpose of the communication, and in order to make it easier for them to respond without fear of humiliation.

Stories can help here too.

Firstly, we can **share learner success stories**. This might involve the following:

- Highlight individual learner achievements.

- Share success stories of academic performance.

- Share success stories of extracurricular activities.

- Share success stories of personal growth.

- Use positive stories to inspire and reassure parents that their children are in good hands.

Secondly, we can **use personal anecdotes**. This might involve the following:

- Share personal anecdotes from our own school days and educational journey.

- Share reminisces from our own experiences as a teacher and school leader.

- Use personal stories to make school staff seem more relatable.

- Use personal stories to show parents that we understand their concerns and aspirations.

We'll explore more on the use of personal stories later.

What have we learned?

In this chapter, we have discovered that:

Stories – because they have the power to engage emotions and foster a shared understanding – can convey much more than bare facts and statistics. School leaders can therefore use stories to bolster their communications with colleagues and parents, and to create cohesion and shared purpose. Stories can also enhance school leaders' interactions with governors.

Stories enable school leaders to share school success stories in a more personal and relatable way, including by humanising dry data and by utilising metaphors and analogies.

Storytelling is a great way to build trust and engage stakeholders such as parents because stories have the ability to connect people to the school's history and to articulate a shared vision for the future.

What can we do?

To put the advice contained in this chapter into practice, it might be helpful to consider the following questions:

1. Do you use stories when consulting with colleagues in order to build empathy and understanding and to exemplify intended outcomes?

2. Do you use stories when communicating with colleagues in order to convey your vision for the future and be authentic and transparent?

3. Do you use stories when collaborating with stakeholders in order to establish a shared identity and involve others in creating a better future, thus investing others in the outcomes?

13 Using story to articulate a vision and foster shared values

In my experience, a great school leader is someone who:

- **Tells a gripping story about their hopes for the future**, a narrative which is consistent, fair, and honest; these leaders are transparent and above reproach, they *stick to the story* in the best possible sense of the phrase.

- **Listens attentively to other people's stories**: they care about and respond to other people's wants and needs and motivations.

As gifted storytellers, great school leaders are:

- **Sensitive**, able to show warmth and to empathise with people's concerns and worries.

- **Assertive**, able to show determination and a strength of response, yet be kind and calm and courageous.

- **Communicative**, able to express themselves through a variety of means and in an appropriate manner, always with enthusiasm, passion, and drive.

There are many ways in which we could define effective school leadership, but I think it is reasonable and practical to meld the myriad activities in which leaders engage into five broad categories or 'stories'.

The five 'stories' of school leadership

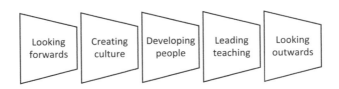

DOI: 10.4324/9781003465492-16

1. Looking forwards

Looking forwards is about setting a vision for the future and agreeing a set of shared values the school will embody to achieve that vision. This is an important facet because school leaders need to have a clear vision for their school which articulates what they want their school to look and feel like, as well as what they want it to achieve for their learners and the community – and they need to communicate this clearly, repeatedly, and with enthusiasm to stakeholders.

The vision should guide leaders' daily decision-making. School leaders should take account of their school's local and national context, not only in terms of their vision but also in their everyday actions. They should think strategically and involve their stakeholders in their decisions.

Leaders need to show conviction of purpose too. This means they must be driven by their vision and not be distracted by setbacks or conflicts.

After vision come values. Values articulate the behaviours and attitudes that all stakeholders must embody and exhibit daily if their shared vision is to be achieved. Values make explicit 'the way we do things around here'. At the heart of most values is a moral code and a commitment to ethical behaviour leading to inclusion and diversity.

Looking forwards is the 'why?' of school leadership.

2. Creating culture

Creating culture comes next. It is about having high expectations of every adult who works for or with the school, and it's about demanding the best for every learner at the school.

One of the best ways to create the culture is to define a set of social norms for what constitutes good behaviour, and this is about much more than the reduction or elimination of poor behaviour. Social norms are found most clearly in the routines of the school. Any aspect of behaviour that can be standardised because it is always expected from all learners should indeed be standardised. For example, walking on the left or right of the corridor, entering the classroom in single file and silence, clearing tables at lunchtime, and so on. These routines should be communicated to, and practised by, staff and learners until they become automatic. This then frees up time, mental effort, and energy towards more useful areas, such as study.

Next, school leaders need to build the culture in practice with as much detail and clarity as possible. Staff and learners need to know how to achieve this and what the culture looks like in practice, from behaviour on buses to corridor and canteen conduct, and behaviour in the workplace or community when on work experience or educational visits. This means demonstrating it, communicating it thoroughly, and ensuring that every aspect of school life feeds into and reinforces that culture.

One way to build the culture is to design routines that learners and staff should follow. Any behaviour that should be performed identically, most or all of the time, should be made into a routine.

Once built, school systems require regular maintenance. This is often where good cultures break down. It is reasonably straightforward to identify what a good culture might look like but, like a diet, the difficulty lies in embedding and maintaining it. This requires visible and consistent leadership, the provision of staff training and mentoring, the effective use of learner rewards and sanctions processes, rigorous data monitoring, staff and learner surveys, and so on.

Creating culture is the 'how?' of school leadership.

What follows – developing people, leading teaching, and looking outwards – constitutes the 'what?' of school leadership – they are about the daily actions leaders take to bring about school improvement and achieve the best outcomes for all their learners.

3. Developing people

School leaders need to foster a collaborative culture and provide learning opportunities for all their staff. They should share responsibility through effective delegation. School leaders also need to value the importance of continuing professional development, including through performance management and appraisal objectives. They should have high expectations of everyone in their school and should, again, lead by example and take their own professional development seriously. They should be well informed and up to date with the latest educational thinking and research, as well as statutory obligations and education policy.

School leaders should take full responsibility for their decisions and for the performance of their school. They should ensure clear accountability at all levels through effective line management structures and by drawing clear links between the school improvement plan and what is happening in school. They should analyse performance regularly and robustly and give clear feedback and performance reports to stakeholders, including governors.

School leaders have legal accountability for what happens in their school as well as moral accountability. They should do what they think is right and should take advice from others – including their local authority and professional associations – wherever possible. But above all they should take decisions that will stand up to scrutiny over the long term.

4. Leading teaching

Schools are seats of learning, and so leading teaching is a key role for school leaders. School leaders are lead teachers, after all. This means leading by example by continuing to be an excellent classroom practitioner who can engage and enthuse learners, and by being up to date with the latest pedagogical research. This also means evaluating teaching and learning effectively – through a variety of means including an analysis of planning documentation, lesson observations, learning walks, work sampling, conversations with learners, and the scrutiny of assessment records – and working with others to improve the quality of teaching and learning and to challenge underachievement (by working with data and investing in intervention and support).

Further, school leaders should demonstrate good judgement, be decisive but thoughtful, and should manage school resources effectively. They should manage their school's finances (although the day-to-day management of school finances will likely be delegated to a bursar, finance manager, or similar, school leaders should fully understand school finances and be accountable for fiscal decisions) in order to ensure their school achieves quality and value for money. It is a school leader's duty to use the public purse wisely. This is achieved by being prudent, by planning ahead (including detailed costs in the school improvement plan), and by prioritising spending according to greatest need and according to the impact that spending will have on learners. In fact, these actions constitute my 3Ps of school finance: prudence, planning, prioritisation.

School leaders should also manage the site, ensuring it complies with health and safety regulations, child protection, and safeguarding. School leaders need to ensure that resources match the curriculum too. Finally, school leaders should manage their school's most important — and costly — resource: staff. This means ensuring that supply meets demand and that all staff have the tools and skills they need to do their jobs well.

Managing school finances, the site, and health and safety is often a part of the job that school leaders, particularly those new to the post, find most challenging because they have trained as teachers not managers, but it is also a key part of the job if a school is to move forwards and achieve sustainable improvements.

5. Looking outwards

School leaders need to look beyond the school gates and act as custodians of their school for the benefit of the local community. They should develop and encourage effective partnerships with other schools, external agencies such as the NHS, and the community they serve. Community cohesion is not solely about offering the school site to the local community — although enabling community use is certainly important, be that by leasing the fields to the local football team or by running adult education classes in the evenings. Rather, community cohesion is about respecting diversity and protecting vulnerable learners. It is about understanding the local community and taking account of where learners come from. It is about working with parents too. Ultimately, it is about bringing the world into schools and taking learners out into the world in order to raise learners' awareness of that world and their place in it. Furthermore, community cohesion is about respecting diversity and inclusion of all types, ensuring a personalised learning programme in which every child can fulfil their potential irrespective of gender, socioeconomic or ethnic background, and additional and different learning needs.

Storytelling the vision

The first 'story' of school leadership, then, was *looking forwards* and this is where storytelling techniques can be particularly helpful, so let's explore this further.

The words *vision* and *values* are often glued together like knife and fork, salt and pepper, day and night, etc. I find it useful to think of the two terms, which are often used interchangeably, in the following way: vision is your destination; values are your means of transport.

In other words, a vision sets out what you want your school to be like, whereas a set of shared values articulates the behaviours and attitudes you expect all stakeholders in your school to adopt in order to get there.

One of the five dimensions of what Vivianne Robinson[1] calls 'student-centred leadership' is establishing goals and expectations which enable leaders to establish the relative importance of various competing demands and thus provide a clear steer.

Goal setting in education, Robinson argues, is not about deciding what is and is not important. It works because it forces decisions about relative importance – about what is more important in this context, at this time, than all the other important things.

Establishing and articulating a clear vision is crucial for any organisation but particularly important for schools which – you might say – sail on such troubled waters, tugged back and forth on a tide of policy from successive governments and their quangos. A vision makes explicit what an organisation stands for and what its people want it to achieve; it binds people (staff, learners, governors, the community, and so on) together in the pursuit of a common goal and reminds them why they do what they do every day. A vision provides a focus for decision-making and conveys a picture of what the future will look like.

According to John Kotter in his book *Leading Change*,[2] an effective vision is **desirable** in that it appeals to the long-term interests of stakeholders. It is **feasible** in that it comprises realistic, attainable goals. It is **focused** in that it is clear enough to provide guidance in decision-making. And an effective vision is **flexible** in that it is general enough to allow individual initiative and alternative responses in light of changing conditions. It is also – more pertinently for our present purposes – **communicable**. In other words, it is easy to communicate and can be successfully explained within five minutes. And this is where story plays such a crucial role. We'll return to this shortly. But first, back to Kotter ...

The most effective vision statements, Kotter says, share the following characteristics: they are ambitious enough to force people out of comfortable routines. For example, becoming 5% better is not the goal; becoming the best at something is often the goal. They aim in a general way at providing better and better products or services at lower and lower costs, thus appealing greatly to customers and stockholders. They take advantage of fundamental trends, especially globalisation and new technology. And they make no attempt to exploit anyone and thus have a certain moral power.

For my part, I believe an effective vision is one which is shared – not just in the sense that it is communicated but that it is understood and owned by most (if not all) of the people in school. It is all well and good for a leader to have a clear vision of what they want to achieve but it will forever remain an aspiration and will never be achieved if it is not understood and shared by everyone else in school.

A vision should express what is unique about a school. What are the unique challenges the school needs to overcome? What will success look like for that institution? What makes its community and stakeholders different?

A good starting point when writing a vision, therefore, is the school's existing vision or, if it does not have one, its motto or values. Why? Because although a vision is about the future, it should have solid foundations in the past, in the school's history, in what the school stands for, and in the very reason it exists. Continuity is important to all those with a stake in the place. No one likes the process of change; it is uncomfortable. People like to know that what they have built, what they have worked hard for, what they believe in, is to be retained and protected. A vision which refers to what the school already does well, as well as articulates what it hopes to do better in the future, keeps all stakeholders happy. Moreover, it is balanced, fair and, above all, cohesive: it connects stakeholders along a path which leads from the past, through the present, to the future …

… And this is where story comes in. Vision creation, after all, is about telling the story of the school – reminding everyone of past success, present challenges, and future promises. It is about weaving a golden thread, a journey of collective improvement, rather than unsettling people with talk of different ways of working and of a new broom sweeping the past away.

Vision creation, put simply, is about *plot*. Here, then, it might be instructive to return to Freytag's Pyramid. You will recall that Freytag's Pyramid consists of five parts:

1. **Exposition:** This is the beginning of the story where the setting, characters, and background information are introduced.

2. **Rising action:** This is where the conflict of the story is introduced, and events begin to unfold, leading up to the climax.

3. **Climax:** This is the turning point of the story, where the conflict reaches its highest point, and the protagonist faces their greatest challenge.

4. **Falling action:** This is where the events following the climax begin to unfold, and loose ends are tied up.

5. **Resolution:** This is the end of the story, where the conflict is resolved, and the story concludes.

A good vision has a similar structure:

1. **Exposition:** Talk of past success – what were the school's beginnings, what has it always stood for, what has it achieved to date?

2. **Rising action:** What is the school's current position, where is it now, and where does it need to be in the future? Why does it need to change and how is change built upon existing foundations; how will the future be built on the past?

3. **Climax:** What will success look like at the end and why is this important? What will it look and feel like for all stakeholders when the vision has been achieved?

4. **Falling action:** What part must everyone play in the process of change? How will colleagues be consulted and involved (not just informed) along the journey of improvement? What will be the benefits of change for all those involved?

5. **Resolution:** What are the first steps, the quick wins? What challenges must be overcome in order to proceed?

This story of the future, like all good stories, should be a shared one. In other words, all stakeholders need to be involved in agreeing the vision. But this does not have to be a long and convoluted process of wrangling over every word and nuance. The consultation should be clearly framed: what aspects of the vision are leaders consulting on, what are the dividing lines?

Leaders need to make it clear what is open for debate and what is not. Leaders need to make clear how they will respond to feedback. People need to feel listened to but, equally, leaders should not promise something they cannot deliver.

Robinson says that, in terms of creating a vision, three conditions need to be in place.[3] The first is that people need to feel personally committed to the goal and believe they have the capacity to achieve it. The goal also needs to be specific so people can monitor their progress towards it.

As we've already discovered, the best stories pique readers' interest by posing big philosophical questions or by signposting knowledge gaps. We yearn for answers. And a good vision is no different. Vision creation works by creating a discrepancy between the current situation and an attractive future. This discrepancy is what motivates people to focus their effort and attention on the activities required to reach the goal and to persist until they achieve it. People commit to a vision that they believe is important. The vision therefore needs to provide an opportunity to achieve what is valued, and people need to accept that the current situation falls sufficiently short of that vision to warrant pursuit of the goal. This is why it is important that a vision is a collective goal rather than that of a single leader and that it emerges through discussion rather than being imposed, and why it is important to tell the story of school improvement.

The second aspect of gaining commitment, according to Robinson, is acceptance of the gap between the goal and the existing state of affairs. Many leaders, she argues, focus only on the desirability of the goal and not on the difference between what they envisage and the present situation. One solution, Robinson says, is to engage in 'constructive problem talk', which involves analysing problems to reveal the possibilities for change.

Here, story can be a powerful tool again. Problem talk works best if it is specific, and so telling stories about individual learners can help bring a challenge to light and make it real and relatable. The learner can be invented as an example, and so too can the situation described, so long as the problem being highlighted is genuine and feels authentic to stakeholders.

Fostering shared values

That's the vision, let us now turn to consider values.

As I say above, the vision is the destination and the values are the means of transport. The values are necessarily longer than the vision because they are a detailed declaration of what an organisation will do in order to achieve its vision. A set of shared values should try to cover all the important aspects of a school's working practices.

As a starting point, consider the following statements:

Our school is a place where ...

- *There is a shared vision of what the school is trying to achieve and a clear strategy to help it get there.*

- *There is a positive whole-school culture of high expectations and effective systems of behaviour management that are known, understood, and adhered to by all staff for all learners.*

- *There is a rich and ambitious curriculum which is taught by skilled, well-motivated teachers to all learners irrespective of background and starting point, ensuring equality.*

- *There is a wide-ranging programme of interesting extracurricular provision which is targeted at those who need it most.*

- *Learners' needs are known, and learning is adapted to meet these needs; more is done for those who start with less, ensuring equity.*

- *Learners make good progress within each year and key stage, academically, emotionally, and socially so that they are prepared for the next steps in their journey.*

- *There is a purposeful, organised working atmosphere, learners are valued, and their contributions are appreciated and rewarded.*

- *Resources are well matched to the curriculum and targeted at those who need them most.*

- *Learners are engaged in learning, are challenged by hard work, and are encouraged to do their very best.*

- *Vulnerable children are identified early, and effective support mechanisms are put in place in a timely manner and are monitored contemporaneously to ensure impact.*

- *Parents and carers are kept fully informed and involved in school life; they are treated as welcomed contributors in their child's education.*

- *There is a strong sense of involvement in the local community, and visitors and outside agencies provide contributions to the school.*

- *All staff are valued and are supported in their own personal and professional development; the school values collaboration over competition and creates a culture of high trust, no blame.*

These act as detailed statements of intent – attitudes and behaviours. They are underpinned by values such as trust, fairness, integrity, and so on.

Once consulted upon and agreed, the vision and values need to be communicated and, once again, this is where story can be utilised.

A vision can easily get lost in the clutter of everyday working life if leaders fail to communicate it effectively. To communicate the vision more effectively, leaders need to ensure communications are simple – all jargon and technobabble must be eliminated. Leaders need to make use of metaphor, analogy, and example. Repetition is also key: ideas sink in deeply only after they have been heard many times – seven times in seven different ways is a good rule of thumb taken from the world of marketing.

The vision should frame every conversation and speech, provide a focus for every meeting, and inform every decision. It should be used as a mantra. It will remind people of their goal and refocus them on what's most important; it will convince them that they are playing a crucial role in helping to make the school's vision a reality and reassure them that they are helping to shape the future.

Daniel Coyle, in his book *The Culture Code*,[4] argues that there are four types of 'catchphrase', which he calls the North Star, Do's, Don'ts, and Identity. The *North Star* provides the Why. It has the highest priority because it carries the aim or objective. In other words, the North Star is the vision. The *Do's* and *Don'ts*, meanwhile, describe the How. In other words, they articulate how to achieve the aim or objective. The *Identity* outlines the qualities or traits that distinguish the organisation from the rest of the world. In other words, they articulate the Who – the personality, morals, beliefs, and attitudes of the organisation, and what makes it unique. Taken together, these four types of 'catchphrase' create what Coyle calls the 'culture story'.

In other words, a vision shouldn't be cliched or corny; it should be about inspiration and navigation. Having a shared purpose is about building a vivid, accessible roadmap with a set of emotional GPS signals that define the organisation's identity and guide the behaviour of its staff. Story and storytelling techniques enable us to do just this.

Into practice
Writing your story

Storytelling the future

Using storytelling to articulate a vision for the future of your school and to foster a set of shared values among stakeholders is a powerful way to inspire and unite people on the journey of improvement. Stories can make abstract concepts more relatable, emotionally engaging, and memorable. Here are some suggestions of how you might use storytelling to effectively communicate your school's vision and values:

1. **Tell a compelling story of the future**

   ○ **Start with a problem or challenge:** Begin the story by highlighting a problem or challenge that your school faces. This creates a context for your vision.

   ○ **Introduce the vision:** Introduce your vision as the solution to this problem or challenge. Describe how things could be better if the vision were realised.

   ○ **Use metaphors and other imagery:** Paint a vivid picture of what the future will look like once the vision is achieved. Use descriptive language to help your audience visualise the outcome. Show colleagues what's in it for them.

   ○ **Demonstrate impact:** Share stories of how individual members of staff or teams will benefit from the vision coming to fruition.

   ○ **Bring it back to learners:** Highlight the positive impact the change will have on learners and outcomes.

2. **Connect your vision to your shared values**

   ○ **Highlight your values:** Identify the behaviours and attitudes that align with your vision and will help make it a reality. These values should resonate with your stake-holders and reflect the principles, morals, and ethics that guide your school – 'the way we do things around here'.

○ **Share stories of your values in action:** Share stories that illustrate how these values have been embodied and embedded within the school. Highlight real-life examples that showcase these values in action.

○ **Show alignment:** Demonstrate how your vision is directly aligned with these shared values. Explain how achieving the vision will uphold and strengthen the values.

○ **Humanise the values:** Use personal anecdotes that humanise your school's values and show how they impact individuals' lives, both within and outside the school gates.

3. **Engage emotions**

○ **Tell emotive stories:** Craft stories that evoke people's emotions related to your vision and values. Emotional engagement helps people connect on a deeper level.

○ **Show empathy:** Share stories that demonstrate empathy and understanding of the challenges your school and its stakeholders face. This shows that you care about their concerns.

○ **Appeal to aspirations:** Share stories that resonate with the aspirations and desires of your school and stakeholders. Tap into their dreams and ambitions.

4. **Make it personal**

○ **Share your own journey:** Personal anecdotes about your journey, struggles, and growth can make your vision and values more relatable and inspiring.

○ **Be authentic:** Be genuine in sharing your passion and conviction for your school's vision and values. Authenticity lends credibility.

5. **Use analogies and symbolism**

○ **Analogies:** Use analogies to help explain complex concepts related to the vision and values, making the abstract seem concrete and the new seem familiar.

○ **Symbolism:** Use symbolic imagery that represents the vision and values. This can create a lasting impression.

6. **Repeat and reinforce**

○ **Retell stories:** Continuously share and reinforce your school's vision and values stories. Repetition helps embed them in the minds of your stakeholders.

○ **Align your communications:** Ensure that all communications, from official announcements to daily interactions, reflect and reinforce your school's vision and values.

Using story and storytelling techniques to articulate your school's vision and foster shared values makes your communications more relatable, meaningful, and compelling. These stories create a sense of purpose, unity, and motivation among your stakeholders, driving them towards a collective goal and embodying your school's values.

What have we learned?

In this chapter, we have discovered that:

A vision is the story of a school, and the best stories remind stakeholders of past success, present challenges, and future promises. The best stories articulate a journey of collective improvement so as not to unsettle people. In short, vision creation is *plot*.

A good vision – like all the best stories – piques interest by posing big philosophical questions, thus creating a discrepancy between the current situation and a better future. It's this discrepancy that motivates people to change.

What can we do?

To put the advice contained in this chapter into practice, it might be helpful to consider the following questions:

1. Do you tell the story of the kind of school you want your school to be and weave a golden thread from past success, through present challenges, to future promise?

2. Do you share this story, involving others in your vision creation?

3. Do you connect your vision to a set of shared values, identifying the behaviours and attitudes that everyone must exhibit if the vision is to be achieved?

Notes

1 Robinson, V (2011). *Student-Centered Leadership*. Jossey-Bass.

2 Kotter, J (1996). *Leading Change*. Harvard Business Review Press.

3 Robinson, V (2011). *Student-Centered Leadership*. Jossey-Bass.

4 Coyle, D (2018). *The Culture Code: The Secrets of Highly Successful Groups*. Random House Business.

Using story to build trust and create a no-blame culture

On the one hand, teaching is a profession (as opposed to a job) and teachers are professionals (as opposed to workers). It follows, therefore, that teachers should be afforded autonomy in the classroom rather than be dictated to by school leaders.

On the other hand, in order to raise learners' aspirations and improve outcomes, sometimes school leaders need to balance their defence of teacher autonomy with their need to achieve school-wide consistency; sometimes leaders need to insist upon every teacher following a set of common working practices so that they can be sure that every learner is in receipt of the same high standards of teaching because a child's birth should not be their destiny.

At the heart of this debate about autonomy is a moral conundrum: should school leaders trust every teacher every day to use their good judgement and expertise in order to do their best for every learner? Or do they need to insist upon systems of collaboration and compliance that would ensure they will do so?

Trust is, of course, vital in any organisation and the first step towards someone being trustworthy is to trust them. But when you're a school leader responsible for the education of hundreds if not thousands of learners, you're left with a tough choice: do you have complete trust in every one of your teachers or do you create systems of accountability which ensure no learner is left behind? The honest answer, I think, is yes *and* yes: yes, you have trust in all your teachers, and yes, you create systems of accountability.

In the sense of professional practice, one size does fit all. Although there is no question that increased coherence means reduced autonomy, it does not necessarily imply decreased professionalism. Doctors are seen as professionals because they have mastered complex sets of shared diagnostic and treatment practices. They exercise their judgement about how those procedures are to be applied in any individual case and are held accountable for those judgements. Teachers need sufficient autonomy to exercise their professional judgement about how to use the framework and to contribute to evaluative discussions about its adequacy. But that autonomy should also be constrained by the need to ensure effective teaching practice – that is, practice under which all learners achieve to a high level.

DOI: 10.4324/9781003465492-17

Professional freedom comes with responsibilities

Inspiration
Telling my story

I teach on an initial teacher training course. One of my first lessons is on professionalism. I ask my trainees what it means to be a professional – as in the member of a profession, not to be slick and assured. We conclude that being a professional requires the following elements:

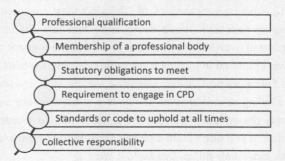

- Professional qualification
- Membership of a professional body
- Statutory obligations to meet
- Requirement to engage in CPD
- Standards or code to uphold at all times
- Collective responsibility

Being a member of a profession means taking collective responsibility for what happens in that profession; it requires collaboration.

Standard professional practice provides the scaffolding that's required for the exercise of truly professional rather than idiosyncratic judgement. In other words, although school leaders should not seek to eradicate individuality, they should eliminate individualism (habitual or enforced patterns of working alone). Eliminating individualism should not be about making everyone the same and plunging them into groupthink; it should be about achieving collective responsibility.

Being a professional is about what you do and how you behave. In their book *Professional Capital*,[1] Andy Hargreaves and Michael Fullan say that being professional is about "being impartial and upholding high standards of conduct and performance. Being professional is about quality and character". Being professional, they say, has more to do with how other people regard you and how this affects the regard you have for yourself. Moreover, being a professional means having collective – rather than individual – autonomy. Hargreaves and Fullan refer to members of the teaching profession – and indeed any profession – as having 'collective autonomy' over their actions as opposed to individual autonomy. In other words, teachers – like doctors and lawyers – need to work within set systems and structures and follow a consistent approach to their teaching practice, rather than work in isolation and have complete autonomy over what they do and how they do it.

In his book *Good to Great*,[2] Jim Collins expounds the importance of having a set of consistent systems and structures which dictate what staff can and cannot do and which governs how they should and should not operate. He uses the analogy of an airline pilot. A pilot, he says, operates within a very strict system and does not have the freedom to go outside of that system. Yet at the same time, the crucial decisions – whether to take off, whether to land, whether to abort, whether to land elsewhere – rest with the pilot. Collins says that great organisations have a culture of discipline which involves a duality.

On the one hand, it requires people to adhere to a consistent system; yet, on the other hand, it gives people freedom and responsibility within the framework of that system.

School improvement is about getting everyone on the same page. In *Leverage Leadership*,[3] Paul Bambrick-Santoyo talks about the challenge of building a rich and supportive staff culture, something which is "one of the critical components to [a school's] success". He refers to Brian Sims, director of high schools for the Academy for Urban School Leadership (AUSL), who transformed 14 of Chicago's least successful district schools into "solid community bedrocks". In so doing, Sims' first job was to get everyone 'on the same page'. In other words, he made sure all his teachers knew the "school's core mission ... and [were] unified in putting it into practice". He explains as follows: "What most undermines failing schools is that everyone on the staff is doing his or her own thing ... turning a failing school around demands a culture where everyone is on the same page, supports the school's mission, and accepts what is needed to get back on track." Sims says that "if you don't build a strong expectation and shared culture early in the turnaround, it's extremely difficult to build it later".

Being a professional, then, means working within the scaffold of standard practice, assuming *collective* rather than *individual* autonomy; being a member of a profession rather than being idiosyncratic. It requires the building of a shared culture – a culture of high trust and low threat; a no-blame culture.

In his book *Deliverology 101*,[4] Michael Barber calls these shared standards of practice 'routines' and he argues that routines are the engine of delivery:

Routines ... follow the clock, with no excuses for delay. They can come in many forms, depending on information, frequency, audience, and format. But the purpose of each is the same: to create a sense of urgency, to sustain focus and momentum, and to track progress. One of the main benefits of routines is their ability to focus the delivery effort despite the multitude of distractions that will plague any system. Routines play a large part in overcoming barriers by forcing the system to regularly check its progress on a consistent set of priorities.

In other words, great schools excel at what they do because they do so in a consistent manner. They have strong values and high expectations. Their achievements do not happen by chance but through highly reflective, carefully planned strategies. There is a high degree of internal consistency. Leadership is well distributed and ambitious to move the school forward.

What needs to emerge, then, is the 'standard operation', a phrase Roy Blatchford borrows from the medical profession:[5]

As a patient entering an established hospital for an appendectomy, a hip replacement, or a kidney transplant – operations of increasing complexity – wherever in the world we are, doctors will swing into action with 'the standard operation'. Barring complications and assuming competent physicians, the patient will leave hospital with a body refreshed.

Blatchford goes on to say that schools are a people business:

> The inner belief and commitment to realising excellence by those who lead schools is the starting point. At its beating heart the excellent school is a place where people care more than others think is wise, risk more than others think is safe, dream more than others think is practical, and expect more than others think is possible ... The particular skills and knowledge required of teachers, therefore, must be non-negotiable and so too must the attitudes, dispositions and high service standards.

Bambrick-Santoyo also talks about the importance of getting to 'teamlyness': "To boost achievement [schools] need to craft the right staff culture", which is one of coherence.[6]

And this leads me on to the importance of collaboration...

At the heart of any true profession are expectations and frameworks that are challenging and open enough for teachers to be able to innovate and enquire into their practice together. Mindfulness must be cultivated, and the norms and conditions of work must deliberately foster it. Practice, especially collective reflective practice, is integral to what Hargreaves and Fullan call 'decisional capital' and, by that token, to professional capital as a whole. Like medicine, teaching is an imperfect science, and it requires thinking professionals working together to maximise its effectiveness.

Judith Little of the University of Berkeley devised a useful continuum of collaboration – from weaker to stronger forms – which comprised the following:[7]

1. Scanning and storytelling – exchanging ideas, anecdotes, and gossip.

2. Help and assistance – usually when asked.

3. Sharing – of materials and teaching strategies.

4. Joint work – where teachers teach, plan, or inquire into teaching together.

The quality of teaching in our schools will best be improved by engaging in quality, collaborative professional development that is sustained over the long term, focused on students' learning, and continually and formatively evaluated.

What is needed, then, is a "community of teachers ... to work together to ask questions, evaluate their impact, and decide on the optimal next steps", says John Hattie in *Visible Learning for Teachers*.[8] He begins that book with a medical analogy and refers to the doctors he's witnessed first-hand "following scripts" and working with set procedures: "Throughout the treatment, the impact of [doctors'] interventions was monitored, changed, and led to the critical decisions ... Teams [of doctors] worked to understand the consequences of treatments and evidence was the key to adaptive professional decision-making – all aiming to maximise the impact."

Culture: it grows on you

In *Rule Makers, Rule Breakers*,[9] the psychologist Michele Gelfand asks what ultimately drives human behaviour. Do ideals, symbols, and beliefs lead people to act as they do? Or are our motivators less ethereal: money, fear, thirst for power, circumstance, and opportunity, with culture only an afterthought?

Gelfand comes down firmly on the side on the culturalists, and the most important ingredients of culture, she argues, are the social norms, the often-informal rules of conduct, the dos and don'ts that emerge whenever people band together.

And it is this notion of 'people banding together' that is so crucial to the kind of culture we need in our schools to help the process of school improvement flourish. The kind of workplace environment we want to foster is one of collaboration not competition.

In a paper pithily entitled 'Organisational blueprints for success in high-tech start-ups: Lessons from the Stanford Project on Emerging Companies' by James N. Baron and Michael T. Hannan, published in the *California Management Review* in 2002,[10] the authors proposed five different models of organisational structure: the star model; the engineering model; the commitment model; the bureaucratic model; and the autocratic model.

The only culture that was a consistent winner – lasting the course and sustaining success – was the one built on *commitment*. In fact, 'commitment' organisations outperformed every other type of organisation in almost every meaningful way. Organisations which followed the *commitment* model were focused on creating a culture in which people happily worked for the same company their whole careers.

Leaders in *commitment* cultures want to create a strong family-like environment. They want employees to be bound to their organisation by a sense of personal belonging and identification; in other words, by a love of their school and what they do.

In commitment cultures, there is a sense of trust among staff and leaders that entices everyone to work harder and stick together through the setbacks that are inevitable. There are also higher levels of teamwork and psychological safety in these cultures.

So, what does 'commitment' look like in practice in schools?

In the best schools I've visited, the staffroom remains a hub – it is busy with staff sharing and listening, offloading, and laughing. Conversely, in the least successful institutions, the staffroom is either non-existent or deserted; instead, staff work in departmental silos or, worse, alone in their classrooms.

In the best schools I've visited, the canteen and corridors are calm, friendly places – respected and kept clean by everyone. People are polite, greeting you with a smile; and they are purposeful, focused on learning and teaching. In the least successful institutions, meanwhile, there's a threatening atmosphere of chaos and confusion. There are no-go areas, behaviour isn't tackled because there is no leadership from the top: rather, behaviour is regarded as a teacher's responsibility and if they can't manage it, they alone are to blame.

In the best schools I've visited, leaders develop a 'no-blame' culture. They believe that just because someone has made a mistake, this doesn't mean they should forget the important contribution the same colleague makes every day. In fact, in such situations, they know that staff need to feel supported and trusted to learn from their mistake and to move on. When things are going well, meanwhile, the best leaders are generous with their praise and recognition.

No-blame cultures have proven vital to the success of organisations. In *Black Box Thinking*,[11] Matthew Syed says that the most successful organisations in the world – and he uses the example of aviation – show a willingness and tenacity to investigate the lessons that often exist when we fail, but which we rarely exploit. A no-blame culture, Syed argues, is about creating systems and cultures that enable organisations to learn from errors, rather than being threatened by them.

After all, practice – which we teachers tell our learners is a vital part of the learning process – is all about harnessing the benefits of learning from failure while reducing its cost. Syed says that it is better to fail in practice than on the big stage. Or, as Eleanor Roosevelt put it, we should "learn from the mistakes of others [because we] can't live long enough to make them all [ourselves]".

Syed says the 'paradox of success' is that it is built upon failure. Everything we know in, say, aviation, every rule in the rulebook, every procedure we have, we know because someone somewhere died.

And yet we can only learn from failure if there is an openness to admit to mistakes. If staff feel threatened by owning up to errors, they are less likely to do so and so that rich seam of intelligence will be lost to us, and we'll keep on making the same mistakes over and again. Only if we operate a no-blame culture will colleagues willingly admit when they get it wrong and then we can work together to get it right next time.

This is why the best teams seemingly make the most mistakes. They don't; they just admit and record them more willingly and more often. Closeted teams who fear failure and blame don't record their mistakes and so they appear, to the outside, to be more successful. This is why the world of medicine appears more infallible than the world of aviation: doctors, particularly in the US where there is a litigious culture, rarely admit to making surgical mistakes. Rather, whenever things go wrong in the operating theatre, it's about inherent risk and factors outside their control. Pilots, meanwhile, alive through testimony and dead through black boxes, openly articulate what they did wrong so that the profession can learn from it and make flying safer and safer.

Leaders in the best schools build trust and openness, and thus develop autonomy, mastery, and purpose. They build for the future; they develop sustainable models by investing in their people and reducing attrition.

Great school leaders create a culture in which middle leaders and teachers are encouraged to honestly self-reflect and admit to mistakes. They review their effectiveness and make tweaks without fear.

Into practice
Writing your story

Strategies to build trust through stories

The best way to build trust and create a no-blame culture is, of course, through story and storytelling because stories have the ability to humanise leaders, as well as to convey vulnerability. Stories can demonstrate a commitment to learning and improvement.

Here are some ways in which school leaders can use storytelling to achieve these goals:

1. **Sharing personal stories:**

   ○ School leaders can share stories that showcase their own mistakes, failures, and lessons learned. This vulnerability shows that leaders are human and that everyone makes errors.

   ○ School leaders can narrate how they turned challenges into opportunities for growth and learning. These stories help to highlight the journey from mistakes to improvement.

2. **Highlighting collective failures:**

   ○ School leaders can share stories about situations where their team faced difficulties collectively. These stories work best when they emphasise the lessons learned and articulate how the team worked together to address challenges.

   ○ School leaders can use stories to explore how these challenges led to positive outcomes, innovation, or the strengthening of team dynamics.

3. **Celebrating learning moments:**

   ○ School leaders can share stories of situations in which mistakes were made but became valuable learning experiences. These work best when they emphasise the importance of extracting lessons from failures.

   ○ School leaders can narrate instances where the school made changes based on feedback or errors, leading to better processes or products.

4. **Demonstrating open communication:**

   ○ School leaders can share stories of instances when they encouraged open dialogue about errors or problems. These stories work best when they show how these conversations led to constructive solutions.

   ○ School leaders can narrate how they empowered colleagues to voice their concerns, or to ask questions, and to express doubts without fear of retribution, thus encouraging others to do likewise and demonstrating the no-blame culture that exists.

5. **Highlighting positive intent:**

   ○ School leaders can share stories that illustrate the importance of assuming positive intent. These stories work best when they emphasise how misunderstandings can be avoided by assuming the best in others.

   ○ School leaders can narrate instances where conflicts were resolved by focusing on the problem rather than blaming individuals.

6. **Promoting collective accountability:**

   ○ School leaders can tell stories that emphasise collective responsibility for out-comes. Such stories show how everyone has a role in success or challenges.

   ○ School leaders can highlight how a no-blame culture encourages accountability and ownership without finger-pointing.

7. **Showcasing mentorship and coaching:**

   ○ School leaders can share stories of mentorship or coaching experiences, where constructive feedback was provided in a supportive manner.

   ○ School leaders can highlight how feedback and guidance contributed to personal and professional growth.

8. **Addressing missteps transparently:**

   ○ School leaders can narrate instances where they communicated setbacks or is-sues transparently. Such stories work best when they show how open communication fosters trust.

   ○ School leaders can share stories that demonstrate the school's emphasis on find-ing solutions rather than assigning blame.

9. **Encouraging others to share:**

   ○ School leaders can foster an environment where team members feel comfortable sharing their own stories of mistakes and learning.

   ○ School leaders can acknowledge and appreciate individuals who openly share their experiences and insights.

Using stories and storytelling techniques to build trust and create a no-blame culture shows that leaders are committed to learning, growth, and creating an environment where mistakes are viewed as opportunities for improvement. These stories can also help humanise leaders, encourage open communication, and foster a culture of account-ability and collaboration.

Motivation = autonomy + mastery + purpose

Once they have fostered trust and created a no-blame culture, how can school leaders keep their staff motivated and focused on the school improvement journey?

In *Smarter, Faster, Better*,[12] Charles Duhigg offers several tips to improve organisational ef-fectiveness. Below, paraphrasing Duhigg, I offer nine such tips:

1. To increase staff motivation, leaders must allow colleagues choices that put them in greater control of their roles. This might involve connecting something they do to something they

care about, explaining to them why a task will help them get closer to a meaningful goal. In short, staff need to know why their work matters.

2. Staff need clear goals – ideally, stretch goals which reflect their ambitions and aspirations. But such goals need breaking down into sub-goals and SMART objectives.

3. Staff need to stay focused. This involves planning ahead, considering the order in which tasks need to be undertaken, foreseeing potential barriers.

4. Staff need to be helped to make better decisions. In other words, they need to imagine various possibilities – some of which might be contradictory – so that they're better equipped to make wise choices.

5. Leaders need to foster effective teams by managing the 'how' not the 'who'. In other words, leaders need to help develop staff's psychological safety by ensuring that everyone in a team feels that they can speak in roughly equal measure and that teammates show they are sensitive to how each other feels. As school leaders, we need to think about the message our decisions reveal. Are we encouraging equality in speaking or rewarding the loudest people? Are we showing we are listening by repeating what people say and replying to questions and thoughts? Are we demonstrating sensitivity by reacting when someone seems upset or flustered? Are we showcasing that sensitivity so that other people will follow our lead?

6. In order to improve staff's productivity, leaders need to develop lean and agile management techniques and delegate control because staff work smarter and better when they believe they have more decision-making authority and when they believe their colleagues are also committed to their success. By pushing decision-making to whoever is closest to a problem, we can take advantage of everyone's expertise and unlock innovation. A sense of control can also fuel motivation, but for that drive to produce insights and solutions, staff need to know that their contributions won't be ignored and that their mistakes won't be held against them.

7. Also, in order to encourage greater innovation, leaders need to become a broker – because creativity often emerges by combining old ideas in new ways – and encourage brokerage within their organisation. This entails being sensitive to our own experiences, paying attention to how things make us think and feel, which will help us to distinguish clichés from real insights. Leaders need to study their own emotional reactions and recognise that the stress that emerges amid the creative process isn't a sign that everything is falling apart; rather, creative desperation is often critical. Anxiety can be what often pushes people to see old ideas in new ways.

8. Leaders also need to remember that the relief that accompanies a creative breakthrough, while rewarding, can also blind us to alternatives. By forcing ourselves to critique what we've already done, by making ourselves look at working practices from different perspectives, by giving new authority to someone who didn't have it before, we can retain a clear perspective and oversight.

9. Finally, in order to improve organisational effectiveness, leaders need to help staff to understand and use data better. When people encounter new information, they should force themselves to do something with it. For example, they should write a note explaining what they just learned, or identify a means of testing out an idea. Every choice we make in life is an experiment – the trick is getting people to see the data embedded in those decisions, and then to use it somehow so they can learn from it.

Charles Duhigg echoes an argument espoused in the book *Drive* by Daniel Pink.[13] Intrinsic motivation, Pink argues, is three-fold:

1. Autonomy: the desire to direct our own lives.

2. Mastery: the urge to get better and better at something that matters.

3. Purpose: the yearning to do what we do in the service of something larger than ourselves.

Taken together, this is the power to write your own story, to narrate your own journey through life.

Firstly, Pink says that "people need autonomy over task (what they do), time (when they do it), team (who they do it with), and technique (how they do it)". The theory behind it is as follows: if someone is in control of their activities, they are more likely to be motivated by them and more likely to excel at them.

Secondly, Pink says that "only engagement can produce mastery – becoming better at something that matters". He goes on to say that "mastery begins with 'flow' – optimal experiences when the challenges we face are exquisitely matched to our abilities – [and] requires the capacity to see your abilities not as finite, but as infinitely improvable". Again, this is about the desire to improve, to want to get better and better at something. People are only motivated to get better at something they are engaged in and enjoy. Pink goes on to say that "Mastery is a pain: it demands effort, grit and deliberate practice. And mastery is asymptote: it's impossible to fully realise, which makes it simultaneously frustrating and alluring".

And, thirdly, Pink says that humans seek purpose, "a cause greater and more enduring than themselves". This is to say that people need to feel that what they are doing will have a long-term purpose and meaning in the world. It's the desire to leave your mark on the world, to do something worthwhile and with impact.

Pink provides a useful example of the power of autonomy, mastery, and purpose in action. He takes us back to 1995 and asks an economist to consider two business models, each concerned with developing a new encyclopaedia: the first model comes from Microsoft, a multi-million-pound global organisation; the other is the result of a not-for-profit 'hobby'. Microsoft's encyclopaedia involves a band of paid professional writers and editors working for well-paid managers who oversee a project which is delivered on time and on budget. Microsoft sell the encyclopaedia on CD-ROMs and online. The hobbyists, meanwhile, do not belong to a company and are not paid. Instead, tens of thousands of people write and edit entries in the encyclopaedia just for fun. Contributors offer their time and expertise for nothing and the encyclopaedia itself is offered free of charge to anyone who wants it via the internet.

Clearly, any economist worth their salt would predict that the first business model led by Microsoft would go on to thrive, while the second model would falter. But by 2009, Microsoft had discontinued *Encarta* while *Wikipedia* continued to thrive – with 13 million entries in 260 languages, it had become the largest and most popular encyclopaedia in the world. The business model that relied on traditional rewards to motivate its employees and customers had failed; the one that relied on intrinsic motivation (doing something simply for the fun of it) had succeeded; in the battle for supremacy, money had lost to the love of learning.

The most successful school leaders, once they've fostered trust and created a no-blame culture, ensure their colleagues have autonomy, mastery, and purpose – the ability and opportunity to write their own story.

What have we learned?

In this chapter, we have discovered that:

Stories and storytelling are great ways to build trust and to create no-blame cultures because they can humanise leaders. Stories demonstrate a commitment to improvement.

Next, stories can help keep staff motivated and focused on the school improvement journey because they can foster autonomy, mastery, and purpose.

What can we do?

To put the advice contained in this chapter into practice, it might be helpful to consider the following questions:

1. Do you build a no-blame culture by sharing personal stories, highlighting collective failures, and celebrating learning moments?

2. Do you ensure your colleagues have autonomy, mastery, and purpose?

Notes

1 Hargreaves, A & Fullan, M (2012). *Professional Capital: Transforming Teaching in Every School*. Routledge, p. 80.
2 Collins, J (2001). *Good to Great: Why Some Companies Make the Leap and Others Don't*. Random House Business.
3 Bambrick-Santoyo, P, Peiser, B, & Lemov, D (2012). *Leverage Leadership: A Practical Guide to Building Exceptional Schools*. Jossey-Bass, p. 215.
4 Barber, M (2010). *Deliverology 101: A Field Guide for Educational Leaders*. Corwin, p. 129.
5 Blatchford, R (2014). *The Restless School*. John Catt, pp. 89, 91.
6 Bambrick-Santoyo, P, Peiser, B, & Lemov, D (2012). *Leverage Leadership: A Practical Guide to Building Exceptional Schools*. Jossey-Bass, p. 217.
7 Little, J W (1990). The persistence of privacy: Autonomy and initiative in teachers' Professional relations. *Teachers College Record*, 91(4), 509–536.
8 Hattie, J (2012). *Visible Learning for Teachers*. Routledge, pp. viii, vii.
9 Gelfand, M (2018). *Rule Makers, Rule Breakers: How Culture Wires Our Minds, Shapes Our Nations, and Drives Our Differences: Tight and Loose Cultures and the Secret Signals That Direct Our Lives*. Robinson.

10 Baron, J N & Hannan, M T (2002). Organizational blueprints for success in high-tech start-ups: Lessons from the Stanford Project on Emerging Companies. *California Management Review*, 44(3), 8–36.
11 Syed, M (2015). *Black Box Thinking: The Surprising Truth About Success*. John Murray.
12 Duhigg, C (2016). *Smarter Faster Better: The Secrets of Being Productive in Life and Business*. Random House.
13 Pink, D (2011). *Drive: The Surprising Truth About What Motivates Us*. Canongate Books Ltd., pp. 94, 111, 120, 126, 133.

Using story to resolve conflict

Sir Tim Brighouse – former Chief Advisor to London Schools – had wise words to share on what makes a school leader successful. In *Essential Pieces: Jigsaw of a Successful School*,[1] he argues that successful school leaders have three qualities in common: energy, enthusiasm, and hope. To this excellent list I'd add 'kindness'.

Four school leadership qualities

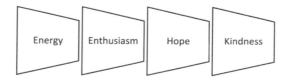

Energy

To my mind, school leaders possess determination, plus an indomitable will and passion for success. They show an interest in every aspect of their school, visiting all areas and speaking to all staff as often as possible. For example, standing in the foyer first thing in the morning allows leaders to greet staff, who can then book a meeting later in the day if they need to talk.

Walking the corridors at break and lunchtime and during lesson changeovers can make leaders seem omniscient and give confidence to teachers that they are not alone, that their leaders have got their backs. This requires excellent time management skills, using the diary effectively and delegating where appropriate to protect their precious time.

Shadowing a learner once a term allows a school leader to see their school from the learner's point of view – an invaluable and humbling exercise which can really inform a school leader's actions and priorities. Walking the floor enables leaders to collect stories of success too, and stories can prove powerful tools when enthusing colleagues and inspiring effort.

DOI: 10.4324/9781003465492-18

Great leaders stay calm during moments of crisis, and at such times are willing to acknowledge mistakes that have been made and then learn from them. They tell positive stories of resilience to remind colleagues of what's important and to steady the ship.

Enthusiasm

Great leaders exude positivity, especially when communicating their school's vision and values, and when reminding staff of past success as well as future promise. Such positivity is best communicated through stories which act as 'state of the nation' addresses told in assemblies, staff briefings, professional development events, and open evenings in which a school leader gives a Henry V-style speech (in Shakespeare's play, Henry V rouses his army as they go into battle at Agincourt with the words "We few, we happy few, we band of brothers; / For he today that shed his blood with me / Shall be my brother"). This is where great leaders really harness the power of stories – and utilise the stories they've collected by walking the floor – to flesh out their ideas and hopes and to galvanise and unite people behind an improvement effort.

Great leaders have an intellectual curiosity too, reading widely and sharing research with colleagues. They also lead by example, as a great practitioner where appropriate, but always as someone who loves to learn and strives to know more and be more effective. Great leaders can also be role models by performing well in assemblies, by visiting tutorials and lessons to talk to learners, and by covering lessons for colleagues to allow them to engage in quality professional development.

Hope

Great leaders display a certainty that their vision will be realised, as if they expect it to be achieved rather than just wish it to be so. They always seek positive change and keep colleagues focused on the process of improvement by telling stories that describe the journey from the past to the present (what have colleagues already achieved?) and from the present to the future (what is their next challenge?).

Hope is also about displaying a boundless optimism and resilience in the face of setbacks. Great leaders can pick themselves up after experiencing a setback, dust themselves down, and keep walking forwards. Yes, they learn from past mistakes rather than airbrushing them out of existence, but they are not deterred by mistakes, regarding them as an integral part of the improvement journey and of growth. They focus on the future and tell stories of recovery and rebirth, of the successes that were born of repeated failure.

Kindness

Great leaders routinely recognise and reward success in a way favoured by each member of staff (some people like public adulation; others melt to a puddle at the mere thought of it). Celebrating others' achievements is an everyday part of what these leaders do rather than an afterthought or rarity. And these celebrations also act as stories of success which inspire others to emulate these achievements and give oxygen to the good and virtuous.

Success stories foster a positive culture and a sense of collective triumph. They also keep people moving forwards in the right direction and starve negative thoughts of air, muffling naysayers and nit-pickers.

Great leaders also give quality time to people. Having an open-door policy does not mean being available 24 hours a day, but it does mean being able to meet with staff as soon as possible and listening and responding to what they have to say.

Great leaders are protective of their staff, showing empathy, respecting people's privacy, remembering birthdays, and granting personal leave – without question – when staff have important or urgent personal matters to attend to such as family funerals. They also set as their default position a genuine belief that everybody wishes to do well and will try their best, rather than assuming the worst of people.

And that, in my opinion, is what makes a great leader. But great leaders are also great because they are human. And as humans they are fallible. They make mistakes. They do not always get it right. Do not look to leaders for perfection or expect it of yourself because, where you ostensibly find it, it may mask duplicity or inaction. Instead, look for humanity, for people who are energetic, enthusiastic, hopeful, and kind, and people who are also prone to making mistakes from time to time because they are willing to take risks, to try new things, and to challenge and reform working practices in the hope of improving their provision. What sets these people out from the ineffectual is their willingness to admit their mistakes and their ability to learn from them, to – as I say – dust themselves down, pick themselves up, and keep moving forwards with energy, enthusiasm, hope, and kindness.

Using story and storytelling to resolve conflict

Like all human beings, school leaders are controlled by their instincts. In fact, in every human brain there is a constant battle being fought between, in the red corner, the frontal cortex and, in the blue corner, the limbic system. The frontal cortex is the rational side; the limbic system is irrational. The limbic system has been called 'the chimp' (by, for example, Professor Steve Peters in his book *The Chimp Paradox*[2]) because it is the primitive part of our brain and often tries to control our actions with pure, naked instincts. It asks, 'How do I feel?' rather than 'What do I think?' It seeks an emotional *fight or flight* response to conflict. The frontal cortex, meanwhile, is the rational side which is concerned with thoughts rather than feelings. It asks, 'What is logical?'

Unfortunately, the limbic system – because it works on instinct – is faster to act than the frontal cortex, which takes time to consider what is rational under the circumstances and seeks to place events in context. This is why there is a constant war being waged in our heads. Our frontal cortex is always trying to wrest back control from the limbic system. Professor Daniel Kahneman calls the limbic system System A and the frontal cortex System B, arguing – including in the title of his book – that there is a conflict between these systems which can be summarised as *Thinking, Fast and Slow*.[3]

We therefore need to control the narrative and tell ourselves a positive story about our abilities and capabilities, not allow our chimp to tell our story for us.

Permit me an example …

Inspiration
Telling my story

Stage fright

I engage in a lot of public speaking. Indeed, it's my bread and butter these days. But no matter how often I stand up in front of a large audience, I still feel nervous beforehand. I don't mind this. In fact, the day I no longer feel apprehensive before addressing a conference is the day I hang up my mic because nervousness means I produce lots of adrenaline and adrenaline makes me alert and helps me to perform better. But when I'm in the spotlight, immediately before I speak, my frontal cortex is doing battle with my limbic system in an internal power struggle. My limbic system is telling me that I'm an imposter, totally unprepared and ill-equipped to speak on whatever subject I've been asked to tackle. My limbic system tells me I won't remember a word of what I'm about to say, and that the audience doesn't respect me and is going to be a tough crowd. My frontal cortex, meanwhile, is trying its best to be rational and stop my limbic system from taking control. It reminds me that I'm prepared and have rehearsed, that the audience will be willing me to do well and will forgive – or not notice – any minor missteps or mistakes I make. It reminds me I do this all the time and always get good feedback, so there's no reason to believe this time will be any different.

Whenever we face conflict, our frontal cortex and our limbic system do battle in this way. The chimp goes into fight or flight mode and makes us emotional and irrational. It gets our blood pumping, our heart racing, and our dander up! But this is the worst possible way to respond to conflict. It's important, therefore, to acknowledge the chimp's existence and be mindful of how it's trying to shape our response. And then we need to put the chimp back in its cage and allow our frontal cortex to take control and provide a logical, rational response that stands up to scrutiny.

EQ trumps IQ

Great school leaders care about other people's feelings, are empathetic, and give time and support to people when they need it most. But because they're human, they are also controlled by their feelings and are, therefore, fallible and imperfect. Sometimes they will make mistakes. What's important is that they acknowledge their mistakes and seek to make amends. And, moreover, that they work hard to avoid making the same mistakes again by wresting control of their chimp.

The best way to take control of the limbic system is to mentally compartmentalise the personal from the professional. Conflict in the workplace is never – or at least very rarely – personal. In the workplace I have never raised my voice at a colleague and indeed, as a teacher and headteacher, hardly ever did so with learners. I modelled patience and diplomacy. At home, however, I often lose my temper with my own children and – let me whisper this confidentially – have even been known to shout! That's because my home life is personal, and my work life is professional. I separate them cleanly in my mind. Whenever I face conflict at work, I remind myself that it isn't personal and that I must be professional. If I lose my patience, I have lost the argument and relinquished some moral standing.

So, how can school leaders control their emotions, remain professional, and either prevent conflict or deal with it effectively when it arises?

One answer is to start with the self, to soul-search in order to become more self-aware, and developing a sense of emotional intelligence is one way to do this. Daniel Goleman developed a three-step model of emotional intelligence:[4]

1. Know yourself (what he called self-mastery).

2. Know others (what he called social radar).

3. Control your response.

Emotional intelligence is commonly defined as the ability to understand ourselves and other people. This comprises the ability to manage and express our emotions, and respond to other people's emotions, in ways that are productive.

In his book *Emotional Intelligence*, Goleman posited five skill domains that are particularly pertinent to school leadership:

1. Self-awareness

2. Managing feelings

3. Motivation

4. Empathy

5. Social skills

Emotional intelligence allows us to model the sorts of behavioural responses we expect to see from others, and this is no more important than when dealing with difficult people. If we don't model the desired behaviours, then we cannot expect these difficult people to mirror them and to behave more appropriately towards us. We also need to be aware of our own ongoing emotional state and conduct a realistic assessment of our own strengths and weaknesses. We need to be aware of the emotional state of our colleagues too and deploy appropriate and measured responses – in a calm and considered way – in what can be highly charged emotional situations.

To be confident of accurately self-assessing, we need to be aware of our strengths and weaknesses; we need to be reflective and learn from our experiences; and we need to be open to candid feedback, to new perspectives, and to continuous learning and self-development.

To be self-confident, we need to present ourselves with self-assurance; we need presence; we need to be able to voice our views even if those views may be unpopular; we need to be willing to fight for what we believe and for what is right; and we need to be decisive, able to make sound decisions despite uncertainties and external pressures.

To be emotionally aware, we need to know which emotions we are feeling and why; realise the links between our feelings and what we think, do, and say; recognise how our feelings affect our performance; and never lose sight of our values and goals.

All of this is about telling ourselves a positive story about our abilities, taking control of the narrative of our lives.

When confronted with difficult people or difficult situations, it is common to try to avoid conflict or deny that conflict exists. We may wait until conflict goes away or we may try to change the subject. It is also common, when accepting that conflict exists, to react emotionally, to become aggressive, abusive, or even hysterical. It is common, too, to find someone else to blame for conflict, to make excuses or to let someone else deal with it. But avoiding or denying conflict will only exacerbate the situation and make us look like weak leaders.

Leaders do not deny conflict; they deal with it and do so effectively.

The story of breakdown

In dealing with conflict, school leaders need to remember that it is a story told over several chapters, not a singular event. In other words, conflict is not – or is rarely – a one-off occurrence that has emerged out of a clear blue sky and will dissipate just as quickly. Rather, conflict builds over time, like the plot of an engaging story. There is, if we look back, a narrative arc that led to conflict and, broadly speaking, there are five chapters along in that story of breakdown:

Chapter 1: Discussion

This is when both people are interested in the other's view of the world and are prepared to share ideas, opinions, and feelings. This stage is simply a meeting of minds with no intention to get the other person to think or feel anything different. Discussion is usually characterised by a respect for each other's viewpoint, an acceptance of the other's values, and a broadening of perspectives.

Chapter 2: Debate

This is when there are different viewpoints and one person would like the other to see things their way, but only if it is right for them. This stage is usually characterised by an openness to each other's ideas and by a respect for the other's viewpoint.

Chapter 3: Argument

At this stage, one person wants the other to 'buy' their ideas, regardless of what they may be thinking. One person believes they are 'right' and the other person is 'wrong'. The other person should be doing it their way. This stage is characterised by a disregard for the other's viewpoint by arguing from one perspective only and therefore a polarisation of opinions, and by the use of lots of 'yes ... buts'.

Chapter 4: Conflict

At this stage, not only does one person believe they are 'right' and the other person is 'wrong' but that person insists they do it their way, that the other person acts according to their values and beliefs. Conflict is characterised by demands that 'you behave as I want you to', through increasingly personalised arguments and the use of lots of 'shoulds', as well as by blame, accusation, and put-downs.

Chapter 5: Breakdown

At this stage the dynamic is so difficult that each person involved feels the need to protect themselves or distance themselves in order to recover from confrontation. One person may act as if the other no longer exists or matters. There may be silence or disdain.

This 'road to breakdown' is characterised by a desire for one person to change the other, or by one person blaming the other. However, as school leaders dealing with conflict in the workplace, we should remember that trying to change someone rarely results in change. Change is more likely to come about from understanding. Wanting to change someone implies there is something wrong with that person and, naturally, this only leads to them becoming defensive and argumentative. Seeking to understand, however, suggests the other person's point of view is valid and reasonable. This is the approach that creates collaboration and mutual problem-solving.

What's more, as school leaders, we should remember that trying to blame someone is reactive and looks to the past in an attempt to discern who was right and who was wrong. A better approach if our goal is a resolution that allows us to move forwards is to focus on the future and on how the situation can be resolved. This is the difference between arguing who left the stable door open after the horse has bolted and going out to try to find the horse! One approach is reactive, futile, and damaging; the other is proactive and solution focused.

Sometimes, no matter how honourable our intentions and no matter how well we deal with conflict, we will encounter someone who is angry and whose anger is expressed inappropriately. In order to disarm that anger, we should listen to what they have to say and stay silent if necessary. This will allow them a right of reply and enable them to vent their anger. They may simply burn out and feel better for having said what they needed to say.

Throughout an angry exchange, we should maintain rapport in both body and voice. We should try to feed back what we hear. It may be possible to change what the person is focused on by asking questions. We should certainly attempt to make empathetic statements that show we understand even if we disagree. Being empathetic is not the same as agreeing with their point of view or saying they are right. When feeding back what the person has said, it may be helpful to take notes and to number their concerns as a list to be acted upon. Feeding back what we think the person has said, and asking them to confirm or clarify if we've understood correctly, helps move the conversation towards action and is much more solution oriented than simply sitting silently and impassively, and it is certainly more helpful than arguing back.

Another useful strategy to employ when dealing with angry people is to use *bridging* language rather than *barrier* language. Conflict can be escalated or defused depending on the way we respond to it. People react to what we say and do, so whether we attack or defend, advance or retreat, anger or appease, we affect how the other person responds. What starts as a discussion can escalate without proper management.

We should not avoid conflict and anger. That may simply escalate the situation. However, we *should* avoid being defensive – it is rarely personal. We should also avoid over-generalising about how someone feels and why they feel that way. Rather, we should listen and seek to understand the person's point of view, and we should remember that we don't have to 'win'. What matters is that communication channels remain open.

A 'barrier' mindset, then, is characterised by the following attitudes:

- I am right.

- You should change.

- You are the problem not me.

- I want to win.

- I want to be right.

- I want to prove you wrong.

- I am indifferent to your needs and feelings.

- My needs and feelings are more important than yours.

These attitudes are often articulated by using the following words and phrases:

- I/me

- You should

- Waste of time

- Your problem is

- That won't work

- Out of the question

- That's my final word

- This is non-negotiable

- You don't understand

- I've heard all this before

- You wouldn't understand

And by the following actions:

- Frowning

- Lip-biting

- Raised voice

- Arms crossed

- Hands on hips

- Hands in pockets

- Hands over mouth

- Avoiding eye contact

- Narrowing of the eyes

A 'bridging' mindset, by contrast, is characterised by the following attitudes:

- I respect you and your views.

- Let's work together.

- I want us both to win.

- Your needs and feelings are important to me.

- Let's work together and problem-solve rather than argue.

- We have a shared interest here.

And these attitudes are often articulated via the frequent use of the following words and phrases:

- Us/our

- We can

- Let's talk

- I appreciate

- Alternatives

- What do you need?

- What do you think?

- Help me understand ...

- What would you say to ...?

... and through the following actions:

- Open posture

- Eye contact

- Low and slow voice

- Looking and acting approachable

- Using open hand gestures

When confronted with difficult people, I try to remember to sail on a calm SEA, which means I stay in control of:

- The **situation** by putting clear boundaries in place.

- My **emotions** by staying calm and professional, thus giving myself the confidence to face whatever problem comes my way.

- The **action** I plan to take, moving the discussion forward.

When a situation calls for more assertive action, I remember to make eye contact in order to indicate interest and sincerity. I remember to take care of my posture, which can be used to emphasise what I am saying. I remember gestures, which can also give emphasis to what I am saying. I remember my voice, using tone and timbre to convince rather than dominate or intimidate. And I remember the golden rules of listening which are:

- Give the other person your undivided attention. Don't do other work or take calls while you are listening.

- Find a quiet place to listen. Avoid places that are noisy or have other distractions.

- Listen to be influenced. Don't allow your mind to be distracted with trying to think up rebuttals.

- Don't interrupt. Let people finish their point.

- Show that you are interested. Do this by nodding or saying 'yes'.

- Maintain eye contact without staring.

- Maintain an open posture; avoid folding your arms.

To conclude, here are my top ten strategies for managing conflict and dealing with difficult people:

1. **Listen:** Say nothing; don't interrupt; don't hurry.

2. **Empathise:** Put yourself in the other person's shoes; validate their feelings.

3. **De-personalise:** Put your feelings to one side – it's not about you.

4. **Be informed:** Understand school policies and procedures, as well as school staff roles and responsibilities.

5. **Defuse or decamp:** Apply calming techniques or remove yourself from harm.

6. **Focus:** Keep the resolution (or the learner) at the centre of conversation.

7. **Take responsibility:** You're not to blame but you are responsible. Say you'll take responsibility and you'll resolve it.

8. **Apologise:** Admitting to mistakes is a sign of strength not weakness; show honesty and courage in learning from past errors.

9. **Resolve:** Seek quick resolutions and explain them and their timescales.

10. **Communication:** Keep the other person 'in the loop'; follow up on promises.

Strategies for resolving conflict through story

Into practice
Writing your story

All of which might beg the question: what part can story and storytelling techniques play in the process of managing conflict? Well, using storytelling to resolve workplace conflict can help leaders facilitate understanding, empathy, and collaboration. Stories also have the power to convey emotions, different perspectives, and the potential for positive outcomes. Here's how leaders can use storytelling to effectively address workplace conflicts:

1. **Choose the right story:**

   ○ **Relevance:** Select a story that relates to the themes, emotions, or issues at the heart of the conflict.

   ○ **Positive outcome:** Choose a story that highlights successful resolution, growth, collaboration, or improved relationships.

2. **Create a safe space:**

   ○ **Open dialogue:** Set up a safe and confidential environment for the individuals involved in a conflict so that they can share their perspectives and feelings without fear or favour.

   ○ **Encourage listening:** Ensure that both parties involved in a conflict actively listen to each other's viewpoints.

3. **Introduce the story:**

   ○ **Neutral introduction:** Present the selected story as a neutral example that relates to the conflict.

   ○ **Analogous elements:** Point out elements in the story that are similar to the current conflict being experienced but without directly relating it to the individuals involved.

4. **Highlight different perspectives:**

   ○ **Multiple characters:** If the story features different characters, highlight how each one has a unique perspective and motivation.

   ○ **Empathy:** Encourage individuals to empathise with the characters' feelings and perspectives.

5. **Find the common ground:**

   ○ **Shared struggles:** Emphasise shared challenges or struggles that the characters in the story face.

   ○ **Common emotions:** Highlight emotions experienced by characters that mirror the emotions felt by the parties in conflict.

6. **Show transformation and resolution:**

   ○ **Conflict resolution:** Narrate how the characters in the story work through their conflicts and find positive resolutions.

   ○ **Growth and learning:** Highlight how the characters grow and learn from the experience, showing resilience and strength of character.

7. **Relate to real situations:**

   ○ **Analogous situations:** Relate elements of the story to the real workplace conflict being experienced, emphasising how the story's resolution can be applied in real life.

   ○ **Suggest possibilities:** Invite the people involved in a conflict to consider how the story's strategies could be adapted to their situation.

8. **Encourage dialogue:**

   ○ **Discussion:** Prompt individuals to discuss how the story relates to their conflict, identifying parallels and differences.

   ○ **Possible solutions:** Encourage the people involved in a conflict to explore possible solutions inspired by the story.

9. **Empower individuals:**

   ○ **Ownership:** Invite individuals to take ownership of their roles in the conflict and the responsibility to contribute to resolution.

   ○ **Future focus:** Highlight that the goal is to learn from the story and work collaboratively towards a positive outcome.

10. **Follow up:**

    ○ **Check-in:** Follow up with the individuals involved to see how the insights from the story influenced their perceptions and actions.

    ○ **Additional support:** Offer additional resources or strategies if and when needed to move towards a lasting resolution.

Using story and storytelling to resolve workplace conflict can bridge gaps, foster empathy, and create a shared understanding among conflicting parties. Stories provide a non-confrontational way to explore potential solutions and encourage positive behavioural changes.

What have we learned?

In this chapter, we have discovered that:

The best school leaders care about other people's feeling and are empathetic. They use stories and storytelling techniques to help them facilitate understanding, empathy, and collaboration because stories have the power to convey emotions and different perspectives. Stories can help leaders manage conflict too because they can help identify a common goal and encourage dialogue.

What can we do?

To put the advice contained in this chapter into practice, it might be helpful to consider the following questions:

1. Do you use story and storytelling to resolve workplace conflict when it arises?

2. Do you use story to highlight different perspectives and help colleagues find some common ground?

3. Do you use story to encourage dialogue?

Notes

1 Brighouse, T (2006). *Essential Pieces: The Jigsaw of a Successful School*. Research Machines.
2 Peters, S (2012). *The Chimp Paradox*. Vermilion.
3 Kahneman, D (2012). *Thinking, Fast and Slow*. Penguin.
4 Goleman, D (1996). *Emotional Intelligence: Why It Can Matter More Than IQ*. Bloomsbury Publishing PLC.

16 Using story to lead change

Any process of school improvement – whichever leg of the journey you are on – necessarily involves change because, if a school is to improve, it must, by definition, change. Managing change, therefore, is an important skill for school leaders. Many senior leaders enjoy working against a backdrop of continuous change because it makes their jobs interesting, challenging, and varied. It gives them a chance to stamp their mark on the organisation, to show what they are capable of. But it's important to remember that not everyone shares this passion for change.

Leaders should start with the knowledge that change can be uncomfortable, particularly for those who feel that change is being done to them not by them. Leaders should also bear in mind that many staff will resent change and will either refuse to engage with it or, worse, act to prevent it from happening. And, as I say above, a school can only improve if everyone works together. So, what is the best way to lead change? Firstly, it is important to understand why people are resistant to it.

People are resistant to change because:

- They are anxious about the impact it will have on their jobs.

- They feel they have tried it before and it didn't work.

- They fear it will mean more work for them.

- They do not understand the need for change; they like the status quo.

- They fear failure.

- They are scared by the pace of change and by being out of their comfort zone.

- They fear change will prove too costly or a waste of time and money.

People are resistant to change because change implies that the status quo isn't good enough, that the way people work now is in some way inadequate. People also resent change because it signals the destruction of all they have worked hard to achieve. Change means abandoning what they know and what they like. All of these things may be true, of course: the status quo may not be good enough; the way people work now may indeed be inadequate. But it is un-likely your school is so thoroughly broken that it requires a total transformation. It is more likely that there will be lots of things about your school that should be retained, preserved, protected. Even if it is so utterly broken that it needs wholesale change, the process of mend-ing it should be done gradually and with the support of staff: this means careful management, a lot of tact, and patience.

Once you understand people's resistance to change, you should begin to engage them in the story of change. As a starting point, it is important to:

1. **Be open and honest** about the need for change: Involve your staff as early as possible; ideally, involve them in the process of identifying the need for change in the first place.

2. **Explain the rationale** behind change: On what evidence have you based your decision to change? What do you hope this change will achieve and why is that important?

3. **Outline the benefits** of change for everyone: What is it in for staff, learners, parents, and governors? How will change make their lives easier and more rewarding?

School leaders might use the following skills when managing change:

- **Patience and self-control**
  Leaders always need to stay calm and considered, and they need to think and behave rationally.

- **Balance**
  Leaders need to balance the needs of learners with the needs of staff, as well as balance the need to improve teaching and learning with the school's financial needs.

- **Communication**
  Leaders need to keep others informed and involved at all times, and ensure communication is genuinely two-way.

- **Problem-solving**
  Leaders need to think through the options and find appropriate solutions.

- **Personal ownership**
  Leaders need to show initiative and be conscientious; they need to take responsibility for their decisions and actions and for the consequences of those decisions and actions.

Leaders of change also need enthusiasm, flexibility, energy, and tenacity if they are to succeed in bringing about lasting, positive change which, in turn, leads to genuine and sustainable school improvement.

I find a change management cycle useful in planning for change. The cycle I use is as follows:

1. Mobilise

Firstly, it is important to understand why some colleagues may resist change. You need to tackle this head on by explaining why change is necessary (where is the need, what is the rationale?) and by outlining the benefits of change for everyone involved. Then you need to involve your staff in the process of change: don't let them see change as something being done to them by the senior team; let them feel genuinely a part of the process and able to contribute to it and affect it. A good way to mobilise staff is to establish 'change teams' or working parties which will be the driving force behind change. Change teams should be representative of all staff.

2. Discover

One of the first jobs for the change team is to identify and acknowledge the issues involved in change. It means developing a deeper understanding of what change will involve and how barriers will be overcome. This might involve members of the change team consulting with others and bringing ideas and issues back to the table. For example, your change team may include a member of each department or faculty, a member of support staff, and a teaching assistant. It may include a member of the admin team and/or site staff. Discovering the issues may be as simple as conducting a SWOT analysis or may be more complex.

3. Deepen

The change team then needs to develop a deeper knowledge and understanding of the scale and scope of the changes that are required. They also need to know and understand the root causes of the issues that led to change being needed in the first place, as well as the issues that will inevitably arise while change is being enacted. This stage is about being forewarned and forearmed, about being prepared for the road ahead. It is also about setting the boundaries – knowing what will be included in the project and what will not – and setting appropriate timescales.

4. Develop

This stage is about suggesting solutions, coming up with improvements to the way people work. It is about the change team taking action, trialling new methods of working, and finding out what is effective and what isn't. It is important at this stage to prioritise those actions which will have the biggest impact. Start with a splash not a ripple. You want other staff to see the impact of what you're doing; you want them to see that change is for the better, that you are getting results and making life easier. You want to win over your detractors and those most resistant to change; you want to convince them that what you're doing is right. For example, your change team may trial a new teaching method – let's say the use of daily low-stakes quizzes as a form of retrieval practice – and this may be videoed and played at a faculty meeting or on a training day in order to show all your staff that such an approach works in your school. This may then encourage others to try it out too.

5. Deliver

This stage is about making change happen. The change team now rolls out the changes they have developed and refined to the whole school. The plans formed in the 'develop' stage are now fully agreed and everyone begins to implement them, again starting with the high-impact actions or 'quick wins'.

In summary, change requires:

Effective leadership

Effective leadership is democratic, it acts as a role model, it supports and encourages others. Why? Because effective leadership leads to people feeling involved and valued, provides broader, richer insights and ideas, and helps improve staff morale, as well as recruitment and retention. Effective leadership also shares responsibility, leads to less stress, higher standards of teaching, effective collaboration, and more honest relationships in which problems are aired and resolved faster.

An inclusive culture

An inclusive culture is one in which people know they can contribute and overcome barriers together, in which everyone is encouraged to play a part in driving the school's change agenda.

Broad collaboration

This means collaboration between schools, stakeholders, and other organisations which helps embed a culture of openness to positive change.

Change teams

Change teams are working parties which are inclusive and representative of all areas of school. They act as a communication channel between the senior team and the workforce, which makes staff feel involved in their school.

Using story to narrate the change process

Here, in my view, are two of the starting principles of effective change management inspired by story and storytelling techniques.

1. Talk isn't cheap – tell your story

Leaders of school improvement talk to their staff and stakeholders and tell them the story of change – communicating the narrative is the key to their success. Staff must feel informed *and* involved in the process of improvement. Leaders should therefore be open and honest with colleagues and should seek to reach agreement where possible, but should not be afraid to make difficult – perhaps unpopular – decisions when this is right for their school.

Leaders must not abdicate responsibility, but they should share it. Where a decision is taken which is not consensual, the rationale should be clearly explained, and staff should understand the benefits of that decision to them, and for the school and its learners.

This involves telling staff the story of change and presenting a positive narrative about the future.

Leaders should not see it as a weakness to ask for help or advice from colleagues or others; nor should they be afraid to admit when they get it wrong. It is a strength, not a weakness, to be self-aware and pragmatic, to adapt to changing circumstances and respond to evolving situations – to ask for assistance.

2. Tweak don't transform – allow the narrative to build chapter by chapter

Change is uncomfortable and unsettling. People are not at their best when experiencing change. Not only should leaders be open and honest about the changes that are needed, not only should they communicate the rationale behind change and outline the benefits of change, but they should also try to avoid unnecessary change.

It is important to understand the status quo, to know what works well and what should be protected and retained. It is important to identify the foundations on which to build. People do not like change because it can be challenging. People like to know their hard work has purpose and meaning. Change needs to be incremental; the future needs to be built on the foundations of the past.

This involves preserving other people's stories, passing those stories baton-like down the line.

The United Tweakers of Great Britain and Northern Ireland

 Inspiration
Telling my story

Here's a story about 'tweaking' rather than transforming.

One of the great puzzles of the Industrial Revolution is why it began in Britain and not, say, France or Germany. The economists Ralf Meisenzahl and Joel Mokyr believe that Britain's advantage was in its human capital.[1] They argue that Britain had a great group of 'tweakers' that gave it the edge. These tweakers were resourceful and creative people who took the signature inventions of the industrial age and tweaked them. In other words, like great school leaders, they took existing ideas and refined and perfected them, and made them work. They retold other people's stories, the myths and legends of their time, and passed them on, making them better.

In 1779, Samuel Crompton of Lancashire invented the spinning mule, which made the mechanisation of cotton manufacture possible. And yet England's real advantage over other industrialising nations was that it also had Henry Stones of Horwich who added metal rollers to Crompton's mule. England also had James Hargreaves of Tottington who worked out how to smooth the acceleration and deceleration of the spinning wheel. Then William Kelly of Glasgow worked out how to add waterpower to the draw stroke, and John Kennedy of Manchester adapted the wheel to turn out fine counts. And, finally, Richard Roberts, also of Manchester and a master of precision machine tooling, created the 'automatic' spinning mule: an exacting, high-speed, reliable rethinking of Crompton's original creation.

All these men, the economists argue, provided the small inventions that enabled the big inventions to happen.

The crux of Meisenzahl and Mokyr's argument is that this sort of tweaking was what made Britain the world leader in the nineteenth century. And it remains this sort of tweaking that is essential if we are to make progress in our schools today.

James Watt invented the modern steam engine, doubling the efficiency of the engines that had come before. But when the so-called 'tweakers' got involved, the efficiency of the steam engine quadrupled.

Samuel Crompton was responsible for arguably the most productive invention of the Industrial Revolution, but the key moment in the history of the mule came a few years later when there was a strike of cotton workers. The mill owners were looking for a way to replace the workers with unskilled labour and needed an automatic mule which did not need to be controlled by the spinner. And who solved the problem? Not Crompton but the tweaker's tweaker, Richard Roberts, who in 1825 produced a prototype and in 1830 manufactured an even better solution. As a result, the number of spindles on a typical mule jumped from 400 to 1,000.

The tweakers are what put Britain at the epicentre of the Industrial Revolution. And the best school leaders have learned the lesson of history. They know that the best way to achieve genuine, sustainable improvements is to tweak and not transform. They know that change should be incremental, and that the future should be built on the foundations of the past.

As such, great school leaders **narrate the change process**. Their stories of future promise start with tales of past success. They tell stories about what others have already achieved, about how far their school has come, what is good about it and should therefore be preserved and protected. They involve others in their stories, prizing collaboration over competition. And their stories are enacted in increments, tweak by tweak.

Strategies for using story to narrate change

Into practice
Writing your story

Here are some tangible tips for using story to narrate *your* change process:

1. Define the takeaway message

Every story of school improvement should begin by asking: Who is my audience and what takeaway message do I want to share with them? How can I boil this message down to a compelling single statement?

2. Use your own experiences

The best storytellers illustrate their messages with their own memories and life experiences. Ask: What events in my life made me believe in the idea I am trying to share?

Although it can be uncomfortable sharing personal details at work, anecdotes that illustrate struggle, failure, and barriers that have been overcome are what make leaders appear authentic and accessible.

3. Don't be a hero

As I said above, the best storytellers involve others in their stories, prizing collaboration or teamwork over individual achievement or egotism. They don't make themselves the star of their own stories. The storyteller can be a central figure in the narrative, sharing their own experiences as I say above, but the ultimate focus should be on the lessons learned or the events witnessed. And the audience should be the protagonists of the story in order to increase their engagement and willingness to invest in the message.

4. Highlight a conflict

A story without a conflict or challenge isn't very engaging. All good stories have a problem to be solved or a conflict to be resolved at their heart. Storytellers aren't afraid to suggest the road ahead will be difficult. The best leaders tell their colleagues that the school improvement journey is going to be tough but if everybody pulls together and perseveres, they'll achieve their vision in the end. A well-crafted story embodies a rallying cry, a call to arms.

5. Keep it simple

Not every story has to be an epic. Indeed, some of the most successful and memorable stories are relatively simple and straightforward. And short stories are often the most impactful because they are so tightly plotted. Good storytellers don't let distracting details detract from their takeaway message. Abide by the principle 'less is more'.

How to avoid common change management mistakes

But even with the best will in the world and a prevailing wind, mistakes can and will be made, and your best-laid schemes will not always go to plan. Some mistakes can be foreseen, however; and thus they can be avoided or mitigated.

In an article for the *Harvard Business Review* in 1995 called 'Leading change',[2] John Kotter explained why some attempts to change the way organisations work are unsuccessful.

The first mistake many organisations make when seeking to improve the way they work is to lack a sense of urgency. Effective change requires the aggressive cooperation of many individuals and yet, without motivation, these people will not help and the effort will go nowhere. Many organisations fail to establish a sense of urgency because they worry that their staff will become defensive and that morale will drop. They worry that events will spiral out of control and short-term results will be jeopardised.

A sense of urgency is created when a frank discussion is had about some potentially unpleasant or uncomfortable realities: namely, that the organisation's performance isn't as good as people think it is and/or that the tectonic plates on which the organisation is built are shifting and sliding at a rapid pace, and the organisation is losing its footing. The purpose of such discussions is to make it clear that the status quo is more dangerous than change.

You will know when the sense of urgency is at the right level when over 75% of school staff know that operating on a business-as-usual basis is inadvisable, unacceptable, and unsustainable.

The second mistake many organisations make when seeking to improve is failing to create a powerful coalition of senior staff. A successful team might only consist of four or five people in the first phase, but it needs to grow quickly before real progress can be made.

A guiding coalition develops a shared commitment to improving performance through change. Although not every senior member of staff will buy into the transformation effort to begin with, the coalition must be appropriately powerful in terms of job titles and status, reputations and relationships in order to effect change.

The third mistake is lacking a clear vision – the most successful guiding coalitions develop an image of the future that is easy to communicate and appeals to all its organisation's stakeholders. The vision clearly articulates the direction of travel the organisation will take in order to become successful. Often the first draft of the vision comes from an individual who drives change, but it is later refined by many others.

Without a clear and positive vision for the future of the organisation, impetus can be lost and the purpose of change can become muddy and confused. A successful vision can be communicated in less than five minutes and can garner a reaction that shows that the audience both understand it and are interested in working towards it.

The fourth mistake is not communicating the vision effectively enough or frequently enough. Without a lot of effective communication, hearts and minds cannot be won. And the vision must be communicated repeatedly; it must be incorporated into everything the organisation says and does. Emails, newsletters, staff meetings, and appraisals are all focused on articulating and achieving the vision.

The vision is communicated in both words and actions too: no one's behaviour must undermine the vision and senior staff must behave in a way that is wholly consistent with the vision.

The fifth mistake is failing to remove the barriers that stand in the way of achieving the vision. Although senior staff can empower others to take action simply by communicating the vision, this is not enough on its own. Instead, effective change requires the removal of any barriers to change.

Often, a member of staff understands and agrees with the vision but is prevented from helping to achieve it because there is a road block in their way. Sometimes this block is a process and sometimes it is a person. Sometimes people are fearful for their jobs, and/or appraisal systems make them act out of self-interest rather than in the best interests of the organisation.

The guiding coalition, therefore, needs to understand what the barriers to their vision are and then actively work to remove them – this might mean changing policies and procedures and it might mean removing some rogue staff.

The sixth mistake is failing to plan for and create 'quick wins'. Most people need compelling evidence that change will be successful within a year or less before they will commit to it. Creating short-term 'wins', therefore, is important as a means of motivating staff and convincing them that change will work.

Creating quick wins is not the same as simply hoping for a win – a successful transformation effort involves leaders actively seeking out ways of improving performance. They establish short-term goals that act as checkpoints on the journey towards achieving the long-term vision, and they work hard to ensure that those goals are scored. And once they are scored, they reward their staff accordingly.

The seventh mistake is to declare victory too soon. It is good to set short-term goals along the way and to celebrate when you achieve them – but never forget that these are small battles in a much bigger war. It is important not to declare the war to be won too soon. Instead, use the credibility afforded by achieving short-term goals as a means of tackling the bigger issues. Start work on abolishing systems and structures that are inconsistent with the vision or that stand in the way of achieving that vision.

The final mistake is failing to reconcile the new vision with the organisation's established culture. Transformation is only successful and sustainable when it becomes the norm, the accepted culture, 'the way we do things around here'.

The vision has to become the expected and established way of working. There are two key factors to consider here:

Firstly, you need to signpost for staff how the new ways of working have explicitly led to improvements, making clear that the changes you've introduced have been successful in achieving better performance. If you are not explicit about this, people are likely to make different connections or no connections at all. Communication is the key here: tell a story linking your vision and your changes to the successes you're subsequently enjoying, and tell that story relentlessly. Dedicate meetings and emails to explaining how success was achieved.

Secondly, you need to make sure that any new appointments, particularly new leaders, are well matched to the vision and model the behaviours you need. A poor appointment at a senior level can undermine the vision and the transformation you have worked hard to achieve.

In conclusion, if we are to learn from these common mistakes, we might infer that an effective change management process – as well as following a cycle such as the one I set out in the previous chapter – follows these eight steps:

1. Establishing a sense of urgency

2. Forming a powerful guiding coalition

3. Creating a vision

4. Communicating the vision

5. Empowering others to act on the vision

6. Planning for and creating short-term wins

7. Consolidating improvements and producing still more change

8. Institutionalising new approaches

More strategies for using story to narrate change

Into practice
Writing your story

As we've seen, story and storytelling techniques can help with the change management process. Stories can help school leaders navigate any resistance to change, as well as inspire buy-in and create a sense of purpose and direction among staff. Stories can also illustrate the reasons behind the change, address any concerns, and paint a compelling picture of the future.

Here's how leaders can use storytelling to effectively manage the process of change:

1. **Craft a compelling narrative:**

   ○ **The need for change:** Start with a story that highlights the reasons and context for the change that's being proposed. Explain the challenges or opportunities that necessitate this shift in working practices.

   ○ **The vision:** Narrate how the change aligns with your shared vision for the future. Paint a vivid picture of the positive outcomes that the change aims to achieve. Use the learner experience to bring this narrative to life, to give it meaning, and to anchor it in reality.

2. **Humanise the change:**

   ○ **Personal anecdotes:** Share personal anecdotes or stories from those colleagues who have experienced similar changes in the past. This makes the change more relatable.

   ○ **Challenges and successes:** Highlight stories that illustrate how overcoming challenges led to growth and success during previous periods of change.

3. **Address concerns and resistance:**

   ○ **Acknowledge concerns:** Use stories to address potential concerns, doubts, or fears that colleagues might have about the proposed change.

   ○ **Past successes:** Share stories of how similar changes have been successfully implemented in the past, reassuring the team that change can lead to positive outcomes.

4. **Showcase colleagues' contributions:**

   ○ **Success stories:** Highlight stories of colleagues who have contributed to positive change initiatives in the past. Celebrate their efforts and results. Talk about how this improved their working lives as well as learner outcomes.

   ○ **Collaborative efforts:** Narrate stories of cross-functional collaboration and how diverse perspectives have contributed to successful changes in the past.

5. **Create a sense of urgency:**

   ○ **Impactful stories:** Share stories that emphasise the consequences of not implementing a change. Show how delaying action can lead to missed opportunities or challenges. Explain how the landscape is shifting and schools that stand still fall through the cracks.

   ○ **Positive outcomes:** Highlight how early adopters of change have reaped bigger benefits, motivating others to embrace the change sooner.

6. **Celebrate progress:**

   ○ **Milestones:** Share stories that celebrate the achievements and milestones reached during the change process. Recognise team efforts and individual commitments.

   ○ **Overcoming barriers:** Highlight stories of how the team collectively overcame obstacles, showcasing resilience and determination and learning more about themselves in the process.

7. **Inspire a growth mindset:**

   ○ **Learning from challenges:** Share stories that demonstrate the value of learning from setbacks and failures. Show how challenges can lead to personal and organisational growth, deepening the collective intelligence.

   ○ **Adaptation and innovation:** Highlight stories that showcase the team's ability to adapt to change and come up with innovative solutions.

8. **Encourage ownership:**

   ○ **Shared vision:** Use stories to emphasise how each member of the team contributes to the overall vision and success of the change.

   ○ **Individual impact:** Narrate stories that showcase how individual efforts align with the broader change goals and bring value to the team, fostering intrinsic motivation and lending purpose and direction.

9. **Create a continuing narrative:**

   ○ **Regular updates:** Provide ongoing updates through stories that track the progress of the change initiative and highlight achievements.

   ○ **Learning journeys:** Share stories of how colleagues are learning and growing as they navigate the change process.

Using storytelling to manage the process of change helps leaders connect with their team emotionally, alleviate fears, and rally support for the change effort. Stories provide a relatable and memorable way to communicate the purpose, benefits, and journey of change, ultimately fostering a smoother transition from the old to the new.

What have we learned?

In this chapter, we have discovered that:

Stories can help school leaders to narrate the change management process, as well as navigate any resistance to change and create a sense of collective purpose. Stories are able to craft a compelling description of the future and create a sense of urgency. They are also excellent means of celebrating progress and of highlighting colleagues' contributions.

What can we do?

To put the advice contained in this chapter into practice, it might be helpful to consider the following questions:

1. Do you use story to narrate the change process? Do you define the takeaway message and use your own experiences, telling personal anecdotes, to convince colleagues your plan for the future is right and worthwhile?

2. Do you craft a compelling narrative to highlight the need for change and to set out a vision for the future?

3. Do you use story to humanise change, to highlight stories of success and of people overcoming similar challenges?

4. Do you tell stories that showcase colleagues' contributions to the change process, as well as their past success?

Notes

1 Meisenzahl, R & Mokyr, J (2011). The rate and direction of invention in the British Industrial Revolution: Incentives and institutions. In Lerner, J & Stern, S (Eds.), *The Rate and Direction of Inventive Activity Revisited* (pp. 443-479). National Bureau of Economic Research Conference. University of Chicago Press.
2 Kotter, J (1995). Leading change: Why transformation efforts fail. *Harvard Business Review*, May–June 1995. https://hbr.org/1995/05/leading-change-why-transformation-efforts-fail-2

The end of the beginning

The end of this story is nigh. The resolution is upon us. So, let's take stock. What have we learned along the journey?

Stories make sense of our lives, make meaning of the world, and make connections with other people, and thus can be a powerful tool in education.

Stories and storytelling can play a crucial role in teaching. They can help teachers to organise the curriculum and structure lessons; aid learners' memorisation; pique learners' curiosity and wonder; relate the curriculum to the real world; help promote inclusion; and prepare learners for future success.

And stories can give meaning and structure to the process of school improvement. They can help school leaders to consult, communicate, and collaborate with stakeholders on the school improvement journey; articulate a vision for the future of their school and foster a set of shared values; build trust and embed ethical leadership behaviours to create a no-blame culture that encourages risk-taking; and resolve conflict and manage people, lead change, and manage processes.

Our self-story influences our day-to-day life. It is our unique take on the 'good' and 'bad' experiences we've had, the choices we've made, and the significance of the different people we've met along the way. Stories provide structure and meaning to our lives; stories order the arbitrary and impose logic on the haphazard. In order to harness the power of story, we must learn to read and write. We must do more, therefore, to get children reading. One way to do this is by using story and storytelling in our teaching, making great stories an everyday part of school life.

The stories we tell our children play a crucial role in shaping their understanding of the world and their place in it. One of the primary functions of storytelling for children is to help them make sense of their emotions. It's important, therefore, that the stories we tell reflect children's own *lived experiences*, that children see themselves and their heritage represented in stories. Stories are important for language development; imagination and creativity; emotional development; bonding time; and relaxation and sleep. As well as getting children to read, we must also help them to read with speed, accuracy, and fluency.

Children who have had stories read to them during the first years of their lives are exposed to a much broader and richer vocabulary than those contained in everyday conversations and,

DOI: 10.4324/9781003465492-20

as such, arrive at school better prepared for reading. Vocabulary is complex but also vital to developing reading comprehension. Young people who develop reading skills early in their lives by reading frequently add to their vocabularies exponentially over time.

Broadly, there are four behaviours associated with good reading comprehension: good readers understand the purpose of reading; good readers understand the purpose of the text; good readers review their comprehension; and good readers adjust their reading strategies.

Fluency is the ability to read text quickly and accurately, adopting the appropriate intonation. It requires some background knowledge about the text, as well as an ability to rapidly retrieve the requisite vocabulary. Fluency also requires a knowledge of syntax and grammar in order to predict the words that are likely to appear next. One of the best ways for teachers to help learners develop fluency is to read aloud to them in an engaging and motivating way to model fluency for them.

Stories are easy to understand and remember. As such, stories can be used as a structure for the curriculum and for individual lessons rather than just as a tool employed within lessons. Using story to structure learning helps create a sense of continuity between lessons, and it helps learners remember key concepts and ideas.

We should rethink the school curriculum not as set of objectives to be met but as a good story to be told. In practice, we might find the 'lead'; locate the 'hook'; discover the 'binary opposites'; tell the 'story'; and define the 'learning'.

Storytelling can also be used as a framework for teacher explanations and modelling – which can be an effective way to make complex or abstract concepts more accessible and relatable for learners. By framing our explanations as stories, we can help learners understand how different pieces of information fit together and how they relate to real-world situations.

Storytelling techniques such as flashback and flashforward can be useful when giving feedback to learners because the best feedback does not compare a learner with other learners in a class but, rather, compares each learner with their earlier self by articulating the 'story arc' the learner is following. Feedback is twofold: it is *feeding back* on the progress made so far and *feeding forward* to what needs to be done next to make continued or expedited progress. Feedback thus makes use of the storytelling techniques of flashback and flashforward to inform a learner's narrative.

By structuring learning according to storytelling rules, such as Freytag's Pyramid, we can create a compelling narrative that engages learners and helps them retain information. This, in turn, can help learners stay focused and motivated, and it can also make our lessons more memorable and impactful.

Story and storytelling provide an excellent means of aiding learners' memory because the story format has psychological significance, which leads to better comprehension and better memory because we know what to expect in a story, and these expectations are driven by a mental representation for story structure. Stories have 'stickability' because they make ideas real; they make ideas satisfying; they make ideas concrete; and they make ideas clear.

Using stories in our teaching can also help learners develop schemas – which is a reader's background knowledge and experience – because narratives help to create a sense of context and meaning around information. Good readers often draw upon prior knowledge and experience to help them understand what they are reading and are thus able to use that knowledge to make connections.

Storytelling helps to engage learners, make learning more enjoyable, and enhance their understanding of complex concepts. Using stories in the classroom can help make abstract concepts concrete and turn the theoretical into the tangible. There are many ways in which stories can be used in the classroom to pique learners' curiosity and engage their interest, including by teaching story-based lessons; telling personal stories; using role-playing and simulations; engaging in creative writing; and using digital storytelling.

Stories can help create vivid mental images, a cue for recall. Some learners may be intimidated by abstract concepts or may doubt their ability to master or understand new material. A story may provide a non-threatening way to ease learners into learning.

Ultimately, the best way to pique learners' curiosity and wonder is to pose a big question – a mystery that demands a solution. Whether this take the form of a case study, a personal anecdote, or an imagined story, the key is to captivate learners' attention by leaving an enquiry unanswered. A story's 'big question' can take various forms, such as a question of conflict; a question of mystery; a question of character; a question of themes; a question of speculation; a question of morals; a question of desire; and a question of identity.

Stories are 'psychologically privileged' because our minds treat stories differently to other types of material. Stories can be used to convey information, ideas, and technical language through engaging learners' imaginations. They can also be used to create a context, providing a mental map and a visualisation of a past situation.

The best stories hold a mirror up to learners' lives. Stories can help our curriculum become more representative of our school community and talk to learners' lived experiences and to their family traditions and cultures. Stories can also celebrate diversity beyond our school community so that we can broaden our learners' horizons.

Storytelling is universal: we all tell stories, and stories are integral to our recollections of the past and to our plans for the future; stories carry our hopes and our fears. The stories we hear when we're young teach us how to feel and how to talk; through stories we inherit our morals and values, our truths and beliefs.

One of the best ways of fostering inclusion is to help disadvantaged learners build cultural capital, and stories are a means of doing this. By reading stories, we can help our learners to develop the language skills they need to access and understand the school curriculum, and then to achieve at school and in later life. Stories open a door to future success.

The use of stories in teaching can help make abstract concepts more accessible and relatable to learners, particularly those who may not have had the same experiences or cultural background as their teachers or peers. By connecting these abstract concepts to concrete examples and personal experiences, we can help to make learning more engaging and meaningful for learners and mitigate the disadvantages faced by those who do not have access to the elaborated code. Stories also have a familiar language, which makes them easy to follow and which helps learners to make meaningful inferences whenever unfamiliar words are used. But stories don't just help learners to avoid using an elaborated code by simplifying the curriculum into more accessible narratives. Rather, they help learners to learn and use that elaborated code because, by exposing disadvantaged learners to a wider range of vocabulary, sentence structures, and abstract concepts, we can help to bridge the gap between their existing restricted code and the more elaborated code of academic and professional settings.

To use stories as a means of improving our learners' language and literacy skills, we must first teach them how to read. Reading is about developing the ability to decode increasingly complex and challenging words across the curriculum; read for meaning; understand a writer's craft; read and engage with a wide variety of texts; and research for a wide range of purposes.

Stories are not only a means of teaching reading, but they can also help teach learners how to write. Writing is about developing the ability to generate, plan and draft ideas for composition; select, shape, and construct language for expression and effect in composition; proofread and redraft written work, drawing on conventions and structures; and use accurate grammar, punctuation, and spelling.

Using story to deliver the school curriculum is helpful not just in terms of boosting learning and academic outcomes but also as a preparation for later life, including the world of work. There are three ways of using story to prepare learners for future success: stories for the world of work; stories for a sense of self; and stories for skills development.

Stories have the power to engage emotions, convey complex information, and create a shared understanding among diverse groups. Thus, stories possess a power that bare facts and statistics do not have, and stories can weave magic into our interactions with colleagues and parents. They help create cohesion and a shared purpose, bonding the whole school community together in common cause.

School leaders can leverage stories and storytelling techniques to enhance their interactions with school governors by sharing school success stories; creating a narrative for the school; personalising data; using metaphors and analogies; narrating challenges and their solutions; leveraging visual storytelling techniques; using personal stories; inviting feedback through stories; using stories in governing body meetings and reports; and celebrating milestones and achievements.

Storytelling can help school leaders build trust, engage parents, and create a strong partnership between the school and families, including by narrating school progress; connecting with the school's history; personalising data and outcomes; inviting parents' stories; providing a vision through stories; using stories in parent–teacher meetings; and using stories in the school newsletter or other communications.

Creating a vision is about telling the story of a school – reminding everyone of past success, present challenges, and future promises. It is about weaving a golden thread, a journey of collective improvement, rather than unsettling people with talk of different ways of working and of a new broom sweeping the past away. Creating a vision is about *plot*, and this story of the future, like all good stories, should be a shared one. In other words, all stakeholders need to be involved in agreeing the vision.

The best stories pique readers' interest by posing big philosophical questions or by signposting knowledge gaps. And a good vision is no different: vision creation works by creating a discrepancy between the current situation and an attractive future. This discrepancy is what motivates people to focus their effort and attention on the activities required to reach the goal and to persist until they achieve it.

Using storytelling to articulate a vision for the future of your school and to foster a set of shared values among stakeholders is a powerful way to inspire and unite people on the journey of improvement. Stories can make abstract concepts more relatable, emotionally engaging, and memorable. We might use storytelling to effectively communicate our school's vision and values by telling a compelling story of the future; connecting our vision to our shared values; engaging emotions; making it personal; using analogies and symbolism; and repeating and reinforcing.

The best way to build trust and create a no-blame culture is through story and storytelling because stories have the ability to humanise leaders, as well as to convey vulnerability. Stories can demonstrate a commitment to learning and improvement. We can do this by sharing personal stories; highlighting collective failures; celebrating learning moments; demonstrating open communication; highlighting positive intent; promoting collective accountability; showcasing mentorship and coaching; addressing missteps transparently; and encouraging others to share.

Once we have fostered trust and created a no-blame culture, we need to keep staff motivated and focused on the school improvement journey by ensuring they have autonomy, mastery, and purpose.

Great school leaders care about other people's feelings, are empathetic, and give time and support to people when they need it most. But because they're human, they are also controlled by their feelings and are, therefore, fallible and imperfect. Sometimes they will make mistakes. What's important is that they acknowledge their mistakes and seek to make amends. And, moreover, they work hard to avoid making the same mistakes again by wresting control of their chimp. But they will, from time to time, have to deal with workplace conflict and, at such times, storytelling can help leaders facilitate understanding, empathy, and collaboration. Stories have the power to convey emotions, different perspectives, and the potential for positive outcomes, including by choosing the right story; creating a safe space; introducing the story; highlighting different perspectives; finding the common ground; showing transformation and resolution; relating to real situations; encouraging dialogue; empowering individuals; and following up.

School leaders can use story to narrate the change management process by defining the takeaway message; using their own experiences; not trying to be a hero; highlighting a conflict; and keeping it simple.

Stories can also help school leaders navigate any resistance to change, as well as inspire buy-in and create a sense of purpose and direction among staff. Stories can also illustrate the reasons behind the change, address any concerns, and paint a compelling picture of the future, including by crafting a compelling narrative; humanising the change; addressing concerns and resistance; showcasing colleagues' contributions; creating a sense of urgency; celebrating progress; inspiring a growth mindset; encouraging ownership; and creating a continuing narrative.

And so, this story reaches its denouement. But it is not the end, nor even the beginning of the end; it is merely the end of the beginning. The storyteller's baton is passed from me to you, for your story begins here. Make it a good one.

Index